THE CULTURED MAN

ASHLEY MONTAGU

The Cultured Man

THE WORLD PUBLISHING COMPANY

CLEVELAND AND NEW YORK

PUBLISHED BY The World Publishing Company

2231 West 110th Street, Cleveland 2, Ohio

PUBLISHED SIMULTANEOUSLY IN CANADA BY

Nelson, Foster & Scott Ltd.

Library of Congress Catalog Card Number: 58-5779

SECOND PRINTING

For many of the definitions contained in the "Answers" I am indebted to *Webster's New World Dictionary of the American Language, College Edition,* and to The World Publishing Company for permission to use them.

The quotation on pages 47-48 is from *The Cocktail Party,* copyright, 1950, by T. S. Eliot. Reprinted by permission of Harcourt, Brace and Company, Inc.

2WP858

To

Lee and Edmund Spaeth

affectionately

CONTENTS

THE ANSWERS

Under the heading for each group of questions will be found the number of the page on which the answers to those questions begin.

PREFACE

As AN anthropologist I had perhaps better explain at once what kind of culture this book is about. When the anthropologist speaks of culture what he has in mind is the way of life of a people, its ideas, habits, skills, arts, instruments, and institutions. I am not directly concerned with that kind of culture in this volume, but rather with the kind of culture that is expressed in the refinement of thought, emotion, conduct, manners, taste, and attitudes of the person.

In the Western world we talk about the educated man and frequently identify him with the cultured man. But an educated man is not necessarily a cultured man. The distinction requires clarification, as does the reason for embarking upon such a distinction at all. It is the function of the first part of the book to make this clear. The marks that distinguish the cultured man are discussed and set out in the first part. In the second part of the book there is added a means by which the reader may evaluate himself with respect to his status as a cultured person in each of a total of fifty categories of knowledge and experience. This is achieved through fifteen hundred questions (with answers following), thirty in each of the fifty different categories, most of which questions test knowledge, while the remainder test attitudes.

The questions are so devised that anyone able to answer any question would almost certainly be able to answer a great many of the unasked questions relating to it. A simple scoring method is provided by means of which the reader may appraise his status as a cultured person in any one category.

The book thus enables the reader not only to take a survey of his own cultural status, but tells him where he needs to devote some additional attention to making the necessary modifications. The one thing the book is not intended to do is to give anyone a feeling of inferiority. It should be made perfectly clear that most cultivated men would find it difficult to answer the majority of the questions. But that is not the point. The whole purpose of this book will be lost if it is conceived to be a game in which the reader pits his wits against the author to win, or if the author is made to compete with the reader for victory. That is not any part of the purpose of this book. Its purpose is to tell you what a cultivated person is, what the value of the cultured person is to himself, his fellows, and his society, and finally, the *kind* of things the cultured person knows, thinks, and feels. The point of the book is that it may succeed in giving you a fair idea of where you stand in relation to the continuum of culture, and help you understand in what further direction you need to proceed. If this book succeeds in propelling you in that direction I shall be more than amply repaid for the labor of making it.

It is hardly necessary to say that it would ill become any man to set himself up as an *arbiter elegantiae* of culture. It is a position that any man in his senses would readily forgo. Yet all of us must have some opinion upon the subject, and it is no more than that that I have attempted to present in this book.

A.M.

Princeton, New Jersey.
May 1958

The Cultured Man

THE distinguishing quality of humanity, its most precious possession, is the human mind, and the quality that distinguishes the human from all other kinds of mind is the unique degree to which its capacity for learning is developed—its educability. Man is the most plastic, the most malleable, the most educable creature in the world. It is because of this trait that he has achieved the conquest of the earth, the air, the sea—of virtually everything but himself.

He is equally capable of achieving the conquest of himself. That he has not thus far done so has not been for want of trying; it has been for want of knowing how to try. Man has left the study of himself to the last of the sciences, now collectively called the behavioral sciences. These are increasingly serving to reveal something of the nature of man. When we understand our own nature better it is probable that we shall be able to deal with it more wisely and effectively than we have in the past.

But however much such knowledge of ourselves may help us to become what it is within us to become, it will always remain true that the culture of certain essential qualities of mind should constitute a basic fulfillment of the birthright of every human being. The capital tragedy of humanity lies in the failure to achieve that fulfillment. The deepest personal defeat suffered by human beings is constituted by the difference between what one was capable of becoming and what one has in fact become.

What are the essential qualities of mind that will always remain so fundamentally necessary to human fulfillment? The answer to that question is one of the objects of this essay, indeed, the principal object of this essay, for there are certain qualities of the mind that distinguish the cultured man, and it is these that we are here concerned to discover, to discuss, and to describe. In brief: What are the marks that distinguish the cultured man?

If it is true that the human mind is humanity's most distinctive and precious possession, then I think it may be agreed that it deserves the most devoted cultivation and attention. For the mind is the medium in which our lives grow and from which we function as human beings. The manner in which we cultivate the potentialities of that medium will largely determine the kind of human beings we shall become. The process of cultivating the potentialities of mind we call *education*. The purpose of education, as generally conceived, is to enable human beings to behave more efficiently than they would do otherwise. The word education originates in the Latin *educare*,* which literally means "to cause to grow, to nourish." Mind is the behaving organism. Any act of the organism is behavior, and in virtually every act some aspect of the mind is involved. Learning is the increase in the facility or strength of any act through training. By virtue of the fact that man is the most educable of all creatures, he is the creature capable of learning more about the world in which he lives, and the life that has its being in that world, than any other creature. This, in effect, means that he is not only capable of learning what is sound but that he is also capable of learning many things that are, in fact, unsound. And when one puts together the sound and the unsound that he has learned, the result is not intelligence but confusion. And as Francis Bacon long ago remarked, truth grows more readily out of error than it does out of confusion.

The culture of the human mind is the finest of all the arts— and one of the most neglected. Neglected, not because we are uninterested but because we are confused. Confused about the direction we ought to take and confused about the goals we should pursue. And so, with the best will in the world, we busy ourselves perfecting means to realize a confusion of goals.

In the Western world, but particularly in America (at least, so our critics tell us), this confusion has achieved threatening

* Not from its cognate *educere*, "to draw out," which is the oft-given incorrect etymology.

dimensions. The things we are interested in, the things we want, our attitudes of mind—in sum, our values—are touchingly clear, touching because of our naive faith that the achievement of these values will bring us happiness and that happiness constitutes the be-all and end-all of existence. Is it not written in the Declaration of Independence that life, liberty, and the pursuit of happiness are the endowed rights of every American? What is not there written is *what* kind of life, *what* kind of liberty, and *what* kind of happiness Americans ought to aim for. But we Americans have written the answer into what we so proudly hail as The American Way of Life. We all know the answer, since we are all exposed to it from the moment of birth. And what is that answer? What is The American Way of Life? If we could find a single word for it, it would be "Success." But what kind of success?

Some of our critics have equated our conception of "success" with "money." We have been accused of being a nation of money-theists, interested in money as an end in itself or as a means toward the achievement of "a high standard of living." It is seldom added that since the greater part of the rest of mankind lives in comparative poverty the rest of the world is preoccupied with the problems of poverty, while Americans who are blessed with comparative abundance are preoccupied with making the best use of their riches. This preoccupation with abundance has given rise to the accusation of "materialism." As a blanket indictment this is silly, but it is nonetheless true of some Americans as it is true of men elsewhere. It is quite true that for many Americans "a high standard of living" means principally physical creature comforts and conspicuous consumption or "keeping up with the Joneses." For such Americans—and there are only too many of them—these are the principal ways in which one demonstrates to the world that one is a success—whether one has in fact been a success or not in the American understanding of that word. We have only to ask ourselves what meaning many Americans would give to the words "He's a great success," to understand what success is considered to be by such citizens. A man's value, his worth, is measured by many Americans in terms of the number of dollars he appears to have achieved. I say "appears" because this being so generally accepted a measure of success almost everyone wants to be taken for a success. And so all the external evidences of success must be sedulously cultivated, even though by the measure of success one is, in fact, a failure. Hence, the clothes one wears, the house one lives in, the television antenna (whether one has a television set or not), the car one drives, all must conform to the requirements of what William James so appropriately called "the bitch-goddess, Success."

Not all Americans behave in this way. But it is surely not an exaggeration to say that too many do, and that *a* dominant if not *the* dominant value of America is success in terms of material values. This has been said many times before. It will bear repeating—constructively—until that time when it no longer needs to be said. It has been said that as a civilization we are barbarians, that we are crude and coarse, and rough and tough and violent. That we are the one example of a society that has proceeded from barbarism to decadence without any of the intervening benefits of civilization. That we have a talent for *doing*, but not for *being* or *becoming*. The people who have said such things are usually foreigners who have visited these shores for varying periods of time. The criticisms that have been made of us have in large part been superficial and wrongheaded. We have not liked being called names, and we have rejected such unseemly imputations as the superficial judgments they, too often, were.

No one likes being called names especially when there is an element of truth in the names—it is then that we are most likely to resent such criticism. It has been stated with somewhat monotonous frequency that Americans are immature, and one of the evidences cited as supporting this accusation is the manner in which Americans react to criticism. Since we have been the recipients of so much misinformed criticism we have tended to pay little attention to any criticism. This is, perhaps, unwise, for the proper response to criticism of oneself is not rejection of the criticism and resentment of the critic but self-examination. Let us, then, examine something of the worse side of ourselves in the face of the facts: a very necessary procedure, since many of us won't face the facts and therefore are unacquainted with them.

Is it or is it not a fact that we Americans have the highest homicide rates in the world? Is it or is it not a fact that we

Americans have the highest violent crime rates in the world? Is it or is it not a fact that we Americans have a juvenile delinquency rate that far exceeds that of any other nation in the world? Is it not a fact that we have the highest divorce rates in the world? The highest alcoholic rates? One of the highest suicide rates?

These are, indeed, the facts. They can be neither repudiated nor resented. They must be understood, for they are very much a product of The American Way of Life, but a part that we are only too ready to leave out of sight and out of mind in the files of the FBI and the publications of some international agency the name of which we don't care to know. The facts to which I refer are frequently published in the newspapers and weeklies, but most Americans, when they learn them, are as likely as not to say, "Well, what of it? Don't other countries have high crime rates, too? We're just more vigorous than they are. We do things in a big way, and there are so many more of us." Such comments are likely to be uttered with a certain amount of innocent pride, and reveal at once the lack of seriousness with which crime in all its forms is regarded, and the complete lack of understanding of what it means to be a human being. Only a short time ago a United States Congressman described the slaying of a Japanese woman in Japan by an American soldier as "a childish action." It was not childish, it was irresponsible. The sales appeal of crime is known and exploited by every element of the communications industry, and the guardians of our lives and property, the police, openly carry their weapons and ammunition on their belts for every American to see. No wonder we accept the daily calendar of crimes, muggings, and homicides with an equanimity that never ceases to astonish the foreigner.

But, yes, this is our worse side. What of our virtues? All our evidence thus far has been negative. This is not undeliberate, for the reason that in a book on the cultured man it seems necessary to provide an immediately understandable practical argument and justification for the cultured man. That argument may be briefly stated as envisaging in the achievable ideal of the cultured man the greater part of the solution to virtually all the problems which at present bedevil the world. Surely, if we could substantially reduce the frequency of some of the disorders of the type to which I have already referred by means of the proper culture of human beings, this alone would justify every effort toward the production of such persons. But, of course, these are not the only reasons for providing the soil in which the cultivated man can grow. The reason that resumes all the reasons for the cultivation of the cultured man is that he represents, and will always represent, the highest flowering of civilization; that in the cultured man are embodied not alone the highest virtues of his society but the finest values of universal humanity, and that he thus represents the achievable ideal of what every man should be or be as nearly as it is possible within him to be. And since America comprises a fair share of the representatives of all mankind there is more than a chance that we may yet win through to a synthesis of those universal values in every man.

Our virtues in America are sufficiently numerous to make it possible for us to envisage the accomplishment of the cultured man as a national type within several generations. As a people we are powerfully characterized by the desire to do the right thing; we want badly to be good. America, as Scott Fitzgerald put it, is a willingness of the heart. We are anxious to have everyone enjoy life, to enable as many as possible of our children to have a college education, to live at as comfortably high a level as possible. American hospitality is a byword, and no foreigner who has ever experienced it can ever forget it. Courage, ingenuity, inventiveness, enterprise, willingness to try new ideas, idealism, humanitarianism, an extraordinary vitality, and a sort of eternal youthfulness and innocence of spirit, these are some of the outstanding qualities of Americans.

Societies, like persons, must be taken as a whole, with their vices and their virtues. And when those of us who have been born and educated or who have lived for many years abroad and are therefore able to take an objective view of the country ask ourselves how America measures up as a whole, the answer is likely to be a very simple and illuminating one. With all its faults we would rather live in America than in any other country in the world. Einstein looked at America and exclaimed, "This is paradise!" We know exactly what he meant. He was aware of his adopted country's many faults, but he was also aware of its many virtues; and taken all in all the whole represented for him something as near paradise as was practicably realizable upon this earth at the present time. We cannot be sure that this is quite so, but it certainly is so for many of us, and has been so for me for more than a generation. Like so many millions of others I owe a great debt to America for the privileges and opportunities it has provided me for being able to do what I could not have done in any other country—to do the work I like and to live comfortably while doing it.

But it is just these wonderful things about America that have made so many of us increasingly sensitive to the faults of this fabulous land. The difference between what America could be and what it has become leads many of us to a critical attitude which is often misunderstood to be one of dislike, of attack, or, even worse, of contempt. The critics who so often tend to be misunderstood in this way are usually the most valiant defenders of America when abroad, and its most consistent critics when at home in America. Their criticism is not motivated by dislike, but by love of America. Their criticism is calculated to be constructive, *not* destructive. They do not believe that loyalty to one's culture or patriotism consists in conformity or support of the *status quo,* but rather in contributing toward the continuous improvement of social conditions and the perfectibility of human nature. Hence, where they perceive faults they would like to see them corrected, and where they believe they see the remedy they would like to see it applied. They deplore what Brooks Adams called "the degradation of the democratic dogma," the defection from the high ideals envisioned by the founding fathers of this country as achievable realities for the benefit of every one of its citizens and of the state. They deplore the mindless vulgarity to which so many Americans have been reduced, the corrupt brightness of those who pretend to minister to their needs, the extraordinary striving for conformity, and the moral evasiveness by which problems calling for immediate ethical solution are too often worsened. That at this late date such shameful events as occurred at Little Rock should still be possible, that a literate electorate should voluntarily return to office the kind of men represented by Mayor Curley and the late Senator Joseph McCarthy, that so many Americans should of their own free choice subscribe to the meretricious and sensational newspapers and magazines that they do and encourage the kind of radio, television, and movies that they do, that they should have so little sense of the fit and proper as to permit the vulgarization of the human spirit to the extent to which they have done, that they have so unconcernedly permitted the rape and spoliation of the natural beauties of their land, and that they should have thrown together so many towns which must surely be among the ugliest upon the face of the earth, all this and much else suggests that there are still too many of our fellow citizens who are incapable of humanely experiencing and dealing creatively and imaginatively with the life of which they are so much a part.

The insensitiveness to beauty in all its forms exhibited by too many Americans is perhaps the most revealing evidence of the coarsening of the human spirit which inevitably leads to a certain deterioration of the essential qualities which make a human being humane.

Not only are these statements not true of all Americans, but they are almost certainly not true of the majority of Americans. Nevertheless they *are* true of a sufficiently large number to make the implied criticisms worthy of serious consideration, particularly by those to whom they do not apply. Perhaps the most frequent criticism brought against Americans is that they are the most materialistic people in the world. Surely, this represents one of the most superficial judgments ever made about any country. In the first place, in terms of the exploitation of our material resources we are still a young country. We are, fortunately, a land rich in those material resources that contribute to the greater comfort of human beings. We are still busily engaged in exploiting those resources. The frontier spirit is still restlessly at work in most Americans. We are still busy staking out claims and working them to the limit. This it is, in part, that creates that vitality and exuberance of spirit which contrasts so markedly with the comparative apathy of so many Europeans, for example. Americans have, happily, achieved the highest standard of comfortable living in the world. What this means in terms of daily happiness those alone will understand who have had to contend with such things as European plumbing and the lack of those physical amenities of everyday living that every American takes for granted. If Europeans have a passion for making themselves uncomfortable, Americans have a penchant for taking joy in life, for making themselves comfortable; and if they concentrate a good deal more attention upon this than Europeans do, it is not because they are materialistically minded, but because they fortunately enjoy opportunities denied to most Europeans.

The same is true of the American's allegedly materialistic interest in money. Here, again, Americans have greater opportunities to be interested in money than Europeans or other peoples —but they are not interested in money as such or in hoarding it selfishly for themselves. Cupidity constitutes no part of the American character. The truth is that Americans on an individual as well as a national level are the most generous of all peoples with money. What other land has to show as many benefactors on such a scale as Carnegie, Harkness, the Morgans, the Rockefellers, the Fords, the Mellons, and numerous others? With the exception, in recent years, of Lord Nuffield in England—a man whose career parallels that of Henry Ford—what did the many extremely wealthy men of England, France, and Germany do with their money during the past hundred years? Whatever they did with it, the one thing they did not do was to create the kind of beneficent foundations so notably associated with the above-mentioned Americans.

Americans are interested in money as a means of maximizing the experience of life in all its manifold possibilities—within the limits of their knowledge of those possibilities. Not only is there nothing wrong with that, but there is everything right with it. The problem, of course, is to know which experiences are worth maximizing and which are not. Insofar as the really crass selfish interest in money is concerned, compared to the *moyen* Frenchman the average American simply doesn't stack up. For really endemic materialism it would be hard to beat either the French or German bourgeoisie. But national comparisons are proverbially odious—they are being made here simply to obviate any impression that the writer is in any way biased in favor of one nation as against another, and in particular to avoid any impression, in view of his references to the faults of Americans, that taken as a whole when weighed on the scale of cultural development Americans are of less worth than other peoples. In this connection several things require to be said.

In the first place it should be pointed out that a common practice of European critics is to compare the best of their own culture with the worst of American. There are some things in which Europeans decidedly excel us, taken all in all—the good manners, for example, of the average Englishman, the cooking of the French, the cleanliness of German streets, the poetry of English poets, the painting of French painters, and the extraordinary literary ability of so many Germans, the warmth and artistic abilities of Italians, the order and craftsmanship of Scandinavians, to mention some of the outstanding differences. But even in these respects the differences are no longer as great as they once were. There are still other differences, and these are not altogether of a minor kind; but however this may be, the truth is that in the second half of the twentieth century there is more genuine culture in the United States—although there may be great patches in the land that are virtually without it—than in any other country of the Western world. With respect to the cultures of the East I cannot speak with any degree of security, and therefore prefer to omit them from the comparison.

But Broadway should not be compared with the Boulevard St. Germain. I have seen bubble gum in Britain as well as in the Bronx, and I have heard Auden quoted in Brooklynese as well as in the accents of Balliol. Beethoven is no more natural to Europe than be-bop is to the United States. Speaking of music, the truth is that Beethoven is probably performed more frequently, and heard by more people, in the United States than in any other country of the world. Consider such facts as the following:

> There are today about 1,000 symphony orchestras in the United States.
> There are 450 opera-producing groups.
> There are an average of 7 opera performances given in this country every day.

Over 255 educational institutions offer degree courses in music and advanced-level musical training.

There are about 200 music periodicals, most of which are devoted to concert music.

Over 33,000,000 Americans play musical instruments, and in 1954 Americans spent over $30,000,000 on printed music, 84 per cent of which was concert music.

In 1954 Americans spent more money at the box office for concert music than they spent for baseball. And in 1955 they spent more money purchasing recordings of concert music than they paid for admission to all baseball games.

It is estimated that 1 out of every 5 Americans is actively interested in one form or another of concert music.*

These are impressive facts, and they make it clear that America is now one of the great musical centers of the world.

American composers such as Barber, Bernstein, Copland, Ives, Schuman, and Sessions enjoy an appreciative following, and America has become the naturalized home of many a foreign musician.

The new idiom of modern music, jazz, was born, bred, developed, and is most proficiently performed in the United States. The influence of jazz has been world-wide, and there appears to be some reason to believe that jazz constitutes one of the main currents of musical evolution of our century. It is something more than the folk music of our time—among other things it constitutes one of the few universal languages of our day. What polyglot diplomats and their minions cannot do polyphonic jazz can.

As for light music, the compositions of Irving Berlin, George Gershwin, Jerome Kern, Cole Porter, Vincent Youmans, and numerous others are known throughout the world.

As for the "musical," that wonderful art form, "South Pacific," "Oklahoma," and, above all and beyond all others, "My Fair Lady," bear sufficient testimony to the fact that in this field Americans have genuinely established an unchallenged supremacy.

The American theater is as alive as it could possibly be, and is flourishing. American playwrights are renowned throughout

* These facts are based on data printed in *Concert Music U.S.A. 1956*. Broadcast Music, Inc., 1956.

the world: Eugene O'Neill, Marc Connelly, Arthur Miller, Clifford Odets, Robert Sherwood, Tennessee Williams are names most theater-loving Europeans know.

There are several schools of American ballet, and the dance is a most highly popular art form which has followed its own unique development in America. Most modern ballroom dance forms evolved in America.

The whole world has long read American writers, and the favorite authors of, for example, Norway's youth, it has recently been announced, are Ernest Hemingway and John Steinbeck. Since 1930 five Americans have been awarded Nobel prizes for literature.

American poets, from Poe, Longfellow, and Whitman to Robert Frost, William Carlos Williams, E. E. Cummings, T. S. Eliot, and Ezra Pound, have not been without some influence in the world.

And as humanists, the reader may be surprised to learn that no less than twelve Americans have received the Nobel award for peace, far more than the number awarded to the citizens of any other land.

Architecture as an art has received an extraordinary fillip and undergone an astonishing development in the United States, while in painting Whistler, Sargent, Winslow Homer, Georgia O'Keeffe, Alexander Brook, Ben Shahn, and others have achieved distinction.

In England, with a population of 50 million, there is one purely independent literary magazine, *The London Magazine*. In America, with a population of 171 million, there are scores of such magazines. Among the outstanding independent reviews, to name but a few, are *The American Scholar, The Antioch Review, The Yale Review, The Partisan Review, The Kenyon Review, The Sewanee Review, The Hudson Review, The Texas Quarterly,* and *Commentary.*

In America we publish fewer books than do England or France. We are said to read fewer books than Englishmen or Frenchmen. If this is true, and it seems to be, it is possibly because Americans are interested in variety, not only in reading but in all other things, and so limit much of their reading to shorter pieces in forms such as are supplied by the big-circulation magazines, *Life, Time, Look,*

The Saturday Evening Post, and *Reader's Digest* with the largest circulation of them all. However, the advent of the paperback books has greatly increased the number of book readers in the United States and brought them closer to the number, per centum of population, that read books in England and France where paperbacks have been long established. So far as paperbacks are concerned the drugstore now serves the function that the bookstore once served. Indeed, people who would never ordinarily have gone into a bookstore are likely to pick up a book in a drugstore, which they had entered in the first place with the intention of buying something quite other than a book.

The number of bookstores in America is constantly dwindling, and there are many large cities in the United States that cannot boast of a single one. That unacknowledged dispenser of culture and civilization, the secondhand bookseller, is becoming as rare as some of the books he used to sell. The only place remaining in many towns in which the potential reader can purchase a book is in the department store, the five-and-dime, or the drugstore.

There are more institutes of higher learning, colleges, and universities in the United States than the total number taken together to be found in France, England, and Germany. And more American children go to high school and subsequently to college than in all these countries.

In the sciences over thirty Americans have won Nobel prizes, and without falling into the trap of defensive boasting I think it may be fairly said that American scientists can at the very least hold their own, in all branches of science, with the best of any other country. In the practical applications of science, in technological development, the United States is unsurpassed—Sputniks notwithstanding.

It is unnecessary to go on. The point has been made that insofar as cultural comparisons with other lands are concerned Americans need have no fears. What Americans need to be concerned with is the direction in which their culture will go. And this is a matter which they have it in their hands to determine by seeing to it that as many Americans as possible come to understand the true meaning and significance of culture.

That all is not as it should be in America many Americans

know only too well. They wish that these disturbing and unpleasant aspects of American culture could be otherwise, though they are not always clear as to why these things are as they are, or how one might go about changing them. The imperceptible as well as the perceptible erosion of moral and democratic values is a danger with which we are constantly faced. How to deal with that danger?

Perhaps the best way to deal with such dangers is by examining the values by which we live that give rise to them. Values are the measures of the interest we have in things, the esteem with which we invest them. Our values aim at the achievement of goals.

This is today, more than ever, a necessary precaution. The deplorable international rivalries of our time have panicked our leaders into a sudden recognition of the importance of scientific and technical education. A high premium has been placed upon science and technology. The government has raised the salaries of its scientific employees. With such unilaterally directed encouragement there is a very real danger that, in the drive to produce more creators of better and brighter intercontinental and other destructive missiles, we shall succeed in overemphasizing the value of science and technology and diminishing the value of the humanities, and thus virtually render the idea of the cultured man obsolete and unrealistic. This is a danger to which we must constantly remain alive and do everything in our power to surmount.

Success, our supreme value, is not a goal, not a destination, but a journey. The principal purpose of a democratic society should be the cultivation of such values in its citizens as will enable them to realize their own best potentialities, as well as those of their fellow men, for being humane. To be humane originally meant to be possessed of those distinctively human qualities which separate man from the brutes, namely, those which an education in the fine arts brought one. This is what the Romans understood by the word *humanitas,* and the Greeks by *paideia.*

Down to the end of the seventeenth century the word "human" was spelled "humane," but toward the end of that century the latter word came to denote the best qualities of which human beings are capable, such as kindness, compassion, tenderness, mercifulness, considerateness. The humane man was one whose qualities were civilizing, refining, and humanizing. In the older universities the study of the subjects which were designed to produce such qualities in their students was pursued in the school of *Literae humaniores*. These subjects were basically the ancient classics, rhetoric, and literature, and were later increased to include philosophy, history, and sometimes the fine arts—the subjects which we today broadly call the humanities.

The conception of the humane man as characterized by civilizing, refining, and humanizing qualities reached its highest development, perhaps, in the eighteenth century, in the Age of the Enlightenment, as it has been called. This is the age of the voyaging discoverers Captain Cook and Bougainville, of Dr. Johnson, Goldsmith, Boswell, Burke, Voltaire, Rousseau, Diderot, Condorcet, Kant, Herder, Franklin, Jefferson, and Washington. It was the Age of Revolution and of revolutionary ideas—and of revolutionary freedoms. The Age of the American and French Revolutions. The age in which the Industrial Revolution and the machine came into being. An age in which men were still being condemned to the hulks for trivial offenses, in which the death penalty was the law for anyone who stole a loaf of bread. An age of incredible inhumanities, but nevertheless an age of yeasty ferment, the harbinger of progress, of better things to come.

Machines, in replacing the labor of human beings, among their effects somehow manage to diminish rather than increase the qualities of civilization and refinement. The machine tends to coarsen rather than to refine the fiber of human existence, it tends quite simply to mechanize. And, as we have since learned, by the end of the nineteenth century the conception of the humane man had somehow become emptied of the refining and even humanizing qualities that were such conspicuous traits in the character of the humane man of the eighteenth century. What had happened? Why had the humane man largely lost these qualities and been left principally with the quality of civilization —not so much civility as civilization—the tendency of the State or its representatives to determine the values by which the individual shall live? The civilized man in this sense is the person who abides by the rule of the *cives*, who possesses the civic virtues, the virtues of a city-dweller. The civilized man naturally adopts the values, that is to say those qualities that are considered to be the virtues, of his particular State as they are reflected in the practices of the particular town in which he happens to have his being. In the course of acquiring those local civilized virtues he may fail to achieve them with any accompaniment of refinement and with little or no humanity. The reference is not to the ruffians or slum-dwellers of our cities or to the unsophisticated rustics who settle in many of them, but to those who have enjoyed the advantages conferred by being brought up in a city, yet who have somehow failed to acquire the qualities of refinement and humanity. They know *about* them, and they can talk about them, but in their own lives it is only too painfully evident that they are either lacking or not well developed.

Possibly if we go outside our country we may be able to take a more purely objective view of the civilized man than if we commenced with some examples too close to home.

Let us take a city-bred German, born in the year 1900 or thereabouts. In the ordinary schools he would have had the advantage of one of the "best" educations in the world, in the land of Lessing, Hölderlin, Novalis, Kant, Heine, Nietzsche, Wagner, Goethe, "wo die Citronen blühen." In the private schools he would have had one of the finest humanistic educations to be obtained anywhere in the world. In the technical high schools and in the universities he would have obtained an education unsurpassed if not unequaled anywhere else in the world. One would therefore have supposed the average German—as well as the unaverage German —to be a fairly well-educated person. And, indeed, by "civilized" standards he was. He could spout yards of poetry very movingly; he read the classics as well as the moderns; he conducted himself properly, obeyed the law, read good newspapers, honored his father and his mother, took pride in his city, opera house, and *Tiergarten*, and was a loyal and devoted citizen of the State. And yet, in 1933 this same model of a civilized man could join the Nazi Party in his millions, and by 1939 be supporting, if not himself actively participating in, the deliberate extermination of helpless millions of his fellow human beings while worshiping the very image and being of the most brutally abandoned madman the world has ever known.

Of their refinement we need not speak—the Germans were never notorious for that. But what had happened to their sense of humanity? Why did none of the messages of such humanists as those mentioned above take? The answer is that they did not take, except as the most superficial of embellishments, because the dominant motif of German *Kultur* was not humanity, but the so-called military virtues as preached by heroes such as Bismarck, Treitschke, and the blood-and-steel militarists of the type of Bernhardi, Ludendorff, and Hindenburg. (Significantly enough, it was the latter who was directly responsible for putting Hitler into the position of murderous power he came to occupy as Chancellor of Germany.)

The point I am endeavoring to establish here is that the twentieth-century German took on the character not of the great geniuses of the human spirit in whose teachings he had been educated, or better to whose teachings he had been exposed, but rather that he adopted the character of the authoritarian State which demanded of the good German that he be one who can either command or be commanded in the best interests of the military expansionist ideals of his country. This appeared to the German as the real "good," the "Realpolitik" of his country to which everything else must be subordinated. And that is precisely the point: what the civilized man will consider to be "good," "true," and "desirable" is largely or entirely determined by what his civilization, his society, his culture considers to be so.

In an era characterized by the motifs of competition and exploitation civilized man will take over the motivations which drive his society, not the "otherworldly" noble ideals of the great spirits of his culture, but the "thisworldly" attainable idols of competitive success. What men tend to believe in is not what other people have *said,* but what present people *do.* And what their society *does,* not what it *says,* is what men tend to believe in and strive likewise to do. In America we do what we believe and talk about what we don't really believe in. Thus, one of the tests we can immediately apply is this: What do we most talk about? Frequently the things we are inclined to do least about, and the things we really don't believe in—even though we may be much concerned with, if not about, them—such, for example, as "democracy" and "education."

But this is to run somewhat ahead. Our concern thus far has been to discover why the qualities of refinement and humanity virtually disappeared from the structure of Western civilized man's psyche in the nineteenth and twentieth centuries. And as briefly as possible I have tried to suggest that this was a result of those qualities being incompatible with the spirit of nationalism developed by so many countries during the nineteenth and twentieth centuries. That, on the other hand, the opposite qualities appeared to be most highly rewarded, and hence were the very qualities by which the man who desired to be a success could live.

This is all quite understandable and rather sad. But we do not have to stand by and see the human race destroy itself because we don't know what to do to prevent such a catastrophe. For all anyone can know it may already be too late. Who can say that some madman may not take it into his head to start an atomic war? An unrealistic optimism in the face of the facts would be only slightly less worse than the apathy which seems to have overtaken so many millions of Americans with respect to the control of atomic weapons. We have to adopt the view that while there is time there is life, and while there is life there is a sporting chance that we may yet rescue ourselves from the very edge of doom, if we would but do what is required of us.

We must make up our minds that atomic weapons must be universally outlawed, and in whatever ways we possibly can we must work toward such an end. At the same time it is necessary for us to realize that all war, all inhumanity in whatever shape or form it takes, can no longer be tolerated, and that most if not all human problems can be solved by human beings working together, co-operatively rather than in conflict with one another.

Above all we must learn to understand that it is through the cultivation of the human spirit, essentially through the cultivation of the human mind, that the problems which face us as human beings, not only in America but throughout the world, will ultimately be solved. If this is so, and I am unable to see that it can be doubted, then the reason for the being and the making of the cultured man is established. A President of the United States, Mr. Calvin Coolidge, once remarked that the business of a democracy was business. I don't think he could have been more wrong. The prime business of a democracy is not the making of dollars but the making of human beings, and my contention is that, if it is to survive, its business must be the making of cultured human beings, for a society is only as strong as its internal resources of humane understanding and being. The best and most enduring defense against external attack is internal security, and this holds true for nations as well as for persons—and I mean spiritual security, *not* physical security. In recent world history England represents an example of the former: when threatened by the Nazi hordes she stood alone, rallied about Winston Churchill, against a physical force which, lacking the moral force of the British, was in fact afraid to invade their island. On the personal level Gandhi is an outstanding modern example of a man who because of his wonderfully cultivated inner spirit gained freedom for his people from a foreign rule which had lasted for two hundred and fifty years.

At this point, since I have been using the words "spiritual" and "spirit," perhaps I ought to say what I mean by them. By "spirit" or "spiritual" I mean something perfectly natural, and not in the least supernatural, namely, the expression of the inner qualities of a human being that relate him in a humanely cultured manner to everything that he is capable of experiencing or contemplating.

Clearly, it is what we understand by "inner qualities" and "a humanely cultured manner" that is in need of explanation, an explanation which should take us a long way toward the answer to the question: What is a cultured man?

Here we must at once ask ourselves a further question. We have been saying that the cultured man is a desirable and achievable ideal toward which every society should strive so that every one of its citizens shall have the fullest opportunities and encouragements to achieve the highest cultivation of which he is capable. The implicit assumption here is that every individual is capable of becoming a cultured person.

Whether this is in fact so or not, we must be quite clear that the only way by which we may discover whether it is in truth so or not is by affording every individual the necessary stimulations and opportunities to enable him to develop as many of the qualities of the cultured person as it is possible for him to achieve. One thing is highly probable, namely, that individuals will vary in their capacity for culture, but that no individual within the normal range of intelligence is incapable of developing as a cultured human being to a degree that, compared with present levels, is very high indeed. In short, the statement frequently made that some individuals are incapable of education or culture may or may not be true and is, in any event, utterly beside the point, for until we have put the matter to a fair test such a statement is meaningless. Indeed, were we finally to discover that some normally intelligent persons are incapable of culture the situation would not in the least be altered, for every individual has the right to the optimum development of his potentialities as a human being to the limit of which he is capable. That limit may never be reached, but the individual has a right to expect, and it is to every society's advantage to make available, the encouragements and opportunities to develop his capacities to the maximum possible degree. This is an *ethical* right that every human being should enjoy by virtue of the simple fact of being human. Equipped with the proper knowledge and the will to do what we ought, there is more than a hope that what is at present largely an ideal may in good time become a happy reality.

This brings us to another important question: What are the potentialities of human beings? Is there anything in the nature of human nature that would make the cultivation of the human spirit particularly difficult? Such, for example, as the alleged "original" sinfulness of human beings or their alleged innate aggressiveness? These are widely held concepts, and it therefore needs to be clearly stated that there is not the slightest evidence that would withstand a moment's critical examination that any human being has ever been born a sinful or an aggressive creature. If there is any iniquity or aggressiveness in man that here requires special comment, it is the vulgar iniquity of assuming the inherent naughtiness of man. If there is an original sin, it is the sin against man's innate nature, the violence we do to his potentialities for becoming humane. The extraordinary aggressiveness with which the notion of man's inherent brattishness has been maintained suggests that, at least in part, it has an emotional origin. Man has looked about him, and observing the course of history, the internecine warfare, the treachery, the rapine and wholesale murder of millions of innocent human beings, the violence of so many human beings about us, the competitiveness and aggressiveness and unprovoked hostility of many human beings whom we have encountered, all this and much else, not to mention the writings of many "authorities" on the subject, has concluded that all these things confirm the view of man's innate aggressiveness, a view which has been held for at least two thousand years in the Western world. But upon investigation what do we find?

We find that the aggressiveness which men exhibit is not something that is born within them, but is on the contrary something which men acquire as a consequence of being mishandled as human beings during the critical years of their early development. The evidence is all against the assumption that human beings are born aggressive. It is all in favor of the demonstrable fact that human beings are taught to be aggressive by having their need for love frustrated—indeed, that aggression *is* love—love frustrated. Let me explain what this means.

Every human being is born with a group of basic needs, so called because they are basic to the survival of the human being. Everyone is familiar with these needs, which must be satisfied if the organism is to survive. There is the need for oxygen, for food, for liquid, rest, sleep, activity, bowel and bladder elimination, avoidance of pain, and flight from danger. What we have learned about the satisfaction of those needs is that though they may be fully met physically, if during the first half-dozen years of development the satisfying is not accompanied by love, the organism is likely to suffer more or less serious consequences. The organism may suffer serious deprivations in any one or all of the basic needs, but as long as the need for love is adequately satisfied the organism will prosper, even though it may suffer more or less serious physical consequences; its psychic development will not be consequentially affected. But should the organism suffer from a lack of adequate love, then it will experience frustration. Frustration may be defined as the thwarting of expected satisfaction. The child expects to be loved; when its needs for love are not adequately satisfied it experiences frustration of the humanly most important of all the needs—the need for love—and it responds to the situation by crying out, as it were, for the love that has been withheld from it. The child resorts to behavior that is calculated to compel the love of those who have withheld it. In this aggressive behavior there is no element of hostility, of the desire to inflict injury upon the others, but simply the overpowering desire to attract their attention, their loving attention. It is only later that children learn to incorporate the desire to inflict injury into their aggressive behavior, and this they learn from the models that have been provided for them, usually by adults and not infrequently by older children. But the aggressive behavior is at first entirely free of hostile content. Aggressive behavior without hostile content is a natural reaction to the frustration of the need for love. Aggressive behavior that is hostile is learned. With the introduction of the content of hostility into aggression the frustrated child feels momentarily somewhat recompensed for being able to inflict "punishment" upon those who have directly or indirectly been responsible for its suffering the loss of love. But whether the content of the aggressiveness is hostile or non-hostile, aggressive behavior in any and every form signifies a need for attention, a need for love, on the part of the aggressor —a need for the love in the expectation of which the child was originally frustrated. Patterns of frustrated-aggressive behavior established in childhood are likely to be continued into, and compounded, in later life, so that the person becomes easily frustrated and readily reacts with feelings of hostility or aggressively hostile acts.

It is the widespread existence of such feelings and acts of aggression in the societies of the modern world that has caused almost everyone to take it for granted that such aggressive behavior must, of course, be inborn, "in the flesh." But as we cannot too often emphasize, it is precisely upon those things we tend "to take for granted" that we need, from time to time, to hang the biggest question marks; and when we have questioned the theory of innate brattishness, in the light of the scientific evidence, we find that it has not the slightest basis in truth.

Hence, in the making of the cultured man we do not need to begin with the handicapping assumption that man is born a nasty aggressive brat, and that therefore it is necessary to spend a good deal of time on teaching him to develop those internal restraints that will enable him to control that brattishness.

On the other hand, the evidence points very strongly to the fact that human nature is on our side, that not only is it probable that there is not an iota of innate hostile aggressiveness in human beings, but that they are born with a vitally more positive equipment of needs that are powerfully oriented toward growth and development in terms of love.* For the cultured man it is especially important that he fully understand the meaning of these words, for there have been many so-called cultured men who have not, and the consequences for the world have often been serious because of their failure in this respect. The fact is that it is only too easy to overconcentrate on the intellectual aspect of life to the exclusion of virtually every other, just as easy as it is to live like an automaton instead of living one's own life as a thoughtful and principled person. The overintellectualized person may become more or less completely detached not only from the emotional aspects of his own nature, but also in respect to all other things. Such persons may know and use all the appropriate words, but the music, so to speak, in them is wanting. They know the labels, and can, as it were, readily provide a chemical analysis of the paper as well as a spectrographic analysis of the ink with which the words are printed, and they can give you a logical and semantic analysis of the meaning of the words, but the one thing in which they seem to have no interest is the human significance of what is written on the label. These are the atom-bomb makers of the world, who with a hand-washing indifference to the consequences of their intellectual activities may yet succeed in destroying all life upon this planet. But not all intellectuals are like that, and some who were have by the recent course of events recovered

* For a discussion of the evidence in some detail see Ashley Montagu, *The Direction of Human Development,* Harper & Bros., New York, 1955.

themselves to a semblance of effective humanity, for, as one of them remarked after the atom bomb, they had known sin. One *is* sometimes inclined to think that it was more than a casual speculation on Jefferson's part that the other planets use this one as a lunatic asylum! Why, indeed, should cleverness so often be incompatible with goodness? It was Frédéric Amiel who, in his *Journal,* pointed out "the malady of the very cultivated" as a certain moral indifference. "Their refinement consists in their ceasing to have a heart. They remove themselves in this way from true humanity and approach the diabolic. What was it that Mephistopheles lacked? Not wit, surely, but goodness . . ."

In this connection one thinks of the long gray shadow cast by a favorite of our time, the *specialist*—the man who knows more and more about less and less, the narrow technician who as he progresses in his specialty retrogresses in his understanding of everything else. His general knowledge grows in inverse proportion to the growth of his special knowledge. As he grows more expert in his special bit of information the specialist tends to decline in his competence as a human being. In a world in which the technologist is as highly valued as our own, the danger to us all of becoming technologized out of existence is great. Humanity must protect itself from the technologists, and do everything in its power to protect the technologists from themselves. Those who are responsible for our institutes of technology are not unaware of the problem, and several such institutes have sought to remedy the defects of the technologically educated student by exposing him to courses in the humanities. This is a step in the right direction, but it arrives somewhat late in the educational experience of the student. The culture of man begins at birth and cannot be postponed until he gets to college. Indeed, it is the first half-dozen years of a human being's life that are the most important for his growth and development as a humane being. These are the foundation years. These are the years during which the fundamental habits and attitudes of mind are set, and upon the foundations and within the matrix of which all that one subsequently learns is built. Of course such habits and attitudes can later be changed or modified, but it is not easy; only too often, whatever changes are subsequently made, the fundamental pattern of personality remains. The changes, if any, are merely superimposed upon that earlier developed pattern.

The dangers both of overintellectualism and underintellectualism, as of so many other errors in the development of the human being, are best avoided in the foundation years—the first six years. Hence, the importance of understanding as fully as possible the meaning of these years.

First and foremost, as I have already said, what we need to understand is that those years are on our side, that the most important requirement for development of the organism from birth onward is love.

What is love? It is the most important thing in the world. Far more important, for example, than the understanding of the particles of the nucleus of the atom. Love is the demonstratively active involvement in the welfare of another in such manner that one not only contributes to the survival of the other, but does so in a creatively enlarging manner, in a manner calculated to stimulate the potentialities of the other so that they may develop to their optimum capacity. It is to communicate to the other that one is profoundly interested in him, that one is there to offer him all the supports and stimulations he requires for the realization of his potentialities for being a person able to relate himself to others in a creatively enlarging manner, who gives the psychological support and sustenance the other requires, to nourish and enable him to grow not only in his potentialities for being a harmonic human being but also to train him in the development of those inner controls that will make all external ones unnecessary. In brief, to love means to communicate to the other that you are all for him, that you will never fail him or let him down when he needs you, but that you will always be standing by with all the necessary encouragements. It is something one can communicate to another only if one has it.

What the newborn, the infant, the child, and the adolescent require most of all for their healthy growth and development is love. The child develops in its own capacities for love by being loved. Love is not only the most important of all the stimulations toward growth and development of its capacities for love, but also in the growth and development of all its capacities, physical as well as psychological. For the healthy growth and development of the human being love is the most indispensable of necessities. Without the stimulus of love the organism cannot develop properly. The child that has not been adequately loved during the first half-dozen years of its life will be most seriously affected in that capacity which is of such great importance for human beings, namely, the capacity to relate oneself in a warm and engaging manner toward others. The child that has not been adequately loved is likely to grow up trained in an incapacity to love others. He is the "cold fish" whose world is one-dimensional, arid, and virtually completely free of all emotional relationships or tenderness.

Such persons may be completely intellectual or completely unintellectual or a mixture of both, but their one characteristic is the lack of the ability to love. The need for love is overpowering in individuals of this kind, but since they have only the vaguest ideas of what love is they often seek it in the most curious of ways. They frequently make their way into positions of power, by acquiring either money or status. By such means they expect they can command the attention they feel so much in need of. These persons may become great political forces, business tycoons, criminals, ambition-driven seekers after fame, and the like. In the course of their activities they are often capable of working untold harm upon their fellow men. When invested with uncontrolled power they become the Attilas, the Napoleons, the Hitlers, and in lesser degree the Bilbos and the Joseph McCarthys, of this world. On less public stages they play their roles as destructively as they are able. Some manage to live out their lives more damagingly to themselves than to others, and some even manage to leave the world, through their works, in some respects richer than they found it, even though in the course of their activities they work much havoc upon the lives of others. Perhaps the majority of sufferers from a lack-love conditioning in childhood are of the kind who succeed mostly in damaging themselves.

Altogether the damage and the loss to the individual and to humanity of inadequate training in the capacity to love is incalculable. It is for this reason that in any consideration of man it is so important to understand why it is that love must play so fundamental a role in his development as a healthy human being and especially as a cultured man.

So much, then, by way of orienting ourselves on the American scene in relation to the cultured man. We may now proceed to a discussion of the marks of the cultured man.

The Marks of the Cultured Man

The principal mark of the cultured man is not so much knowledge as his attitude of mind in relating his knowledge to the world of experience. It is a common error to equate knowledge with culture, just as education is usually falsely identified with culture—they are not the same things. Knowledge and education are indispensable parts of the cultured man's equipment, but in themselves they do not confer the grace of culture. Television quiz programs have, in recent times, graphically presented to our senses abundant examples of this truth. To know the answers to questions on points of fact may be highly profitable on quiz programs, but not nearly as valuable in terms of the experience of life as being immediately able to feel as one ought and to act as one should in the situations that arise. In the situations of daily life it is not so much factual answers that are required of us as humane acts. Such acts are not usually a function of memory, of the facts we can recall, but they are, rather, an expression of feeling—or at least, they seem to be so. The truth is that such feelings are compounded of acts which are in part the result of training both in emotion and reason, and in part the result, probably, of the organization of other innate tendencies which we as yet scarcely understand, such, for example, as those aesthetic impulses which must be held accountable for the strange necessity of beauty, and those other impulses of sympathy with suffering, and the like.

It would be going beyond the evidence to say that there is nothing instinctive about culture, but so far as we know it is something that human beings have to learn. Certainly human beings are born with a capacity for culture, but unless they receive training in it they do not become cultured. What, then, is culture?

A dictionary definition of culture might read "the training, development, and refinement of mind, tastes, and manners." Observe that the emphasis here is again on "training." But the operative word is "refinement." By refinement is meant the state of delicacy and elegance, of polish, and of freedom from coarseness and vulgarity in character, thought, feelings, speech, and manners.

One of the best definitions of culture I know is Alfred North Whitehead's: "Culture is activity of thought, and receptiveness to beauty and humane feeling." The activity of thought not only of one's self but an interest in that of others, and the humane feeling not only of others but of one's self. The receptiveness to beauty and humane feeling from without, and the capacity for beauty and humane feeling within and as it stems from oneself, these are necessary and essential traits of the cultured man, but alone they are not enough to make a cultured man; the other necessary condition that must be fulfilled is "activity of thought." By "activity of thought" is to be understood several things. The first of these is that the cultured man is characterized by a mind that is *actively interested*; it is a mind that latches on to things, that with some intensity is constantly attentive, because it is very much alive and excited by the nature of things and curious as to their being, because the actively thinking mind constantly wants to know. Curiosity is one of the permanent and certain characteristics of a vigorous mind.

The second aspect of "activity of thought" is the ability to use one's mind as a finely analytic tool, a tool critically capable of probing the evidence and arriving at sound conclusions, sound in terms not alone of a positive or a negative, "Yes" or "No," but also of "I don't know," and of suspended judgment. It was Cardinal Newman who wrote that "A liberal education is the education which gives a man a clear, conscious view of his own opinions and judgment, a truth in developing them, an eloquence in expressing them, and a force in urging them. It teaches him to see things as they are, go right to the point, to disentangle a skein of thought, to detect what is sophistical, and to discard what is irrelevant. It prepares him to fill any post with credit and to master any subject with facility." Well, that is quite an order, but it *is* something to aim for.

Sound thinking contributes to sound health both of mind and body in the individual, and thus contributes to the welfare of society. Indeed, there is good evidence that thinking, the use of the mind, is as necessary an exercise for the mind's health as is the exercise of the muscles of the legs for walking. And just as one has to learn to walk, so, too, one has to learn to think. It is thought, Pascal said, that makes the greatness of man.

All these things the cultured man realizes. The humanely oriented mind, sensitive to beauty and the problems of being human, refined in thought, in speech, and in manner, finely and dispassionately able to examine, analyze, and evaluate whatever impinges upon it: this is the mind of the cultured man. Without the ability to think soundly a man cannot be called truly cultured. Nor could he be so called without those characteristically humane and aesthetic sensibilities which, together with the capacity to think soundly, render him a cultured man. In brief, each of these traits, the humane mind, the sensitiveness to beauty, an intense interest and curiosity, and an ability to think soundly, are the necessary conditions, no one of which minus the presence of the others is sufficient to make a cultured man; but which necessary conditions, occurring together in an individual, constitute the sufficient conditions minimally requisite to make a cultured man. Summed up, the two outstanding qualities of the cultured man are humanity and reason, or, as Jonathan Swift characterized them in his *Battle of the Books,* "sweetness and light."

It is one of the marks of the cultured man that he presents a unity; he is not a humane man *and* a thinking man, but his humanity and his reason seem to be all of a piece, and so much of a piece that it seems impossible to separate the one from the other—so that his humanity never overcomes his reason, nor does his reason ever replace his humanity, but both work in harmony and balance together. I hope I shall not be understood as saying that there have ever been or that there will ever be many human beings who, all their lives, have achieved a perfect balance between their feelings of humanity and their reason. There have undoubtedly been some, and there will undoubtedly be more, but what I am saying is that it is possible to approximate such a balance more or less, and that it should be the principal and the highest function of a society to enable every one of its citizens to achieve this balance with whatever competence is possible for them.

In considering the marks of the cultured man it is to be understood that, as in all other respects, no two individuals are alike and that variability is the rule. So that it is to be expected that there would be fairly considerable variation among human beings for cultural development. Some would undoubtedly be able to advance further than others. We must not, therefore, expect that all men by virtue of cultural development in the sense in which we are here discussing it will become equal in intelligence, culture, or any other traits. They will certainly not become equal in these respects. But what would be likely to happen is that as a consequence of the stimulation of their potentialities for cultural development, in keeping with their individual rates of development and capacity for learning, many human beings would be able to achieve a degree of cultural development that would otherwise have been impossible for them. This is an end toward which we can all engage ourselves.

And this is yet another mark of the cultured man: that he is profoundly interested in bringing the benefits of culture to all his fellow men regardless of their physical or psychological characteristics. It is a mark of the cultured man that he is aware of the fact that equality is an ethical and not a biological principle. What a person's physical or innate psychological potentialities may be has nothing whatever to do with the fact that as a human being he has every right to all the privileges and opportunities that a human being by his birthright requires, namely, the nurture and stimulation of his potentialities for being a cultured human being—no matter how broad or how narrow the limit of those potentialities may be. This, in fact, is the meaning, the original meaning, of the word "education"—as we have already seen.

But a distinction must be made between the educated man and the cultured man. It is unfortunate that such a distinction should at all be possible, but in view of the realities of the situation it is a very necessary one to make, for education has become something far removed from culture. A cultured man is an educated man, but an educated man is not necessarily a cultured man. A man who has graduated from a university is generally agreed to belong to the class of educated men—although that proposition is becoming increasingly doubtful. I think it will be generally agreed that most university graduates of our own time are not cultured men in our understanding of the term. They are *instructed* men—a very different thing.

What passes for education in the Western world today is more accurately described as instruction. The student studies subjects. Almost always the different subjects are taught as if they were unrelated to each other, and as if the principal immediate purpose of learning them was to pass examinations and take a degree. Instead of interrelating every subject with the others into a total functioning whole in the interest of the cultural development of the person in relation to his fellows, education is fragmented and anatomized. For the most part modern education prepares men to live better with machines than with themselves or with other human beings.

One of the results of this kind of education is that it tends to reverse the true order of things, as when men become enslaved by the machines that were originally created to serve them. Thus, there are many among us who appear to be working very hard to support automobiles, television sets, and other such gadgets, in the belief that they are necessary to our existence and because they give us pleasure, without realizing that we are, in fact, no longer in command of them but that they are in command of us. In this way an "educated" populace learns to accept the erosion of its freedoms under the spurious guise of advances in the standard of living. Our education in the art of making ourselves physically comfortable by multiplying the effective distractions ill prepares us for leading a healthy existence—which is what genuine education should help us to do. "Education," as Whitehead put it, should be "the guidance of the individual towards a comprehension of the art of life . . . Each individual embodies an adventure of existence. The art of life is the guidance of this adventure."

At the threshold of the Age of Automation we are about to enter upon the broad expanse of the Age of Leisure. At the time of the Declaration of Independence the average American worked almost ninety hours a week. By the end of the Civil War that stretch was reduced to about seventy hours. In 1900 sixty hours was the average working week. Less than thirty years later it was down to fifty hours a week. And in a similar period since, that is, by 1955 another ten hours had been lopped off the working week to arrive at the standard forty-hour week of the present, with week-ends completely free. Today there is serious talk of a four-day working week, and even a three-day working week; and there can be little doubt that such reductions, and even greater ones, will be achieved in a relatively short time. Millions of Americans will find themselves with a great deal of time on their hands, and squarely faced with the problem of turning it into leisure as opposed to ennui, idleness, or worse. What is leisure? Leisure is free and unoccupied time with which the person may do precisely as he pleases. But it is a great deal more. Leisure is the most challenging responsibility that a man can be offered, for it is when he is free to do what he pleases that he is really called upon to exhibit the quality of his internal resources.

It was the view of Aristotle that "the aim of education is the wise use of leisure." For an aristocrat, as Aristotle was, that was an excellent definition, but for those who are not likely to be overburdened with leisure, education should be a great deal more than that, although certainly one of the functions of education should be to prepare the individual in such manner that he be able to use his leisure wisely. It is never too late to learn, but it is much harder later than earlier. It will be much easier to teach men the wise use of leisure early in life than late. And it is important that we begin doing so immediately, for before we are aware of it the Age of Leisure will be upon us. Received by a people ready to make the best of it, this benison can serve greatly to increase our happiness. Visited, however, upon a people that is not really prepared for it, there is a real danger that many of its citizens may make the worst of it

> . . . and squander time profusely there
> On vulgar arts beneath our care.

It has recently been remarked by Dr. William Russell, President Emeritus of Teachers College, Columbia University, that "Too much leisure with too much money has been the dread of societies across the ages. That is when nations cave in from within. That is when they fall." Too much of a good thing is, of course, never any good, and since work is a necessity of existence, an unhealthy disproportion of one in relation to the other is likely to have undesirable consequences. As every man who has lived long enough to learn it knows, the principal, the most enduring, and the most reliable source of happiness is work. It was John Stuart Mill who wrote that happiness is not something one finds by seeking, but something that comes by the way, usually as a by-product of work. Ruskin added, "When men are rightly occupied, their amusement grows out of their work." Which is exactly what George Eliot made Adam Bede say in her novel of that name, "There's nothing but what's bearable as long as a man can work . . . and the best o' working is, it gives you a grip hold o' things outside your own lot." And, finally, it was Voltaire who wrote, "Labor preserves us from three great evils— weariness, vice, and want." We require no more dramatic testimony to its value than the well-known decay which afflicts men who believe that they can find happiness by retiring from work. Even the playboy who does no work in the usual sense works at being a playboy, otherwise he, too, would wither on the vine.

One must be trained in the art of being a human being in a world so beautiful, so various, and so challenging as this in order to be able to utilize one's leisure fruitfully. The man who does not know how to make the best use of his leisure is likely to find it tiresome—idleness is a most fatiguing disorder, and one that can readily become endemic among a people unprepared for the intelligent use of leisure. Studies of the manner in which Americans spend their leisure indicate that 60 to 80 per cent of that leisure is spent in and around the home, with most of the time going to the watching of television. The number of homes equipped with television is staggering. Thirty-nine million out of the forty-six million American homes have at least one television set in them. In Boston it is said that there are more television sets than bathtubs. The average viewing time devoted by the American family to television amounts to five and a half hours a day. Do-it-yourself activities are a recent development as are non-spectator do-it-yourself sports, at least on the scale in which they are now indulged. At the present time, it is said, not more than 20 per cent of

Americans are reading a book, compared with 55 per cent of the English. However, we have already surmised that Americans are probably reading more magazines.

Some of the devices by which contemporary Americans are attempting to distract themselves, such for example as the do-it-yourself craze, are by no means as bad as some of our pundits are inclined to have us believe, but there can be no doubt that, by and large, the communications industry upon which the contemporary American relies to such a great extent for his entertainment serves not only to debase his taste but also to reduce his experience as a human being. By "communications industry" I mean every form of medium through which information is conveyed to the individual; this includes newspapers, magazines, books, advertising, radio, television, and the like.

The effect of the kind of homogenized pabulum served up by these unacknowledged educators, to a public whose taste has been carefully nurtured (and debased) upon a steady diet of it, constitutes an impoverishment of the quality and a narrowing of the range of humane experience. Instead of developing as an actively thoughtful, humanely interested, and actively participating critic and appreciator of his culture, he becomes a mere passive receptacle, a victim of the inexcusable vulgarities of the purveyors of popular distraction and the manipulations of "the hidden persuaders." Indeed, distraction from the stress of living has become a major industry. Under such conditions values become rapidly debased, and where debased values become the currency of the realm they are reckoned at the prevailing rate of exchange. Gresham's Law, again: the bad currency restricts the availability of the good. This is about where we stand today in the relation of education to culture. Our task, clearly, should be to work toward making education mean what culture is.

Most of us, it is to be feared, are not prepared for the coming advent of leisure. *Now* would be a good time to start thinking about the best ways by which we could adequately prepare ourselves for the coming changes. The possibilities for the perfection and enrichment of human life through the judicious use of leisure are virtually unlimited. I believe that were we to attempt to achieve an approximation to the ideal of the cultured man we would be more than adequately prepared to meet the problems of the Age of Leisure.

Not only is the wise use of leisure a mark of the cultured man, but the value he places upon a certain amount of privacy in the use of it is another, for the cultured man is a contemplative man, one who has learned the proper balance between the active and the contemplative life. Upon occasion, and those occasions may be more than once during each day, he will seek to be alone with himself and his thoughts. Every man, as well as every woman, should have a room of his own to which he may retire in complete privacy, there to contemplate in the serenity of himself and his privacy those matters he wishes to examine and ponder. In our own time privacy is not only difficult to achieve, but for most people has become superannuated and even frightening because it is identified with that one state that almost everyone is anxious to avoid, namely, loneliness.

In recent years the increasing isolation of the individual and the fragmentation of social relationships in an age of anxiety have become matters of frequent comment. In a valuable book published in 1941, *Escape From Freedom,* Erich Fromm pointed out that modern society affects man simultaneously in two distinct, yet related, ways. Man becomes more independent, self-reliant, and critical, and he becomes more isolated, alone, and afraid. Man flees from freedom because freedom has thrown him upon his own resources, to sink or swim by his own efforts—and man in the free Western world has shown that he would rather be supported and maintained in his efforts by his fellow men than be left to his own devices. I am going to suggest that man's flight from this kind of anxious freedom serves to foster the conditions that minister to the shrinkage of his personality and the ever-growing invasion of his privacy.

In T. S. Eliot's *The Cocktail Party,* one of the characters remarks:

> . . . Do you know—
> It no longer seems worth while to *speak* to anyone! . . .
> No . . . it isn't that I *want* to be alone,
> But that everyone's alone—or so it seems to me.

They make noises, and think they are talking to each other,
They make faces, and think they understand each other.
And I'm sure they don't . . .

The fear of being "desocialized," of being alone, is a healthy
fear, for the biosocial nature of man is directed toward *relatedness*
as the process of living. To be or feel alone is both unnatural and
unhealthy. In a society in which so many of its members feel
lonely, cut off from their fellows, any socially sanctioned means
that tends to reduce this feeling is likely to be perfervidly embraced. Hence, the success of the telephone, then the movies, the
radio, and finally television. For all these are means of communication, and communication is the essence of the social process.
Furthermore, if you can have the means of communication on
your own terms by simply picking up the receiver, paying your
admission, or turning a knob, you can enjoy a much wider range
of experience than would ever be possible in face-to-face relationships with your neighbors.

Well might the New Caliban remark:

> You taught me language,
> And my profit on it is
> I know how to read the TV news.

But he doesn't make any such remark. He's glad of his TV schedule,
his television, his radio, and his telephone; they all minister
to his sense of security, and they provide him with a one-way
means of communication that he can turn on and off at will—he'd
rather not turn it off, but fatigue accumulates and one must sleep.

Everyone in the communications industry is out to please the
viewer, the much sought-after consumer and final arbiter of what
he shall consume. So far there is no record of any viewer ever
having been lethally affected by that form of consumption known
as TV. But there is reason to believe that the communicators have
sometimes had the feeling that their sending stations were dis-
charging into a mass of moribund nonconductors; this has been
the case, mostly, when good programs were involved. On the
whole the communicators manage to operate on the same wave
lengths as the communicatees, and all is—communicationally
speaking—well. The communicatee is really a receiver, but that

is the name usually given to the instrument that picks up the physical waves which the recipient then converts into his own coin of the realm—depending upon the state of his treasury. So we had better call the recipient by his proper name, namely, "recipient." To call him a "receiver" might suggest that he is nothing more than a passive mechanical instrument, or even that he was a receiver in bankruptcy, with the hint that somewhere possibly we are dealing with a bankruptcy of the spirit or even of ideas—to all of which, of course, a loud "Perish the thought" might be in order. It depends upon the point of view.

Man is socially the most highly developed of all creatures. Interaction with other human beings is an environmental necessity to him. No man can survive as an island entire of himself. No man wants to be an island. But every human being wants and needs to replenish his resources for being social by having a room of his own—as it were, a sanctuary—to which he may retire, and in which he can be alone with himself, undisturbed by the rumors and alarums of the outside world.

The right to be alone is at least as important as the right to be with others. The delights of occasional periods of solitude have often been celebrated, but by none more notably than the Swiss philosopher Zimmermann, in his famous but now forgotten book *On Solitude,* written toward the end of the eighteenth century. Indeed, it is since the end of the eighteenth century that solitude, or what we should in our own day call privacy, has become increasingly more difficult of achievement. By privacy we mean freedom from social contact and observation when these are not desired.

Toward the end of the eighteenth century man in the Western world, through painful and long-enduring struggle, through hard-earned thought and bloody battles, had won through to the conception of the sacredness of the individual and his right to "life, liberty, and the pursuit of happiness." Man, for the first time, had the vision of a realizable future in which the rights to which men were equally heir would be available in the form of the necessary opportunities to realize their potentialities, their individuality, according to the kingdom that was within them.

In the Western world this belief was enshrined in the doctrine of progress—that heady wine of the past which was so generously poured out as a libation to the future. Man, henceforth, could only go "onward and upward." Expanding freedoms, the franchise, education for all—these were all to contribute to the further development of the individual, for surely a society that made it possible to pursue the right to "life, liberty, and happiness" could not lead to anything other than ever-enlarging orders of freedom for the individual?

To be free of bondage or restraint, to live under a government based on the consent of the citizens, these are basic among all freedoms, because they do, indeed, permit the maximization of the individual's capacity for living. And this is the reason why a democracy is from every possible humane point of view the best form of government for human beings. Providing, as it does, the maximum possibilities for freedom and order, it also provides for the possibility of error and the correction of error.

What so many human beings in the modern world have failed to understand is that freedom is the greatest of all trusts, that it is a great responsibility, not the least important part of which is our responsibility to our fellow men, that freedom does not consist, as Lord Acton pointed out, in the liberty to do what we like, but in the right to be able to do what we ought. Surely, freedom consists in the right to discover what we *ought* to do and in the liberty to be able to do it. All this is to say that freedom does not consist in the right to do anything we please, but in the right to discover those things that we ought to do that would please us because they are the right and the healthiest things to do. Freedom, as Erich Fromm has said, not in the sense of the ability to make arbitrary choices and not freedom from necessity, but freedom to realize what one potentially is, to fulfill the true nature of man according to the laws of his existence.

I am going to suggest that the increasing loss of privacy from which Western man is suffering, particularly in America, serves, among other things, to reduce rather than to increase the chances of the individual being able to discover what those things are that are right and healthy for him, as a human being, to do. And that from this fact spring certain serious psychological consequences.

A genuinely healthy society holds together by the respect which men give to men, by the recognition of the biosocial needs of man for relatedness, and the making available of the means by which that relatedness can be achieved. Such a society, instead of providing men with instruments that make them less than themselves, affords them the means of becoming instruments of something greater than themselves. In spite of the superficial appearances our society lamentably fails to afford such opportunities to the majority of individuals. We teach the three R's, but we teach them as techniques for the achievement of limited objectives. Our educational attitudes are not directed toward "drawing out" but toward "pumping in." Our value system is a conflicting one, in which the worship of God is taught on the one hand and of Mammon on the other. The pursuit of life in reality reduces itself to the pursuit of a living; liberty assumes the form of economic liberty, and happiness resolves itself into getting whatever one can out of life by whatever means one can. In the United States we have achieved the highest standard of living in the world—but it is seldom, if ever, added, at the cost of the highest number of ulcers, mental breakdowns, homicides, violent crimes, juvenile delinquency, alcoholic, and drug addiction rates in the entire world. Can it be that something is somewhere wrong? That there are causes for all this breakdown, death, and destruction of human beings—that these causes are traceable ones?

The question is raised here because in order to understand the conditions that have led to the increasing invasion of our privacy, it is desirable to understand how it has come about that man has become so fragmented, so isolated, and so insecure—for that invasion has been a welcomed one.

It will not for some time be possible to say again, as Byron did a century and a half ago, that

> Society is now one polished horde
> Formed of two tribes, the *bores* and the *bored*.

For the polish has long been transferred from our surfaces to our domestic juggernauts, our chrome-plated amenities and our automobiles; it is they that give us "prestige," and the possibilities of boredom have been reduced to the vanishing point. The world is now amused.

Today, anyone who chooses can cause your phone to ring and invade your privacy whether you like it or not. Whether you like it or not anyone who chooses to do so can know everything—both true and false—that it is possible to know about you, in fact, more than you know about yourself. In this our government has set the example, for the Federal Bureau of Investigation has millions of such records on file in Washington. The files of the Congressional Committee on Un-American Activities are open to anyone who cares to use them. Then there are the manpower lists, the biographical reference works, specialty lists, telephone books, Black Books, Red Books, Who Knows What books, the scandal-mongering yellow press, private eyes, public eyes, FBI's, wire-tapping, Dun and Bradstreet ratings, TV and radio brainwashing, "the hidden persuaders," subliminal conditioning, and so on. Privacy has gone with the waves. "Big Brother" of George Orwell's powerful and prophetic novel, *Nineteen Eighty-Four*, is already watching you. A life of one's own is already well-nigh impossible, and the paradox is observed that, in a world in which the private life of the individual daily shrinks, and his social life with his fellow human beings is reduced to the narrowest dimensions, his life should become increasingly more public. Western Man has become the solitary individual in the lonely crowd.

Small-town gossip was at one time the only medium through which such publicity could be achieved—or rather thrust upon one. But that was a very primitive medium compared with the devices at our disposal in the modern age. Today we have gossip sheets with huge circulations which specialize in the exposure of the most intimate details of the individual's life—whether such details are true or false matters not one bit. Duly elected members of the Congress use their positions for political and private purposes to institute public Congressional inquisitions during which those whose reputations they wish to destroy are nakedly exposed to the public gaze. If the government sets the example for such destructive indecencies, it is not surprising that innumerable individuals have set themselves up in everything ranging from one-man vigilante committees to group organizations dedicated to the investigation of the private life of any and every individual they choose to pillory. These individuals and organizations are more than willing, they are anxious, to supply anyone who asks for it with such information. And if it isn't asked for, they will supply it whenever an opportunity arises. As a consequence of such publicity many persons have been deprived of the right to earn a living.

It has even been suggested that this kind of desecration of man's privacy be put on a "scientific" basis. Dr. W. H. Sheldon, for example, in a book entitled *Varieties of Delinquent Youth* (Harper & Bros., New York, 1949), has suggested that since "we have begun to forget *who are* the biologically best" people, this difficulty could be overcome "if standardized photographic records of even a few hundred thousands of a well-sampled population were to be kept for so short a time as half a dozen generations, together with biographical summaries embracing the physiological, psychiatric, and social adventures of this sample population . . ." And he goes on to suggest that at a very small cost "we could keep central files of standardized photographs of the entire population."

And, of course, these photographs will be in the nude. Thus will the last of our privacies be exposed. Our warts and our wrinkles, not to mention more private parts of our anatomy, would become the vicarious property of the public custodian. The possibilities are very interesting.

Since we are now in the Cinderella-land of photography, it should be mentioned that telephoto lenses are now available that can pick up scenes over great distances, and that it is now possible to do this with television and sound and other recording devices. Such devices have already been used by crime investigators and the military. Their application to civilian life is already creeping in.

In addition to the one-way glass screens through which one can be observed without being aware of it, there are schools in the United States today in which the principal can listen in on the classroom, and hospitals in which the nurses can listen in on the patient. Television for similar purposes is just around the corner. Here, too, the possibilities are very interesting.

In the realm of sound or rather *noise* it must be said that the offenses committed this way in the United States are unparalleled for sheer barbarism anywhere else in the world. Many years ago that disgruntled philosopher Schopenhauer wrote an essay "On

Noise." It is many years since I read it, but I vividly recall how scorching Schopenhauer was on the sudden sharp brain-stopping thought-killing explosive cracking of the whips of coachmen and others. What Schopenhauer would have had to say on the din and discord created by the automobile horns of today, the noises of starting and gear-shifting, the backfiring of trucks and buses, and the whistling and groaning of brakes—all to the accompaniment of a perfusion of essence of gasoline exhaust fumes—can only be surmised.

Public noises, sanctioned and created by public agencies, are among the most barbarous and stupid of destroyers of the individual's inalienable right to quietude. At all times of the day and night their licensed discords are encouraged to break in on one. Consider the piercing shrieks that suddenly fracture the smog-laden air when the police in their cars are bent on getting somewhere in a hurry. The principal function of the sirens, when the police are hurrying to the scene of a crime, often seems to be to announce their impending arrival to the criminals so that the latter may make a leisurely getaway. To these iniquities of the police-car sirens add those of ambulances, rescue squads, and the clanging of fire-engine bells (the least offensive of the noises).

How thick-skinned must one grow in order not to understand that the sudden noise of sirens constitutes a nerve-racking violation of one's privacy, and a damaging assault upon one's nervous system? For nothing is more effective than such noises in producing an unpleasant jumpiness of the nervous system. It is not without significance that in no other civilized land in the world does one encounter such noisome sirens as those of the police cars in the United States. How far gone must one be not to know that the last thing on earth a sick or injured person wants to hear while he is being driven to a hospital is the clanging signal or siren of the ambulance; this only serves to disturb him and contribute to his anxiety—as well as to that of everyone else. Surely, some other means could be devised that would enable such vehicles to gain a speedy right of way—if only by the adoption of more pleasant sounds or signals?

In many towns it is no longer possible to ride in a taxicab without the exacerbating accompaniment of the radio-transmitted directions of the central dispatcher. The cab-driver keeps the din going not only because he has to, but, apparently, because it helps to alleviate his loneliness.

Another iniquitous intrusion is the continuous blasting from automobile horns that wedding caravans feel obliged to perpetrate. Funeral processions indicate their nature by turning on their automobile headlights. Could not the too ebullient friends of the newly wedded be induced to settle for something as civilized?

Urbanites who think to escape these impertinences of noise by moving to the country may find that factory whistles or sirens or both can be uncomfortably annoying, and what is perhaps even more hard to bear, every so often one will be awakened from sleep by the community fire siren, which whines, and moans, and groans until the firemen have appeared—and all sleep has vanished. Effective signals under such conditions are highly necessary, but, again, surely some less barbarous means to summon firemen could be devised? It is done in other parts of the world.

Ah, public-address systems! These are instruments of torture which are at the disposal of anyone who has anything from moth-eaten ratskins to political self-aggrandizement to peddle. Wherever you may be your eardrums may suddenly be assaulted by the inescapable abomination issuing from a mobile public-address unit. Seated in your own home your privacy may be similarly blasted by the outbreak of obstreperousness issuing from such a mobile unit.

When, recently, a well-known railroad attempted to capture its customers as an unconsulted audience for public advertising, the revolt among some of the travelers, led by the late Harold Ross of *The New Yorker,* successfully put the quietus on that profane scheme. But elsewhere, in many parts of the country, the public-address system has successfully established itself in the interest of advertising.

Thus, in whatever environment one may be, the opportunity of being quietly with oneself is inexorably diminishing, for there is no longer any time of the day during which one cannot be broken in on by the uninvited gate-crashers of the sound barrier without so much as a by-your-leave.

In addition to the varieties of noise another widespread technique, developed within the last hundred years for the invasion of privacy, is advertising. Advertising in its proper place is undoubtedly a desirable means of making people acquainted with what they might otherwise fail to know. But when I want to contemplate the beauties of the land I would prefer that contemplation to be uninterrupted by the impertinence of the huckster's misshapen and misplaced art, which like some pathological sequestrum too often suggests that it would be better for not being at all. Certainly, there are some landscapes that are so dreary that they are lent greater interest by almost any kind of hoarding; there can be no criticism here. But where the natural beauty of the land is picturesque enough, we can dispense with the dubious embellishments of the advertisers. Increasingly, however, as one travels about the country one has occasion to observe that no longer is it true that "every prospect pleases," but that it is more than ever true that this is so because "only man is vile." No other creature defaces its natural habitat with such unnatural excrescences as does man. Perhaps we shall some day live to see the whole of nature taken over by the advertising fraternity. The sea alone, I believe, has thus far resisted their efforts—but it is only a matter of time before they will conquer even that element. Skywriting, public addresses from the sky, advertising blimps and planes are no longer novelties. Just think of the advertising possibilities inherent in artificial satellites!

But for the time being let us keep to the earth and the advertisers. One of the most insidious forms the erosion of privacy takes is mail advertising. I am not for a moment suggesting that large numbers of individuals do not like receiving advertising in their mail. On the contrary, it is clear that innumerable persons do enjoy receiving this kind of mail, especially where the other kind is likely to be somewhat thin—better a letter from a company that wants to communicate with you and wants you, earnestly, to communicate with it, than no letter at all. For the advertising people such persons become like so many puppets who can, in certain numbers, be moved in the desired direction. I will not discuss, but only refer to, the untold thousands of acres of beautiful trees that are sacrificed in order to manufacture the paper upon which the advertisers impress their blandishments. Nature and beauty may suffer, but communications must be maintained.

Those of us who are affronted by the time-wasting litter represented by so much of the advertising mail we receive are probably
in the minority, and I shall not dwell upon this kind of invasion
of their privacy, which is after all one of the minor invasions.
But I do think that one of the little-considered consequences of
mail advertising is well worth some attention, and that is the
reducing effect it has upon the reading habits of the population.
There are large numbers of people whose reading is virtually restricted to the advertising they receive through the mail. Such
readers are to be found not only among the isolated rural dwellers,
but also among many who live in the larger urban centers of this
world. What with the telephone, radio, movies, television, and
the other distractions that modern life has to offer, the reading of
the advertising mail fits comfortably into the necessity to be enter-
tained, and will do service for a good deal of the reading of other
kinds which might otherwise have been done. The contribution
thus made to the increasing spiritual illiteracy of the many is, I
believe, a factor to be reckoned with by the few.

The fact that the new advertising technique of "subliminal
conditioning" is being seriously discussed at all is something of a
reflection of the complete lack of respect for the person that
exists in so many quarters in our society, a lack of respect that has
developed at an accelerated pace in recent years. "Subliminal conditioning" is a term taken over from psychology. It has been
familiar to psychologists for forty years. What it practically means
is that anyone can be caused to respond to stimuli which are of
such low intensity that the subject is unaware of the fact that he
has been stimulated. There is talk of "subliminal conditioning"
through the media of TV and the movies. In this manner, without
in any way being consulted, it is proposed to relieve us of the
control of our minds and the right to make our own choices. Thus
inauspiciously is the era of "thought control" to be ushered in.
We can, of course, protest, and see to it that the necessary pro-
visions are made outlawing all such proposed rape of the mind. It
is, in fact, not too early to begin pressing for such unfortunately
necessary legislation.

With the toleration that is increasingly exhibited toward these
encroachments upon our privacy goes an increasing callousness to

them. We grow accustomed to the transgressions upon our being, the violations of our privacy, and the infringement of our right to be alone with ourselves whenever we choose. This is life as we know it, and the harder it grows the more hardened do we become to it. In becoming so hardened we become cut off from the best that is within ourselves and the best that we could make of ourselves and the world in which we live. We become increasingly insensitive to all those things to which we should be most sensitive—above all, to human need. In the crowded cities in which so many of us live in loneliness, we live more and more for ourselves, in environments in which the modes and opportunities for spontaneous and unreserved social participation are reduced to a minimum. The struggle for existence and the gigantism of our cities have largely served to bring this isolation about, and at the same time to produce the state of mind which invites every kind of intrusion that will serve to reduce one's isolation. It is in this way that isolation comes to be confused with privacy, and the privacy of isolation is unwanted. Since in isolation (which is lack of desired social contact) privacy is excessive, the individual is only too glad to sacrifice his privacy for less isolation.

The unsatisfied desire, the longing, for social participation leads to the fear of being alone, and the desire for occasional solitude tends to be overcome by the fear of being alone. In this manner the need for privacy may eventually be completely submerged in the overpowering need to be *with*—overpowering because it has been so inadequately satisfied by normal means. When such an annihilation of privacy is achieved man is, indeed, in danger—he is in danger of self-annihilation, of becoming a living automaton at the mercy of anyone who knows how to make him tick. In such a society one becomes grateful to "Big Brother" for assuming the task of directing the life one is no longer capable of directing oneself. In this way does the annihilation of privacy lead to the annihilation of the person, and of society; for the healthy society depends upon the ability of man to think and reflect upon what a true society is—and without the privacy to think and reflect man and society are lost.

Many men in contemporary society are very much in the state of Browning's *Paracelsus:*

> I give the fight up: let there be an end,
> A privacy, an obscure nook for me.
> I want to be forgotten even by God.

What man needs is not to be forgotten by anyone, but to be remembered as one who needs to be needed, who needs to be neighborly, who needs to be responsible to others, who needs to love and to be loved. As Denis de Rougemont has remarked in his brilliant book, *The Devil's Share,* "Without real neighborliness, you are no longer responsible for anything nor for anyone. But without the feeling of responsibility of each toward others, there is no possible civic freedom: dictatorship becomes inevitable in every society whose maxim is 'each for himself and God for all,' which is the maxim of those who do not believe in God. . . . *The sense of one's neighbor, responsibility* and *liberty* are things intimately linked, they engender one another mutually and can not long subsist without one another. And order is born of their alliance."

The return of privacy will be brought about only when the return to neighborliness has been achieved. The tragic fact is that in a society such as ours in which the individual can enjoy the vicarious society of anyone from kings to criminals, the individual is today more than ever alone. The more, as it were, the world is with us, the more lonely do we become. We live, and work, and spend, and have our being, but become more and more isolated from mankind and from nature.

Shall we ever recover our hearts? It is a question—and it is a question that can be successfully and happily answered only if each of us will do what is required—namely, to return to the fellowship of man. This is the answer to the individual's plaint:

> And how am I to face the odds
> Of man's bedevilment and God's?
> I, a stranger and afraid
> In a world I never made.

"In a world I never made." Quite. But just as the fact that we have ourselves been made by others does not absolve us from the responsibility of attempting to remake and improve ourselves, so we are responsible to the world we never made to do what we can to make it nearer what it should be. It is all very well to take the world as we find it, but it would constitute the most abject confession of failure to leave it so. The cultured man cannot take the world as a matter of course. Unlike the common man he does not pretend to a creed in which he does not believe. He offers up no smoke of incense before an empty shrine. He is not content to say that someone ought to do something about it. *He* does something about it whenever it is possible for him to do so. He is a man of action as well as a contemplative man. As a cultured man he does not subscribe to such Carlylean misconceptions as that life is an act, not a thought. For he perfectly understands that acts which are not soundly based in thought and experience are unlikely to have sound consequences. But there are pleasures of thought without action that are at least as much a part of life as the acts which stem from sound thought. In either case contemplation, meditation, in the quiet refuge of that room of one's own is a necessary requirement in the regimen of the cultured man.

It was Socrates who said that "The unexamined life is not fit for human living." A truth by which the cultured man lives, for the cultured man is an artist, an artist in humanity. His art consists, in part, in the ability and the skill with which he wields the tools of knowledge and experience in the desire to improve himself, in relation to himself, in relation to others, and in relation to the mysteries and the world in which he lives. He contemplates with continuous interest the mysteries of Nature, of Life, Death, Love, Beauty, Mind, Genius, Creation, Time, Destiny, Character, the Sexes, Religion, God, Immortality, and the like. Each of these mysteries is an exciting one, and the cultured man feels that he is indebted to these mysteries for the interest they add to his life. They are worthy of the thought he is ever ready to devote to them. He neither forgets nor ignores them. Nor does he assert that since he can do nothing about them, the best thing is to put them into "the suspense account." There is much that he *can* do about them. He can *think* about them. And think he does.

Upon each of these mysteries cultured men have come to differing conclusions as often as they have come to similar ones—often concluding that conclusions are not yet possible, and that the most appropriate attitude of mind in the face of these mysteries is neither the willingness to believe nor to disbelieve but the willingness to continue dispassionate inquiry and investigation. Certainty for the cultured man, as for the scientist, is measurable in terms of high degrees of probability. He suffers from no compulsive enslavement to destructive certainties, for he knows that absolute certainty is the right of uneducated minds and fanatics, and that the more confused the fanatic becomes the more violence does he put into his absolute certainties. Arrogance is usually in inverse proportion to erudition.

In all such matters it is not knowledge as such that marks the cultured man, but his attitude toward and the use he makes of knowledge in enlarging his own understanding and experience of life as well as that of others, for he knows that to understand is to tend to unify. Almost by definition a cultured man is one who is dissatisfied with the state of his knowledge and is aware of his limitations, and if he does not go so far as to say with Socrates, "One thing only do I know and that is that I know nothing," he cannot, in having a just estimate of his knowledge, take any but the most modest view of it. All that he knows is that human nature is infinitely perfectible and that ultimately all human knowledge— and all knowledge is human—must be brought into the service of that end, the perfection of human nature. He is, however, fully aware of the fact that one cannot know everything, and he is wise enough to know that in this life it is necessary early to determine not only what one shall know but also what one will not know, to determine not only what knowledge one will acquire but also what one will voluntarily forgo. It is obvious that in the complex cultures of the Western world there are literally thousands of bits of technical knowledge that can be safely left in the hands of the specialist and the technician and which need never impinge even upon the periphery of the experience of the cultured man.

Knowledge in itself is not an end, but a means to an end: the living of a full and humane life. Toward that end certain minimum essentials of knowledge are necessary. These are obviously reading, writing, and arithmetic, the basic tools necessary to make one's way about in the world. A basic competence in the use of these tools is indispensable, but here again it is not so much the basic competence that is important as what one has learned in the process of acquiring that competence. What we know about anything is the way we behave about it. It is important to know, but it is even more important to know what to do with what we know. It is for this reason that in teaching it is the method and not the content that is the message. I should say that there are few, if any, subjects which it were right to teach as if they were things in themselves, but that everything a human being learns during his educational years should be taught him as a vital part of the system of co-ordinates that is to form the framework of his personal culture in relation to that of the rest of the world. In short, I would say that virtually all teaching should be contextually cultural, that is to say, placed within the context of the culture, as a going concern, of which the student is a part. The process of imparting and acquiring knowledge—apart from technology—should be inseparable, should, indeed, be one and the same thing, as the process of making a cultured man.

And the process of making a cultured man does not depend upon the transmission of knowledge, but upon the manner in which that knowledge is transmitted by the teacher. The teacher who is enthusiastic about teaching is likely to imbue his teaching with an infectious enthusiasm for the art of sound thinking; he will stimulate the imagination to soar but also to remain in control; he will increase the sensibilities of his students toward the appreciation of beauty and the will to contemplatively approach the mysteries that surround and touch us; he will encourage the student to allow his imagination to play freely upon what he is learning: such a teacher will contribute toward the making of a cultured man, rather than toward the making of a technician. Such teachers are usually deeply interested in the cultural development of their students, and affectionately concerned for the welfare of human beings generally. The attitude encouraged in their classes is not one of simple listening and note-taking, but rather one of adventure, of joint exploration leading to discovery under the guidance not only of one who knows, but who knows what knowledge is for. From such a teacher, as Plato wrote, "After much converse about the matter and a life lived together, suddenly a light, as it were, is kindled in one soul by a flame that leaps to it from another, and thereafter sustains itself." And not only sustains itself, but by that light also helps to kindle the light in others. It is, indeed, in this way that the pure flame of culture serves to increase its power. Thus the good teacher is often the instrument of something greater than himself.

Knowing these things it is, therefore, a further mark of the cultured man that he holds the teacher in high respect. Whenever he thinks, he remembers those who taught him how to think. A man is educated, properly speaking, when he has developed the attitudes of the cultured man as a bearer of the continuity of civilized values.

The cultured man has a sense of humor. That is to say, not only is he able to perceive the comic (as well as the tragic) side of things, including himself, but he knows how to wear his own private crown of thorns gracefully, over one ear, as it were. Indeed, a cultured man without a sense of humor is unimaginable, for the ability to bear one's learning lightly and to enjoy every aspect of it, the ludicrous and amusing as well as the serious and instructive, is one of his outstanding qualities. A sense of humor includes very much more than the ability to see the funny side of things. It implies a certain balanced resilience, a steadiness of mental stance, a certain interior perspective. As Monckton Milnes put it, "The sense of humor is the just balance of all the faculties of man, the best security against the pride of knowledge and the conceits of the imagination, the strongest inducement to submit with a wise . . . patience to the vicissitudes of human existence."

The cultured man is free of prejudices. He does not indulge in prejudgment. He does not believe in the process of supporting emotional judgments with handy reasons. He will not make judgments on insufficient evidence, finding such practice repugnant to everything for which he stands, and he declines to accept any statement as true unless it can be verified. He does not believe that truth is determined by a show of hands. Being aware of the vagaries of the human mind he is particularly careful about checking his "facts" recollected from memory, for he is aware that memory often tends to be a process of retroactive falsification.

The sureness with which we remember often turns out to be in inverse relation to the accuracy with which we recall. The memory of things past is a *re*membrance of things past, a remembrance of things drawn, as it were, through a fine screen overlaid by later memories and experiences, and softened by time. Distance lends enchantment to the view, and time puts a glory round it. In the presence of startling opinions, of opinions based on prejudice, he takes the view that the only sound attitude is the willingness to inquire into the facts, and to share the inquiry as well as the results of it with those who have offered their opinions. The cultured man knows that the truth is more frequently ascertained by asking questions than by giving answers.

He knows that setting oneself in order is the basis for practicing good human relations. He believes that the Socratic injunction, "Know thyself," is the beginning but not the end of wisdom, knowledge of self being a necessary means toward the end of achieving wisdom. Thus, the cultured man has an understanding of the nature of human nature, its structure and dynamics, unconscious and conscious. He is fully aware of the fact that, as Oliver Goldsmith put it,

> Logicians have but ill defined
> As rational the human kind.
> Logic, they say, belongs to man,
> But let them prove it if they can.

He knows that it is neither reason nor logic that motivates the behavior of most human beings. He knows that behavior in himself as well as in others is usually the expression of a complex network of processes, not simply the result of the unconscious and the conscious mind in interaction, but of the chemistry of the body as well. He is aware of the fact that man is an animal, but with the difference that he is the *human* animal, that the human animal is driven not only by his chemistry but by a system of symbols, some of which have been relegated to the unconscious and some of which are conscious, the unconscious symbols being out of the control of the individual and the conscious ones more or less under his control. He understands that the conscious symbols are least under control when the unconscious ones are least under control, and that therefore if one is to achieve a genuine control of oneself it is necessary to be aware of and to understand these things. He knows, as that woman of genius, George Eliot, put it so long ago, "Our mental business is carried on much in the same way as that of the State: a good deal of hard work is done by agents who are not acknowledged." The contributions that depth psychology, psychoanalysis in all its schools, have made to the understanding of human nature he is particularly and critically aware of. He has a sufficient self-respect and self-reverence to take the understanding of himself with all the seriousness that it merits.

The cultured man is a man of integrity, of sound moral principle. To himself being true he cannot be false to any man. The principle of expediency is repugnant to him, and never on any account will he trade with his conscience. He is a just man, but not so just that he is unaware of human frailty. He knows that in order to be kind it is necessary to be just, but he knows also that in order to be just it is necessary to be kind, for the essence of the law is love, justice being love expressed through rational calculation.

As a good citizen the cultured man has a sense of personal responsibility for decency and justice. He knows that the real meaning of civilization is in learning to be kind, and that this involves an active responsibility for the welfare and happiness of his neighbor. Deeply concerned, as the cultured man must be, with the single thread of his own life, he knows that that thread is but one of innumerable others which go to make up the tapestry of human society. He looks upon himself as a small part of the whole. He does not regard himself as the whole and everything else as a mere part of that whole. He is co-operative, believing that mutual aid and working *with* others is a way of life infinitely superior to that of working *against* others to achieve goals; that co-operative competition is a very different thing from competitive competition, and that the greatness of a civilization is not measured by the quantity of its rich men, but by the quality of all those things that money cannot buy—those qualities, especially, that mark the cultured man.

The cultured man is an encourager of the unique in personality, the idiosyncratic and the eccentric appeal to him. He knows, for example, that any institution, whether it be a college, university, research organization, or what not, can, to an illuminating extent, have its measure taken by a tally of the number of eccentrics it has on its staff. "Show me your eccentrics." If they cannot be produced we may be reasonably certain that imagination does not play as prominent a role in the policy of the institution as it ought, and we can be further reasonably certain that its emphases are upon the orthodoxies of knowledge rather than upon the spirit of free inquiry. By an "eccentric" I don't mean a "screwball" or an "oddball" or a whimsical oddity, but one who is bold, original, imaginative, and courageous in his thought, one who is unconventional enough to strike out for himself. One who is inclined to challenge any statement that is repeated with the ritual fidelity of the true believer, and who is tolerant of fools even though he is unwilling to suffer them gladly.

The temperament of the eccentric is often such that it grates upon his colleagues, who find him difficult to take, however offbeat and interesting his mind may be. Hence, the eccentric has a difficult time maintaining a place in any institution for long. The cultured man understands but deplores this, for he knows that human beings have to be accepted as entities, with their faults as well as with their virtues, and that the eccentric calls for greater sympathetic understanding than the uneccentric.

The cultured man does not pretend to possess virtues, and he is suspicious of those who consider themselves virtuous, for he knows that virtue is often more dangerous than vice because it tends to be free of the constraints of the conscience, that the sense of virtue can be as corrupting as the sense of power. The rather unattractive qualities one would expect of a man brought up to be a philosopher king in Plato's Academy are distinctly *not* those of the cultured man.

Finally, the cultured man is a wise man. "Wisdom," Whitehead tells us, "is the way in which knowledge is held. It concerns the handling of knowledge, its selection for the determination of relevant issues, its employment to add value to our immediate experience." It is the art of life—the magnanimity of life. The discipline of the whole man. The cultured man wears his wisdom lightly, knowing full well that wisdom is not a state of being but a process of becoming, of growth, of development, and that the wise man grows from the errors he commits quite as much as from the truths which otherwise accrue to his horizons. He is willing to draw up long-dated bills on the bank of time because he believes that the only philosophically tenable position even for a pessimist in these days is optimism. This, I suppose, is what Mark Twain meant when he said that pessimism is the name that men of weak nerve give to wisdom. The wise man believes in the future because he has put his faith in humanity.

> Ah, love, let us be true
> To one another! for the world, which seems
> To lie before us like a land of dreams,
> So various, so beautiful, so new,
> Hath really neither joy, nor love, nor light,
> Nor certitude, nor peace, nor help for pain:
> And we are here as on a darkling plain
> Swept with confused alarms of struggle and flight,
> Where ignorant armies clash by night.

These words from Matthew Arnold's "Dover Beach" stir a sympathetic chord in the heart of the cultured man, for he fully understands their tragic meaning, but his view remains that, beautiful as they are and true as they must be for so many human beings, in the ultimate analysis they represent a piece of ineffectual melancholy, a confession of defeat to which the cultured man in his wisdom knows that it is stultifying to subscribe. He knows that

> He who would love his fellow men
> Must not expect too much of them.

He knows that human beings are still learning, by trial and error, how to be human, and that many fail by the way. He knows that compassionate understanding and sympathy is the approach of the humane, while blame and censoriousness is the approach of the insufficiently humane. He is a person who having had loving order made in himself makes loving order in the world. Such is the cultured man.

YOUR CULTURE QUOTIENT

THE CULTURED MAN, we have said, is not the merely knowledgeable man, but the man who is knowledgeable and uses his knowledge humanely. He is, of course, much more than that, but in the light of the preceding discussion this brief statement will do. We said that culture was essentially an attitude of mind, a humane state of receptivity toward whatever can in any way be experienced. This being so, it is clear that cultural status cannot be measured in terms of knowledge alone, but is principally measurable in terms of attitudes, plus a certain irreducible minimum of knowledge.

In the pages that follow there are fifty categories of knowledge containing thirty questions each, of which twenty-five are tests of knowledge and (usually) five are tests of attitudes. Each question is assigned a certain numerical value. By totaling the scores for each question you will arrive at a total category score. By adding the totals for all categories you will obtain your total culture score. By dividing the total culture score by fifty you will obtain your CULTURE QUOTIENT.

Before we go a step further let me make one thing clear: no one is expected to know the answers to all the questions in these fifty categories. Obviously, different individuals drawing up similar lists of questions would produce very different ones. I have endeavored to make each question representative of a large number of other questions that might have been asked in its stead. Each question has been selected in such manner that if you are able to answer it correctly the probabilities are high that you would be able to answer a large number of questions related to it, but which have remained unasked.

Since in each category the questions are separated into those testing knowledge and those testing attitudes, by totaling the answers in each group separately you may discover for yourself where, precisely, your strengths and weaknesses lie. The answers to the questions and their score value are provided at the back of the book. Here, too, are provided references to books and other sources designed to assist you not merely to fill in the lacunae in your knowledge, but also to help you in the development of sound attitudes of mind. The function of these questions is not a static one. Their function is both dynamic and constructive: to tell you more or less exactly where you stand as a cultured person, and precisely in what directions you need to move from that position. No one grows who stands still.

In scoring yourself or others, a correct answer rates a full score. An incorrect answer rates a zero. Some questions are in two parts. If your score is correct in only one part give yourself half the total score. Answers which suggest a "Yes" or "No" should be accompanied by the reasons for your answer. In the answers you will usually find full particulars given in reply to the questions asked. Where the questions refer to dates the day and month as well as the year are given in the answer. You are *not* expected to give anything more than the year. Most of the questions are so structured that answers to them are usually either correct or incorrect. But there are some exceptions; the method of scoring these questions will be indicated. There are no "trick" questions. In the scoring of attitudes the same rules apply, but there will often be the possibility of partly correct answers. In the light of the correct answer, as given in the section devoted to answers, you must judge for yourself whether your answer is half correct, one-quarter correct, or three-fourths correct, or more or less, and score yourself accordingly. In scoring yourself you must, of course, be completely honest. When in doubt as to the value of your answer consult someone else.

A good idea is to get someone else to score you first without giving you either the answers or the score, and then score yourself by the measure of the answers and scores at the back of the book. You may then compare your self-score with the independent score. If there are any differences in the scores, and there are likely to be, you might profitably discuss them with the independent scorer.

It is to be understood, of course, that the questions asked in the following pages constitute but a small sample of the thousands of additional questions that could be asked. To have any genuine value such a sampling of questions must be fully representative. I have tried to make it so. This sampling is not the precipitate of research in which many thousands of questions were tried out on as many thousands of persons, with the results then put through a statistical mill which finally yielded the key questions. Such a study would be interesting. Someone may some day make it. I have not. What I *have* done is to draw upon my own experience of the cultured men and women I have known and the kinds of attitudes of mind and knowledge that characterized them. The questions, however, represent one man's view—my own—of a cross-section of what the cultured man should know, and as reflected in the tests of his attitudes—what he should be.

The Questions

AGRICULTURE, BOTANY, AND HORTICULTURE

Answers on page 135

~·~

1. Define agriculture.
2. Define botany.
3. Define horticulture.
4. What is a truck farm?
5. Hydroponics is?
6. Do plants possess hormones?
7. The largest ranch in the United States is?
8. What is agronomy?
9. In what general area were the earliest known sickles found?
10. Name a tree that has to be artificially fertilized if it is to bear fruit.
11. Plant ecology is?
12. The bark of a tree is analogous to what organ in man?
13. What is a cotyledonous plant?
14. What is pomology?
15. What is photosynthesis?
16. What is a stamen?
17. What is a pistil?
18. Name some cultivated grasses.
19. Where is corn believed to have originated?
20. What is a corolla?
21. What is a calyx?
22. The leafless Indian pipes and pinedrops derive their food from?
23. In what region is the white potato believed to have originated?
24. True mahogany comes from?
25. What is silviculture?

26. Do you think that every community ought to have a botanical garden?
27. Do you cultivate or have you ever cultivated plants?
28. When out in the open do you take the greatest care with matches?
29. Do you think that, under the achievable conditions of agriculture, the population is likely to outrun the food supply?
30. The Sunday edition of one metropolitan newspaper requires the cutting of half a square mile of forest trees. Which would you rather have, the Sunday paper every week or the knowledge that the trees were preserved?

AMERICANA

Answers on page 137

1. What is the title of Thomas Paine's most famous work?
2. What are the two best works ever written on America?
3. What American's autograph is regarded as of highest value by collectors?
4. ASCAP is?
5. The first Woman's Rights Convention was held in what year?
6. The *Acushnet* was?
7. New Harmony was?
8. Who was Edward Livingston Youmans?
9. The first American musical composer was?
10. The *Clermont* was?
11. What was the G.A.R.?
12. Why were scientific activities so late in getting started in America?
13. What is the importance of the Fourteenth Amendment?
14. What is the Mason-Dixon Line?
15. The Volstead Act was passed in what year?
16. What is the Nineteenth Amendment?
17. What was the first real graduate school in America?

18. The first telephone was invented by?
19. The first motor-driven plane flew at?
20. Who was Vernon Louis Parrington?
21. Who called Ernest Hemingway the greatest writer since Shakespeare?
22. What do you think of the above statement?
23. Sears, Roebuck & Co. once bought a million copies of what novel?
24. What American was responsible for the destruction of 160 tons of books and pictures?
25. What are the "Big Three" among American universities?
26. What do you think of isolationism?
27. Should Alaska and Hawaii be granted statehood?
28. Should all educators receive a higher rate of pay?
29. Have you any criticisms to make as to the manner in which Americans play games?
30. Why are Americans so often called the most materialistic people in the world?

~·~

AMERICAN HISTORY

Answers on page 140

1. When and by whom was America first discovered?
2. The first white settlement in America was at?
3. The first Negroes were landed in America when and where?
4. The first book printed in English in America was?
5. The oldest university in America is? It was founded in?
6. The Pilgrims arrived at Cape Cod in the year?
7. The oldest learned society in America is?
8. The first missionary to the Indians was?
9. What was King Philip's War?
10. When did New York acquire its name?
11. Who was John Peter Zenger?
12. What is the date of the first Continental Congress?

13. What are the dates of the War of Independence?
14. Articles of Confederation were drawn up in the year?
15. The date of Cornwallis' surrender?
16. The Constitution was signed when?
17. What is the Bill of Rights? When was it adopted by Congress?
18. The first Congress met in what year?
19. What was the date and the purpose of John Brown's raid?
20. Who were the first reigning European sovereigns to set foot on American soil?
21. Who was the first President of the United States to be inaugurated in Washington?
22. The African Slave Trade was abolished when?
23. The War of 1812 was declared on what grounds?
24. What was the Dred Scott decision?
25. On what grounds was the War with Mexico fought?
26. What do you think of the statement that America is still a young country?
27. What do you think of the way we have treated the American Indian?
28. What do you think of Little Rock?
29. If a knowledge of its history is a measure of one's pride in one's country, how would you evaluate most Americans?
30. Are Americans any more capable of learning from history than other peoples?

ANATOMY AND PHYSIOLOGY

Answers on page 142

1. What is the average weight of the human brain?
2. How many milk teeth are there?
3. How many permanent teeth are there in a full set?
4. What is the principal blood-forming organ of the body?
5. Is the esophagus in front of or behind the trachea?
6. What is the hardest substance in the body?

7. Where are the coronary arteries situated?
8. How many chambers does the heart have?
9. What is the aorta?
10. The pupil of the eye is formed by?
11. Do hair and nails continue to grow for a short time after death?
12. In which sex is the metabolic rate higher?
13. Which is the "master gland" of the body?
14. What is an endocrine gland?
15. What is a hormone?
16. Bones are hollow. Would they be stronger if they were solid?
17. What makes some eyes blue and others brown?
18. What is the Babinski reflex?
19. Colostrum is?
20. How does tobacco smoke enter the blood stream?
21. How does saliva get into the mouth?
22. Does shaving cause hair to grow more rapidly or more abundantly?
23. Why is it inadvisable to cross one's knees?
24. What is the behavioral trait most frequently associated with the long-lived?
25. Give some reasons why overweight is bad for health.
26. Do you smoke?
27. Are you a civilized and moderate drinker?
28. Do you take exercise?
29. How often do you see your dentist for a check-up?
30. How often do you see your doctor for a general check-up?

ANTHROPOLOGY

Answers on page 144

1. Define anthropology.
2. How many species of living men are there?
3. What are the three great major groups of mankind?

4. About how long has man been on the earth?
5. Do innately determined mental differences exist between the so-called "races" of mankind?
6. What fossil forms are the closest known relatives of man?
7. Who were the first people to bury their dead?
8. The father of scientific anthropology in America was?
9. Where when they want to rest do people indulge in exercise?
10. Does the size of the forehead bear any relationship to intelligence?
11. What are the principal blood groups?
12. Who wrote *Primitive Culture?*
13. Who wrote *The Mind of Primitive Man?*
14. What peoples have no belief in a supreme god?
15. What twentieth-century people were unable to make fire?
16. What is a matriarchal society? Can you name one?
17. Briefly define "culture."
18. What is meant by "cultural relativism"?
19. What is the principal argument of *Patterns of Culture?*
20. State, in not more than a dozen words or so, the factor principally responsible for the differences in the cultures of the world.
21. What peoples have no chiefs?
22. Are there any objections to the use of the word "race"?
23. Are the languages of nonliterate peoples less complex than those of literate peoples?
24. The principle of equality is based on?
25. The most famous statement on race was issued by?
26. Should anthropology be taught in our schools?
27. Do you think that race prejudice can be significantly reduced by legislation?
28. What recent changes in attitudes can you trace to the influence of anthropology?
29. Do you believe in integration of the schools?
30. What would you say is the principal use of anthropology?

ARCHAEOLOGY

Answers on page 147

1. Define archaeology.
2. What is the oldest known bas-relief?
3. What are the oldest known statuettes?
4. Where, precisely, are the oldest known cave-paintings located?
5. Who was Heinrich Schliemann?
6. The most primitive stone tools are?
7. What is the Rosetta Stone?
8. What is the oldest known village site?
9. What is the earliest known city-state?
10. Who were the principal excavators of Tutankhamen's tomb?
11. What is radiocarbon dating?
12. Who was Champollion?
13. What is the "Kensington Stone"?
14. What is "The Fertile Crescent"?
15. The first appearance of pottery is usually associated with what archaeologic period?
16. Sir Leonard Woolley's name is principally associated with?
17. Our knowledge of Cretan civilization is largely due to?
18. Machu Picchu was discovered by?
19. The earliest writing is found in?
20. What are the earliest evidences of raiding?
21. The earliest record of a king occurs in?
22. Who was Boucher de Perthes?
23. Name two popularly priced recent books on archaeology by V. Gordon Childe.
24. The Palaeolithic period begins and ends . . . when?
25. What is the Piltdown Skull?
26. Should there be laws, within reasonable limits, making all archaeological finds the property of the state?
27. Do you believe that archaeological finds should remain in the country in which they were discovered?
28. What books have you read on archaeology?

29. Would you like to go on an archaeological "dig"? Why?
30. Of what use is archaeology?

~·~

ARCHITECTURE

Answers on page 150

1. Define architecture.
2. What do you understand by the Byzantine style?
3. What is Baroque?
4. What is Perpendicular? Where are the finest examples found?
5. What is one of the best preserved buildings of antiquity?
6. Who wrote *The Stones of Venice?*
7. Who wrote *The Architecture of Humanism?*
8. Who wrote *Sticks and Stones?*
9. What is the Geometric style?
10. Who was Banister Fletcher?
11. Who were the leaders in the Bauhaus movement?
12. What is meant by "thrust"?
13. The Erechtheum is what, and where?
14. The top front of a Greek building is called?
15. A lintel is?
16. What was the duration of the Gothic period in architecture?
17. The first skyscraper in New York was?
18. Sir Christopher Wren's most famous building is?
19. The Imperial Hotel in Tokyo was designed by?
20. Who invented concrete?
21. An architrave is?
22. A wainscot is?
23. An entablature is?
24. A frieze is?
25. The most famous living American architect is?
26. What do you think of the trend toward the ranch-house style?
27. What do you think of the "picture window"?

28. Do you think that the local authorities ought to "approve" the style in which it is proposed to build any structure?
29. Should utility in architecture ever be sacrificed to beauty?
30. The most important quality in an architect is?

~~

ART

Answers on page 152

1. Define art.
2. Who was the father of Impressionism?
3. How did Impressionism receive its name?
4. Who was the originator of pointillism?
5. Who painted "The Madonna of the Rocks" and how many versions by the same painter are there of this picture?
6. Who was the inventor of perspective in painting?
7. Name three of the artists and the names of their works represented in the Loggia dei Lanzi.
8. Who first introduced oil painting?
9. Tempera is?
    Who were the painters of the following works:
10. "La Primavera"
11. "The Last Supper"
12. "La Gioconda"
13. "The Blue Boy"
14. "The Potato Eaters"
15. "A Lady Standing at the Virginals"
    Who were the sculptors of the following works:
16. "David"
17. "Night" and "Day"
18. "Hermes with the Infant Dionysus"
19. "The Thinker"
20. "Rima"
21. The Baptistery Doors at Florence
22. Rembrandt's favorite model was?

23. What great country has never produced a great painter?
24. Picasso is the founder of what school of art?
25. What is Dadaism?
26. Do you occasionally visit art galleries and attend exhibitions?
27. What do you think the function of art is or could be in education?
28. Would you like to see more of our public buildings decorated by artists?
29. Would you like to see more of our private homes decorated by artists?
30. What is the value of the artist to society?

ASTRONOMY

Answers on page 155

1. Define astronomy.
2. The diameter of the sun is?
3. What is the use of an artificial satellite?
4. Stars are?
5. The most distant visible star from the earth is?
6. The geocentric conception of the universe is sometimes called?
7. What is the meaning of aphelion?
8. What is the meaning of ecliptic?
9. What is a penumbra?
10. What is the ether?
11. Which of the planets is characterized by "rings"?
12. What is the circumference of the earth?
13. What is a light year?
14. Name the planets of the solar system.
15. What is a galaxy? Name one.
16. An eclipse is?
17. William Herschel was?
18. What is the principal means of studying the heavens, by eye or by camera?

19. Why is there no possibility of life on the moon?
20. What is the distance of the moon from the earth?
21. The *Almagest* was?
22. The most important book in the history of astronomy is?
23. What are some of the practical uses of astronomy?
24. The distance of the sun from the earth is?
25. A comet is?
26. What value do you think interplanetary travel would have?
27. If you were lost could you orient yourself and map your course by the stars?
28. What do you think of the Russians having beaten us to the launching of the first satellite?
29. What books have you recently read on astronomy?
30. Do you think that astronomy ought to form a more intensive part of the educational curriculum in our schools?

~~

BALLET AND DANCE

Answers on page 157

1. Define ballet.
2. Define dance.
3. Morris dancing is?
4. What is a choral dance?
5. What was the Castle Walk?
6. A choreographer is?
7. *La Boutique Fantasque* is?
8. Who was the greatest impresario of the ballet of the twentieth century?
9. *The House Party* is?
10. Perhaps the most perfect male ballet solo was danced by . . . in . . . ?
    Name the composers of the music for the following:
11. *The Three-Cornered Hat*
12. *The Fire Bird*

13. *Daphnis et Chloé*
14. The most distinguished living English ballet dancer is?
15. A minuet is?
16. The most distinguished English ballet corps is known as?
17. Who was Nijinsky?
18. Who is Serge Lifar?
19. Who was Isadora Duncan?
20. A pavane is?
21. Who is Ted Shawn?
22. Who is Moira Shearer?
23. Who is Martha Graham?
24. Do you think it is *natural* to dance?
25. Who was the outstanding dancer in "The Red Shoes"?
26. Ought all children be taught to dance?
27. How often do you go to a ballet or attend a dance recital?
28. How often do you dance?
29. Ought there to be a national ballet?
30. Ought dancing be taught in the schools?

BIOGRAPHY

Answers on page 159

Identify:
1. Thomas Hobbes
2. Thomas Malthus
3. Thomas Mott Osborne
4. C. S. Peirce
5. Gilbert Murray
6. Henry Thomas Buckle
7. Thomas Masaryk
8. Richard Burbage
9. Alfred Adler
10. Walter B. Cannon
11. Thorstein Veblen

12. Henry Sigerist
13. Harry Stack Sullivan
14. Petr Kropotkin
15. Thomas Hunt Morgan
16. J. M. Keynes
17. Gaetano Salvemini
18. George Sarton
19. Alfred North Whitehead
20. Havelock Ellis
21. Lionel Trilling
22. Paul Tillich
23. Robert Maynard Hutchins
24. Alfred Zimmern
25. Lynn Thorndike
26. Percy Bridgman
27. Martin Buber
28. V. Gordon Childe
29. Niels Bohr
30. Vladimir Zworykin

BIOLOGY

Answers on page 162

1. Define biology.
2. How is sex determined?
3. What is a gene?
4. What is a chromosome?
5. How many chromosomes are there in the human germ cells?
6. How does radiation act upon heredity?
7. What is natural selection?
8. What is an atavism?
9. What is heterosis?
10. Define a race.
11. Of what animal could it be said that it has neither pride of ancestry nor hope of posterity?

12. What is a mammal?
13. If a white person marries a white-appearing person of Negroid ancestry is there any chance that they may have a colored child?
14. Are there any biologically undesirable effects of human race-crossing?
15. What is telegony?
16. To what order of mammals does man belong?
17. Are acquired physical characters heritable?
18. What is meant by "Darwinian fitness"?
19. What is a mutation?
20. Name the man who first induced mutations in an experimental animal.
21. What is an invertebrate?
22. What is a dolphin?
23. The name of Lamarck is identified with the doctrine of?
24. Should close cousins be permitted to marry?
25. If a dark-skinned animal were kept in a dark room for several years would it turn white?
26. What is a fossil?
27. Is war a eugenically good thing?
28. What do you think of eugenics?
29. Which has the greater adaptive value in man, competition or cooperation?
30. Do you think the evolution of man has come to an end?

~~

BOOKS

Answers on page 165

1. What is a book?
2. What is a half title?
3. What is a colophon?
4. What is a signature?
5. What is a duodecimo?

6. What is a leaf?
7. Who said "A good book is the precious life-blood of a master-spirit, embalmed and treasured up on purpose to a life beyond"?
8. What is bibliography?
9. Do publishers print books?
10. Baskerville is the name of?
11. What is meant by the term "edition"?
12. What is a folio?
13. Is it more economical to print in double or single column in a book or periodical?
14. How many copies of a book must a publisher normally sell in order to break even?
15. What is William Morris's most famous printed book?
16. The most beautiful book produced by Eric Gill is?
17. What is the function of the dust jacket?
18. The first printed book was?
19. The first type used was made of?
20. Who is the author of *The Anatomy of Bibliomania*?
21. Paper was first invented by which people?
22. When did cloth bindings first come into use?
23. *The Magnificent Farce* was written by?
24. The gold stamp on the front cover of a book is known as?
25. In a first edition would you prefer a soiled original binding to one in morocco?
26. Do you collect books?
27. Do you prefer paperback to hardcover books?
28. How many books a year do you read?
29. Do you approve of private-press books?
30. Do you think the book clubs a good idea?

CHEMISTRY AND TECHNOLOGY

Answers on page 167

1. Define chemistry.
2. What is technology?
3. What is the composition of water?
4. What is distilled water?
5. Osmosis is?
6. Brass is an alloy of?
7. Bronze is an alloy of?
8. Biochemistry is?
9. A retort is?
10. The irreducible and ever-present substance in all living matter is?
11. Lysis is?
12. The pH of a substance is a measure of its?
13. Sir William Ramsay discovered?
14. Who is the author of *The Nature of the Chemical Bond?*
15. An alembic is?
16. What is steel?
17. Do plastics occur in nature?
18. The great artificial dye industry was made possible by the discovery of?
19. Is CO_2 necessary for the functioning of the human body?
20. What is aluminium?
21. Who was Bessemer?
22. Who was Alfred Nobel?
23. How are diamonds made artificially?
24. Pewter is?
25. Distinguish between technology and science.
26. Should all students of technology receive a basic training in the humanities?
27. Do you think that a knowledge of chemistry ought to be a basic part of education?
28. Can a person be considered cultured who has no working knowledge of chemistry?

29. Do you think we could do with more technical high schools?
30. Is American civilization dominantly a technological one?

~~

CLASSICAL ANTIQUITY

Answers on page 170

1. Who was the Roman historian who first attacked and then embraced Christianity?
2. Who was Marcus Aurelius?
3. The author of *De Rerum Natura* was?
4. Who was Socrates' wife?
5. An amphora was?
6. The stoa was?
7. Zeus was?
8. Who was Nausicaa?
9. *Leucippe and Clitophon* is?
10. Parnassus was?
11. Adonis was?
12. Hetaerae were?
13. The title of Apuleius' best-known work is?
14. Who was the Greek philosopher who lived in a tub?
15. Who is the author and who the translator of "They told me, Heraclitus . . ."?
16. Seneca was?

Name the authors of the following works:
17. *The Nicomachean Ethics*
18. *Poetics*
19. *The Symposium*
20. *The Odyssey*
21. *The Frogs*
22. *Oedipus Rex*
23. Who was Atticus?
24. Archimedes was?
25. What disease is said to have played a significant role in the decline of Greek civilization?

26. What are the advantages of a classical education?
27. Should every ordinarily well-educated person have a knowledge of Greek and Latin?
28. How often do you read a book by a Latin or Greek author (in translation)?
29. What do you think of the attitude of the Greeks toward women?
30. Would you like to see more Greek plays produced?

~~

CULTURE HISTORY

Answers on page 173

1. What is the origin of the romantic conception of love in the Western world?
2. Name a good book on the history of cultural traditions.
3. Darwin's influence upon Western culture has largely been?
4. The cultural traditions of America are mainly of what origin?
5. The first printed English book was?
6. The argument of Godwin's *Political Justice* was?
7. The Royal Society was founded when?
8. The *Académie des Sciences* was founded in what year?
9. Lyric poetry, in the Western world, was largely the creation of?
10. Who was Condorcet?
11. The Philosophes were?
12. The idea of equality received its first major impetus as a result of?
13. When and where did the Industrial Revolution begin?
14. The greatest obstacle to social reform in the centuries preceding the nineteenth was?
15. What were the checks on population increase first stated by Malthus?
16. What is Puritanism?
17. Distinguish between the Gregorian and Julian calendars.
18. What is the argument of *Émile*?

19. Which was the first country to abolish the slave trade?
20. Denis Diderot was?
21. Incunabula means?
22. *The Subjection of Women* was written by?
23. Is "racism" an ancient or a modern development?
24. What kings married their own sisters?
25. What do you think were some of the errors committed on both sides during the nineteenth century in the conflict between science and religion?
26. Name several of the leading nineteenth-century antagonists of revealed religion.
27. In what lies the value of any cultural tradition?
28. Do you read books on cultural history?
29. What should be the purpose of teaching cultural history in our schools?
30. How do you benefit from your knowledge of culture history?

~~

ECONOMICS

Answers on page 178

1. Define economics.
2. What is Gresham's law?
3. What is the "economic interpretation of history"?
4. Who first described economics as "the dismal science"?
5. Is innate nature or economic rivalry or both a principal cause of war?
6. What is the theory of "marginal utility"?
7. Is it true that "competition is the life-blood of a nation"?
    Who are the authors of the following works:
8. *The Wealth of Nations*
9. *The Great Transformation*
10. *An Essay on the Principle of Population*
11. *A Dissertation on the Poor Laws*
12. *The Economic Consequences of the Peace*

13. *Principles of Political Economy*
14. Define money.
15. Henry George was?
16. William Stanley Jevons was?
17. Ricardo was?
18. Vilfredo Pareto was?
19. Define trade.
20. Define barter.
21. Define inflation.
22. What is the gold standard?
23. What is the World Bank?
24. What is the Federal Reserve Bank?
25. Which economist greatly influenced Charles Darwin?
26. Do you read books on economics?
27. Is economics a moral science concerned with human values or not?
28. Should man be in the service of economics, or economics in the service of man?
29. Is necessity the mother of invention?
30. Do you think that economic planning would greatly assist the development of a society?

~~

IN GENERAL

Answers on page 181

1. Stefan George was?
2. Peter Abelard was?
3. A thespian is?
4. Henry Adams was?
5. The Admirable Crichton was?
6. John Knox was?
7. Fridtjof Nansen was?
8. A nautch girl is?
9. Sun Yat-sen was called?

10. Domenico Theotokopoulos was the real name of?
11. What is xenophobia?
12. *Ralph Roister Doister* is?
13. What is the fourth estate?
14. A collage is?
15. What name is given to the Japanese code of chivalry?
16. Jo Mielziner is?
17. Quetzalcoatl is?
18. "Christian" is the hero of what famous book?
19. What is terrazzo?
20. Stendahl's real name was?
21. The great inspiration of Dante's life was?
22. A morganatic marriage is one in which?
23. The ides of March refers to what day in our calendar?
24. Simon Bolivar was?
25. Who said "Every man is his own hell"?
26. Who was Paul Gustave Doré?
27. What are "the dogs of St. Ernulphus"?
28. "Nature abhors a vacuum." Who said it?
29. Who said "Let us cultivate our garden"?
30. Who said "I disapprove of what you say, but I will defend to the death your right to say it"?

GEOGRAPHY AND METEOROLOGY

Answers on page 185

1. Define geography.
2. The Great Divide is?
3. The pole of cold is where?
4. The diameter of the earth is?
5. Graham Land is?
6. Arnhem Land is?
7. Precipitation is?
8. The Admiralty Islands are?

9. What is Phrygia?
10. Innisfail is?
11. Longitude is?
12. The largest desert in the world is?
13. Define meteorology.
14. Ratzel was?
15. The southernmost populated island is?
16. A savannah is?
17. A sirocco is?
18. An isobar is?
19. A tornado is the result of?
20. Cumulus clouds are?
21. Name several of the world's largest lakes.
22. Sir Halford Mackinder's name is associated with what?
23. Topography is?
24. What is the Tropic of Cancer?
25. The Irrawaddy is?
26. Is man adapted to live in all lands and in all climates?
27. Do you think the weather influences our moods?
28. What are the uses of meteorology?
29. Do you think there is any relation between atomic explosions and the weather?
30. Could teaching in geography and meteorology be improved?

~~

GEOLOGY

Answers on page 189

1. Define geology.
2. What is a fault?
3. Distinguish between stalactites and stalagmites.
4. What is the Paleocene?
5. Sandstone is?
6. Feldspar is?
7. Alfred Wegener was?
8. The age of the earth is estimated to be about?
9. A glacier is?

10. Petroleum is thought to be the natural product of?
11. The oldest rocks are known as?
12. A volcanic eruption is due to?
13. A terminal moraine is?
14. What is alluvium?
15. What is the relation of archaeology to geology?
16. A petrologist is?
17. Crater Lake is thought to have been produced by?
18. How does geology help the anthropologist?
19. The name of Laplace is associated with?
20. The famous *Principles of Geology* was written by?
21. A paleontologist is?
22. A diamond consists mainly of?
23. Pumice stone is?
24. Talus is?
25. A meteorite is?
26. Do you think an elementary knowledge of geology an indispensable part of the equipment of the educated man?
27. Are you able to recognize a fair number of rocks and the evidences of glaciation?
28. Do you place much faith in radiocarbon dating?
29. Of what use is seismology?
30. What are some of the uses of geology?

EUROPEAN HISTORY

Answers on page 192

1. Define history.
2. What is Magna Charta?
3. The Peace of Westphalia was?
4. What were The Wars of the Roses?
5. The Crimean War was a fiasco because?
6. Who was Justinian?

7. What German general turned the tide at the Battle of Waterloo?
8. The Heights of Quebec were taken by?
9. The *ancien régime* is?
10. Who was known as *Stupor Mundi?*

Give the dates of the following events:

11. Execution of Charles I
12. The French Revolution
13. The Boston Tea Party
14. The Franco-Prussian War
15. The circumnavigation of the globe was first achieved by?
16. Salimbene was?
17. The Second Empire was?
18. Who was it who defined history as "little else than a picture of human crimes and misfortunes"?
19. Name a reference work on modern history.
20. Who was the father of Elizabeth I of England?
21. Who was called Edward the Peacemaker?
22. Who was the last king to appeal to the doctrine of the divine right of kings?
23. Name several works critical of Arnold Toynbee's *A Study of History.*
24. Have you any criticisms to make of Toynbee's *A Study of History?*
25. What is the relation between history and the historian?
26. What, in your view, is the most important trait that the historian should possess?
27. How could the teaching of general history be improved?
28. Do you read historical works?
29. What are some of the uses of the study of history?
30. Is history true?

HISTORY OF IDEAS

Answers on page 195

1. What is an idea?
2. The idea of the benzene ring first occurred to?
3. The idea of the unity of mankind first occurs in what book?
4. What great thinker thought that the intelligence was situated in the heart?
5. Who was William Paley?
6. Who gave the first account of the circulation of the blood?
7. Who was Democritus?
8. Who was the originator of Social Darwinism?
9. Did T. H. Huxley ever reverse himself on the subject of the cosmic process?
10. Who first developed the idea of the unconscious?
    Who are the authors of the following works:
11. *Protestant Ethic and the Spirit of Capitalism*
12. *The Great Chain of Being*
13. *Gemeinschaft und Gesellschaft*
14. *The Eighteenth Century Background*
15. *The Mediaeval Mind*
16. *Religion and the Rise of Capitalism*
17. *Dialogue on the Two Great World Systems*
18. *A History of the Warfare of Science with Theology in Christendom*
19. *De Revolutionibus Orbium Coelestium*
20. *De Humani Corporis Fabrica*
21. *Ideen zur Philosophie der Geschichte der Menschheit*
22. In what work did Freud first develop the idea of a death instinct?
23. Name a periodical dealing with the history of ideas.
24. Who were the people who first developed the idea of a single god?
25. Is there a scientific basis for astrological ideas?
26. Do you read books on the history of ideas?
27. Is there any genuine ground for a belief in the idea of progress?

28. Are you averse to speculation and conjecture in any discipline or branch of knowledge?
29. Do you think more highly of the man of imagination in science or the steady worker?
30. What are some of the uses of the study of the history of ideas?

HISTORY OF SCIENCE

Answers on page 198

1. What people first independently invented the symbol for zero?
2. Name the two most important source books in English for the history of science.
3. Who discovered the electron?
4. What two books are regarded as ushering in the Renaissance of science?
5. Who was Roger Bacon?
6. Who was William Gilbert?
7. What do you know about phlogiston?
8. Describe the connection between Halley and Halley's comet.
9. Joseph Priestley's most notable discovery was?
10. In what year was *The Origin of Species* published?
11. Who was Gesner?
12. Who were the three independent rediscoverers of Mendel's laws?
13. Who was Clerk Maxwell?
14. Who was Johannes Peter Müller?
15. Who coined the term *vitamine?*
16. Who was Josiah Willard Gibbs?
17. Newton's most important work was?
18. The discoverers of radioactivity were?
19. Leeuwenhoek was?
20. Karl Pearson was?
21. The differential calculus was invented by?
22. The first telescope was made by?

23. Whose motto was "Pauca sed matura" ("Few but mature")?
24. Name one or more periodicals devoted to the history of science.
25. Who was Galois?
26. Is the history of science a branch of the humanities or of the sciences?
27. Should the teaching of the history of science be combined with the teaching of culture history?
28. Should all universities teach the history of science?
29. How should the history of science be taught?
30. What are the uses of the history of science?

LANGUAGE

Answers on page 203

1. Define language.
2. Does any language exist without a grammar?
3. What is an infix?
4. What is a phoneme?
5. Distinguish between speech and language.
6. Linguistics is?
7. What is mood convection?
8. Semantics is?
9. Define a word.
10. *The Meaning of Meaning* is by?
11. Name several good books on language.
12. The best English is spoken at Oxford or Cambridge?
13. Give an example of the subjunctive mood.
14. What is a glottal stop?
15. Distinguish between communication and language.
16. Define slang.
17. To what linguistic stock does English belong?
18. To what linguistic stock does Hungarian belong?
19. What is a morpheme?
20. Does the term *Semitic* refer to a language or linguistic stock or to a race?

21. Mention some of the theories as to the origin of language.
22. What is the best international language thus far developed?
23. In what part of America is the best English spoken?
24. Define dialect.
25. Is American English or English English the more colorful and inventive?
26. How many languages in addition to English do you speak?
27. How many languages in addition to English do you read?
28. Should there be an international language?
29. In learning a foreign language should one begin with grammar or not?
30. Do you take especial care about the manner in which you use language?

~~

THE LAW AND LIBERTY

Answers on page 208

1. Define law.
2. What is the meaning of *Ignorantia legis neminem excusat?*
3. *Amicus curiae* means?
4. Who was the attorney for the defense in the Sacco-Vanzetti case?
5. How many judges are there on the bench of the United States Supreme Court?
6. What is the relation between law and liberty or freedom?
7. What is the meaning of *corpus delicti?*
8. What is statutory law?
9. The earliest preserved code of law is?
10. Who was the attorney for the defense in the "Monkey Trial"?
11. What is the meaning of *habeas corpus?*
12. Jurisprudence is?
13. The author of *Ancient Law* is?
14. The great contribution of the Greeks to the theory of law was?
15. What is wrong with the American law of libel?

16. What was the *jus gentium?*
17. Define liberty or freedom.
18. What is the difference between a barrister and a solicitor?
19. The basic freedoms secured to every American are set out in what document?
20. The greatest safeguard of freedom in the United States is?
21. What is the statute of limitations?
22. During World War II was it legal to intern persons of Japanese ancestry?
23. Who was Elijah Lovejoy?
24. Is capital punishment defensible?
25. What is a free press?
26. Are you a member of the American Civil Liberties Union or a similar organization?
27. What is your attitude to a law with which you do not agree?
28. Is freedom free?
29. Should Congress have the right to investigate the political beliefs of anyone?
30. Do you believe that legislation can bring about changes in public opinion and attitudes?

THE FACTS OF LIFE

Answers on page 211

What is the average duration of:
1. Human pregnancy
2. Menstruation
3. The interval between menstruation and menopause
4. Adolescence in the female
5. Adolescence in the male
6. What is the average age of puberty in the female?
7. What is the average age of puberty in the male?
8. Is the average female capable of procreation at puberty?
9. Do epidemics of flu occur in cycles?

10. Are some babies drug addicts at birth?
11. The expectation of life for the average white female in the United States in 1957 was?
12. The average expectation of life for the white male in the United States in 1957 was?
13. Why do females live longer than males?
14. Are more women or men killed in home accidents?
15. What factors most influence the rate of growth of children?
16. What is cancer?
17. How does cancer kill?
18. Do you think it possible to eliminate a disease like hemophilia (bleeders' disease)?
19. When mulattoes marry what will be the skin color of their offspring?
20. What is meant by physiological age?
21. What is the average rate of respiration in the adult?
22. What are the principal factors influencing blood pressure?
23. At each beat the heart pumps about how much blood?
24. How many quarts of blood are there in the average human body?
25. Does the growth of children vary with the seasons?
26. At what age should children begin to be introduced to the facts of life?
27. Do you occasionally read books on social biology?
28. How well grounded should the cultured man be in the facts of life?
29. What is your opinion on artificial insemination?
30. Should social biology be a school subject?

LITERARY CURIOSITIES

Answers on page 214

Who was the original of:

1. Harold Skimpole
2. Adonais

3. Buck Mulligan
4. Alroy Kear
5. Scythrop
6. Mr. Boythorn
7. What novelist often took a week to find the right word?
8. What novelist wrote over 200 books?
9. What American wrote over 100,000 sonnets?
10. What writer employed an army of helpers to assist him in the writing of his books?
11. Who wrote *Curiosities of Literature?*
12. What is the world's best-seller?
13. What was George Eliot's real name?
14. Who did H. L. Mencken call "the most civilized Englishman alive"?
15. What was George Sand's real name?
16. What is the best all-round English weekly?
17. What was Currer Bell's real name?
18. What painter was a brilliant controversial essayist?
19. What was Saki's real name?
20. What American Nobel laureate in literature never went to college?
21. Of what great writer do we have practically no remnant of writing in his own hand?
22. Name two authors who suffered from serious skin disorders of the face.
23. Why did Gibbon never marry?
24. The largest library in the world is?
25. Who is the author of *Sibyl?*
26. Do you return the books you have borrowed from friends?
27. What is a Little Magazine, and what are its functions?
28. Is style the man?
29. Do you believe that there ought to be a literary censor?
30. Do you read dictionaries?

ENGLISH AND AMERICAN
LITERATURE

Answers on page 216

1. What is literature?
2. What is generally said to be the earliest novel in the English language?
3. Who was The Great Cham?
4. What is the longest American novel?
5. Leopold Bloom is a character in what work?
6. Iambic pentameter was first used by?
7. Who wrote of the influence of the American frontier on American literature?
8. Who wrote the final lines ". . . the play is the tragedy, 'Man,'/ And its hero, the Conqueror Worm"?
9. Who was John Fiske?

Name the authors of the following:

10. *The Hind and the Panther*
11. *The Shoemaker's Holiday*
12. *The Battle of the Books*
13. *Euphues*
14. *A New Way To Pay Old Debts*
15. *A History of the Earth and Animated Nature*
16. *Epithalamion*
17. *The Titan*
18. *The Turn of the Screw*
19. "Benito Cereno"
20. *Manhattan Transfer*
21. *The American Jitters*
22. *Light in August*
23. *The Flowering of New England*
24. *The American*
25. *The Degradation of the Democratic Dogma*
26. Do you read works of literary criticism?
27. Do you subscribe to any literary journals?

28. Should a literary critic himself be competent in the medium he criticizes?
29. Do you read poetry?
30. Are there any areas of human experience which should not be written about?

~~

LITERATURE IN GENERAL

Answers on page 218

Name the authors of the following:

1. *Gil Blas*
2. *The Cloister and the Hearth*
3. *La Comédie Humaine*
4. *Là-Bas*
5. *Fleurs du Mal*
6. *The Wind in the Willows*
7. *The Prince*
8. *The Art of Courtly Love*
9. *A Wreath of Cloud*
10. *Candide*
11. *The Monk*
12. *The Shepheardes Calendar*
13. *The Castle of Otranto*
14. *Orlando*
15. *John Brown's Body*
16. *The River*
17. *Imaginary Conversations*
18. *Conversations with a Cat*
19. *archy and mehitabel*
20. *Don Juan*
21. *Le Père Goriot*
22. *Madame Bovary*
23. *War and Peace*
24. *The Sorrows of Werther*

25. *Paradise Lost*
26. Is it possible to read too much?
27. How many works of literature apart from novels do you read in a year?
28. Should one meet the authors of the books one admires, whenever possible?
29. Do you think we could do with more programs on literature in radio and TV?
30. Do you see any foreign literary reviews?

\~\~

MANNERS

Answers on page 221

1. Define manners.
2. Are there any occasions when good manners are contraindicated?
3. Are you considerate toward those in menial capacities—as well as all others?
4. Are you inclined to pour oil upon troubled waters?
5. Under what, if any conditions, is it permissible to withhold the truth?
6. Are you punctual?
7. Are you a courteous driver—front and backseat?
8. Is the proper word *serviette* or *napkin?*
9. In the ordinary course of events would you read anything that was not intended for your eyes?
10. Do you respect children as persons and "include them in"?
11. Are you capable of swallowing your pride?
12. What did Dr. Johnson mean when he said "A gentleman refrains"?
13. "There is always a best way of doing everything, if it be to boil an egg. Manners are the happy ways of doing things." Who said it?
14. Do you ever lose your temper?

15. Do you tend to pay while others fumble?
16. Do you make way for others?
17. Briefly discuss the words "That lady."
18. Are you a good listener?
19. Do you ever offer a blank contradiction to anyone in conversation?
20. Do you suffer bores gladly?
21. Do you forgo some things that others might have them?
22. Are you inclined to take friends little gifts from time to time?
23. Do you play games to win or for fun?
24. Who defined politeness as fictitious benevolence?
25. Are you gracious in your manner?
26. Do you drop in on people without giving them prior notice of your visitation?
27. Is it fair to judge a person by his manners?
28. Are you aggressive or cooperative in your approach to trespassers?
29. Are you a stickler for form?
30. However much you may disagree with them do you respect the right of others to hold their opinions, and have you ever done anything to defend such rights?

~~

MARRIAGE

Answers on page 223

1. Define marriage.
2. Of all the possible bases for marriage which do you think the soundest: (a) physical attraction, (b) money, (c) family, (d) character?
3. If you believe in an engagement period, how long should it last before marriage?
4. What are the arguments against premarital relations with the betrothed?
5. Should one wait a year or two after marriage before having children?

6. Should a wife work who has small children at home?
7. Should a husband help his wife with domestic chores?
8. Should husband and wife on an occasional evening visit their separate friends separately?
9. May husband and wife have separate friends?
10. Should a young married couple live in the same house with their in-laws?
11. Which sex should be older at marriage?
12. Do the married live longer than the unmarried?
13. What do you think the best age at which to marry for the female?
14. Should husband and wife occupy separate beds?
15. What is endogamy?
16. How many marriages end in divorce in the United States?
17. Should the usual age at marriage for males and females be modified?
18. What was the principal objection to the marriage of Mrs. Simpson to Edward VIII?
19. Are there any societies in which marriage does not exist?
20. Sequential polygamy is a form of marriage practiced in what country?
21. The form of marriage in which a woman may have plural husbands is known as?
22. In what manner may marriages between Catholics be dissolved?
23. The most amusing exchange on marriage occurs in what famous work?
24. Name a good history of marriage.
25. What is polygyny?
26. What is the most important single factor making for success in marriage?
27. What do you think of marriage counseling?
28. Why do you think the divorce rates are so high in the United States?
29. Are you married?
30. Do you think the institution of marriage will ever be abolished?

MEDICINE

Answers on page 226

1. Define medicine.
2. Who is known as the Father of Medicine?
3. Who was Suśruta?
4. Vaccination for smallpox was first proved beneficial by what doctor?
5. Who was Galen?
6. Reduction in the incidence of polio is principally due to?
7. Pellagra is due to?
8. Who was Paracelsus?
9. What is ACTH?
10. A medical eye specialist is called?
11. The normal temperature is?
12. What is the meaning of "diathesis"?
13. Does more or less cyclic enlargement of the tonsils mean that they should be removed?
14. What is the meaning of "constitution"?
15. Is masturbation capable of leading to insanity?
16. Does penicillin act by killing bacteria?
17. Why should you never squeeze a boil?
18. What is a coronary thrombosis?
19. During what period of pregnancy is German measles capable of doing some damage to a certain proportion of fetuses?
20. Who discovered the first antibiotic?
21. A peptic ulcer is?
22. Is there any cure for the normal form of baldness in men?
23. A metastasis is?
24. What is the principal acid secreted by the stomach glands?
25. What are vitamins?
26. Do you believe that there ought to be some form of social medicine?
27. Should babies be born at home?
28. Should the giving of contraceptive advice be limited to physicians?

29. Would you like to see more trained midwives available?
30. Do you have medical insurance?

~·~

MOVIES, RADIO, AND
TELEVISION

Answers on page 229

1. Who was the director of *The Cabinet of Dr. Caligari?*
2. Who was the director and star of *Grand Illusion?*
3. The star of *M* was?
4. Who was the star of *The Last Laugh?*
5. On what social grounds was *The Birth of a Nation* criticized?
6. What is The Hays Code?
7. The star of *The Blue Angel* was?
8. The young female star of *Mädchen in Uniform* was?
9. The best history of the German film is?
10. Who was the producer and director of *Nanook of the North?*
11. The star of *The Circus* was?
12. The first man to make moving pictures was?
13. Name the first sound moving picture.
14. What radio program caused listeners to believe that the earth had been invaded by the inhabitants of another planet?
15. The first commercial television broadcasts in the United States were begun in?
16. The FCC is and does what?
17. What is a teleprompter?
18. Who was the first person to win more than $100,000 on a quiz show?
19. What were early radio sets called?
20. What do NBC, CBS, and BBC stand for?
21. "Omnibus" is a show broadcast when?
22. About how many TV sets do you think are in use in the United States?

23. What do AM and FM stand for?
24. Who was Edward Howard Armstrong?
25. If TV as a form of entertainment ceased to exist would it affect you in any way?
26. What effect has television had upon the character of movies?
27. Why do you think that TV has not ousted radio?
28. Do you think that the violences and crudities of many TV programs for children could be eliminated with advantage?
29. Are you for or against subscription television?
30. What do you think of the general level of radio and TV programs?

~~

MUSIC

Answers on page 232

1. Define music.
2. In what special way does Beethoven's Ninth Symphony differ from his others?
3. Who was Paganini?
4. Who was Henry Purcell?
5. Name some of Kurt Weill's compositions.
6. What is a concerto?
7. A fugue is?
8. What is an oratorio?
9. Who developed a famous test for measuring musical talent?
10. Segovia is?
11. Why can't the English play jazz?
12. What is a lute?
13. Terpsichore is?
14. A cadenza is?
15. A berceuse is?
16. The Guarnieri family was distinguished for?
17. On what play is the musical *Oklahoma* based?
18. On what play is *My Fair Lady* based?

19. What is chamber music?
20. How many Bachs of the same family were there who were composers?

Name the composers of the following:

21. *The Trojans*
22. *The Golden Cockerel*
23. *La Danse Macabre*
24. *Tea For Two*
25. *St. Louis Blues*
26. Do you read books on music?
27. Are you able to read music?
28. Do you play a musical instrument?
29. How often do you attend musical events?
30. Should all children, regardless of musical talent, receive a musical education?

~~

NUMBERS, WEIGHTS, AND MEASURES

Answers on page 234

1. Define number.
2. Define weight.
3. Define measure.
4. Define area.
5. How many feet in a mile?
6. According to tradition how was the yard established?
7. How many pounds in a ton?
8. Define horsepower.
9. What is a calorie? Define it.
10. How many millimeters are there in an inch?
11. How many pints in a liter?
12. How many inches in a meter?
13. What is specific gravity?

14. How is volume determined?
15. How many square yards in an acre?
16. How many feet in a fathom?
17. How many drams in an avoirdupois ounce?
18. How many grains in a troy ounce?
19. In printing a pica is?
20. A ream is?
21. What is meant by "the median"?
22. What does the term "mean" mean?
23. Define value.
24. The letters XL mean?
25. The letters $\overline{\text{XL}}$ mean?
26. Do you think that mathematics is an essential part of the equipment of the well-educated man?
27. Should numbers, weights, and measures be uniform throughout the world?
28. What can statistics tell about the cause of anything?
29. Do you think that giant mechanical brains will someday replace human thought?
30. Do you think we ought to adopt the metric system?

OPERA

Answers on page 236

1. Define opera.
2. What was the first opera?
3. What were the subjects of the earliest operas?
4. Define *opéra comique*.
5. The great reformer of opera was?
6. What is an *opera seria*?
7. "Ruddigore" is a play on what words?
8. What are *intermezzi*?
9. Define grand opera.
10. What is the title of Nietzsche's book in which he jettisoned Wagner?

Name the composers of the following:

11. *Pelléas et Mélisande*
12. *Peter Grimes*
13. *The Consul*
14. *Die Zauberflöte*
15. *Beggar's Opera*
16. *Threepenny Opera*
17. *Hänsel und Gretel*
18. *Dido and Aeneas*
19. *Porgy and Bess*
20. *Oberon*
21. What is an operetta?
22. In what opera does Wagner's "Wedding March" occur?
23. What is an *opéra bouffe*?
24. Name a good biography of Gilbert of Gilbert and Sullivan.
25. Do you understand people who don't like opera?
26. Do you think we ought to have a National Opera House?
27. Do you think there ought to be a State Opera House in each state?
28. About how many operas do you think have been written?
29. Do you enjoy comic opera?
30. How often do you attend the opera?

PARENT-CHILD RELATIONSHIPS

Answers on page 238

1. Do parents determine the fate of their children?
2. Can parents be too loving?
3. Should all frustration of children's needs be avoided?
4. What should parents seek to do for their children?
5. The best way to lay the foundations in childhood for the development of a cultured person is?
6. Should children be permitted to call their parents by their first names?

7. Is sibling rivalry inevitable?

8. Should a child always be given reasons for its parent's demands?

9. What is the Electra complex?

10. What is a "Kibbutz"?

11. Do you think it possible to abolish the institution of the family?

12. Can adoptive parents be just as good parents as biological ones?

13. Should an adopted child be treated as if it were legally the issue of its adoptive parents?

14. Do you think candy consumption should be regulated by the parents?

15. Is it true that "the child is father to the man"?

16. Should potential parents be tested as to their fitness to rear children?

17. Should parents be pals to their children?

18. What is the Oedipus complex?

19. Should parents allow their children to select their own occupations?

20. Are parents the best judges of their children?

21. Do children learn more by precept or by example?

22. Should parent-child organizations be encouraged for the instruction and preparation of prospective parents?

23. What role should grandparents play?

24. Do you think that fathers are adequate to their role in our culture?

25. Have you ever supported your local Parent-Teacher Association?

26. Do you think there ought to be greater cooperation between parents and teachers?

27. What would you recommend to parents who disagree on discipline?

28. Have you given hostages to Fortune?

29. Do you think corporal punishment of children ever permissible?

30. Name a good encyclopaedia on parent-child relationships.

PHILOSOPHY

Answers on page 241

1. Define philosophy.
2. G. E. Moore's most influential book is?
3. Russell and Whitehead are the co-authors of?
4. Empiricism is?
5. The categorical imperative is?
6. The Stoics were?
7. The main subject discussed in *The Symposium* is?
8. Logical positivism is?
9. Existentialism is?
10. Idealism is?
11. Pragmatism is?
12. C. S. Peirce's most representative essays are to be found in what book?
13. What is metaphysics?
14. What is a value judgment?
15. Define ethics.
16. Aristotle was the pupil of?
17. What is the naturalistic fallacy?
18. Name some existentialist philosophers.

   Who are the authors of the following:
19. *Tractatus Logico-Philosophicus*
20. *Die Welt als Wille und Vorstellung*
21. *The Philosophy of 'As If'*
22. *The Critique of Pure Reason*
23. *Either/Or*
24. What is Occam's razor?
25. What is Ernst Cassirer's most important work?
26. Do you read philosophical works?
27. Do you believe in free will?
28. Does knowledge lead to wisdom?
29. What use is the philosophy of science?
30. What are the uses of philosophy?

PHYSICS

Answers on page 245

1. Define physics.
2. Light travels at the rate of?
3. Define heat.
4. What is the boiling point of water?
5. How does one convert the Fahrenheit scale into the centigrade scale?
6. What is the melting point of ice?
7. Name the particles of the nucleus of the atom.
8. What is the periodic table?
9. State the first law of thermodynamics.
10. State the second law of thermodynamics.
11. What are Newton's three laws of motion?
12. What is mass?
13. What is the meaning of $E = mc^2$?
14. Distinguish between a molecule and an atom.
15. Distinguish between centripetal and centrifugal force.
16. Gravity is?
17. Under what conditions could the oceans become a mass of fire as hot and bright as the sun?
18. What is the principle of indeterminacy?
19. The Michelson-Morley experiment is famous for?
20. What is a cloud chamber?
21. What is pressure?
22. The Leaning Tower of Pisa is famous for?
23. When water is frozen does it occupy more or less space?
24. A volt is?
25. An amp. is?
26. Do you think physicists ought to receive a better training in the humanities?
27. Do you think that a moratorium ought to be declared on all work in nuclear physics?
28. What do you think should be done about atom bombs?
29. What do you think of the dangers of fallout?

30. Have you done anything by way of protesting the testing of atom bombs?

~·~

POLITICS AND GOVERNMENT

Answers on page 249

1. Define politics.
2. Define communism.
3. Define democracy.
4. Define republicanism.
5. When was the first English labor government elected?
6. In what year was F. D. Roosevelt elected President of the United States?
7. What is the Electoral College?
8. A ward-heeler is?
9. What country used to be known as "The Sick Man of Europe"?

Name the authors of the following works:

10. *Politics*
11. *The Industrial Revolution*
12. *Physics and Politics*
13. *Behemoth*
14. Who was Lloyd George?
15. What is the Monroe Doctrine?
16. What was the Weimar Republic?
17. What is Pan-Germanism?
18. Who wrote *Human Nature in Politics?*
19. What was the Potsdam Agreement?
20. Is is possible for a naturalized American citizen to be Secretary of State?
21. What is the House of Representatives?
22. Who said "Man is a political animal"?
23. Thomas Hobbes was?
24. Who wrote "For forms of government let fools contest:/ Whate'er is best administered is best"?

25. Who wrote *The Spirit of the Laws*?
26. Do you participate actively in any way in politics?
27. Do you vote regularly in all elections?
28. Do you vote for the party or the man?
29. How do you account for the opprobrium which attaches to the word "politician"?
30. What do you think our attitude should be to the Russians?

PSYCHOLOGY

Answers on page 252

1. Define psychology.
2. Give a one-word synonym for "mind."
3. Behaviorism is?
4. What is the unconscious mind?
5. Why is the mind chiefly in the head, and the brain in the head?
6. Define psychoanalysis.
7. Define behavior.
8. Define intelligence.
9. Alfred Adler's psychology is known as?
10. What is meant by "displacement"?
11. What did Freud mean by "libido"?
12. What is "repression"?
13. Define "cathexis."
14. Who defined mind as "a stream of consciousness"?
15. What is the Weber-Fechner Law?
16. Is the term "insanity" a legal or a medical one?
17. What is the opposite of "love"?
18. What is the Moro reflex?
19. Is it normally possible to overwork the mind so that it breaks down?
20. Does man possess any instincts?
21. Distinguish between "sensation" and "perception."
22. Distinguish between a reflex and an instinct.

23. The best biography of Freud is?
24. Define a neurosis.
25. What is a psychosis?
26. What do you think of the idea of a "death instinct"?
27. What do you think of psychoanalysis?
28. What do you think of extrasensory perception?
29. Should clinical psychologists be licensed just as doctors are?
30. Why is it desirable that all practicing psychoanalysts should themselves have been analysed?

CHECK YOUR REFERENCES

Answers on page 256

1. The standard guide to reference books is?
2. What is the most exhaustive dictionary of the English language?
3. What is the standard work on common English usage?
4. What is the latest work on American-English usage?
5. What is the most up-to-date one-volume American encyclopaedia?
6. Phyllis Hartnot edited what standard reference book on the theatre?
7. What is the best reference work to recent medical literature?
8. Theodore Besterman is associated with what bibliographical work?
9. What is the most exhaustive catalogue of American books?
10. What is the best reference to books in print in the United States?
11. The standard reference work on the social sciences is?
12. What is the standard bibliography of English literature?
13. For brief biographies of English and American worthies of the past the standard compendiums are?
14. Name several books of quotations.
15. William Langer edited what one-volume reference book on world history?

16. Name a reference book useful in tracing specific laws.
17. Harvey and Brewer are names associated with what reference books on literature?
18. What specific kind of reference work is Shepherd's atlas?
19. Name the most exhaustive bibliography of medical literature in the United States.
20. What is the title of Percy Scholes's one-volume encyclopaedia of music?
21. Who compiled the *Oxford Companion to American Literature*?
22. For information about the time of sunrise or sunset you would consult what book?
23. What is the best-known thesaurus in English?
24. Name an exhaustive reference work on the bringing up of children.
25. Name the standard multi-volume reference work on religion.
26. Name the most complete reference work on folklore.
27. Stedman, Gould, and Dorland refer to dictionaries in what field?
28. Name the standard brief dictionary of English literature.
29. Name a modern handbook to classical literature.
30. Do you much use reference works?

RELIGION

Answers on page 259

1. Define religion.
2. About what date did Abraham live?
3. In what locality of what country did Abraham live?
4. About when was the Old Testament written?
5. How old was Jesus when he died?
6. About when was the New Testament written?
7. What are the Dead Sea Scrolls?
8. In what book of the Bible does the Sermon on the Mount occur?

9. In what book of the Bible does the injunction to "Love thy neighbor as thyself" first occur?
10. Who was the founder of Judaism?
11. By whom was Christianity first brought to England?
12. Who was the founder of Protestantism?
13. By whom was Protestantism established in England?
14. What is meant by "The Reformation"?
15. What is "original sin"?
16. Who was responsible for the doctrine of original sin?
17. What is a Unitarian?
18. What do you understand by the doctrine of the separation of Church and State?
19. What is *agape*?
20. Who was the first Pope?
21. St. Ignatius of Loyola founded what religious order?
22. The father and mother of King Solomon were?
23. Who were the Pharisees?
24. What is clericalism?
25. Who were the Philistines?
26. Do you believe in freedom of religious belief and practice?
27. Do you believe that a person has a right to be a nonbeliever?
28. What do you think of the Biblical attitude toward women?
29. Do you think that secular beliefs can adequately replace religious ones?
30. Is a secular religion possible?

SCIENTIFIC METHOD AND LOGIC

Answers on page 263

1. Define science.
2. Define logic.
3. Define truth.

4. What, in one word, best describes the method of science?
5. Is a scientist interested in proving theories or in discovering what is?
6. Distinguish between induction and deduction.
7. What is a fact?
8. Define definition.
9. What is a syllogism?
10. Do recent statistical studies prove that smoking is a cause of cancer?
11. Define cause.
12. A cart-wheel is placed horizontally on a vertical axle. Seated on the wheel and facing each other are a cat and a dog, the former at the center and the latter at the circumference. The wheel is made to rotate. Does the dog go round the cat?
13. What is the Principle of Excluded Middle?
14. What is the operational method?
15. What is observation?
16. What do statistics prove?
17. Who said "Truth grows more readily out of error than it does out of confusion"?
18. What is meant by the phrase *post hoc ergo propter hoc?*
19. What is an experiment?
20. What is a *petitio principii?*
21. What is the principle of parsimony?
22. Define a proposition.
23. What is the philosophy of science?
24. Describe the scientific attitude of mind.
25. What is the difference between the plausible and the probable?
26. Can scientific methods provide a basis for ethics?
27. Do you believe everything you read in the newspapers?
28. What do you understand by "keeping an open mind"?
29. Do you check your "facts"?
30. If man is descended from apelike creatures does it follow that he must have inherited apelike potentialities of behavior?

SEX DIFFERENCES

Answers on page 267

1. Are more boys or girls born?
2. Do the bones harden earlier in boys or girls?
3. The mortality rate for almost all diseases is higher in which sex?
4. Which sex lives longer on the average?
5. Are men stronger than women?
6. What is the sex-determining mechanism in the human species?
7. The relative brain weight is greater in which sex?
8. Which sex is more often color-blind than the other?
9. Are males more often behavior problems than females?
10. Do girls or boys achieve puberty earlier?
11. In which sex is the sickness rate higher?
12. Are men better drivers than women?
13. Are men or women more resistant to emotional stress?
14. Which sex, in general, does better on intelligence tests?
15. Is diabetes more frequent in the male or female?
16. In which sex is the suicide rate higher?
17. Stuttering occurs more frequently in males or females?
18. Do women overdraw their accounts more frequently than men?
19. Which sex is more frequently hospitalized for mental illness?
20. How many times has a woman received the Nobel prize?
21. Which person has received the Nobel prize twice?
22. Are males or females more occupied with sex?
23. Among what animals do the males hatch the eggs or take care of the young?
24. Which sex has the lower metabolic rate?
25. What is "feminine intuition"?
26. Do you believe that individuals ought to be judged as persons and not as members of a group or sex?
27. Should women receive the same education as men?
28. Do you believe that women ought to receive equal pay for equal work?

29. Should women be more fully represented on all bodies having to do with their welfare?
30. Would you vote for a woman President of the United States?

~~

SOCIAL QUESTIONS

Answers on page 271

1. Does our educational system require revision?
2. Is cosmopolitanism a first step in internationalism?
3. Is the use of force or violence ever justified?
4. What do you think of the idea of world disarmament?
5. Should women be required to serve on all juries?
6. Should the voting age be lowered?
7. What do you think of the idea of world federation?
8. Should a pregnancy ever be artificially terminated?
9. Should the approach to the problem of juvenile delinquency be on a community or on an individual level?
10. Do you think we ought to have more leisure first and education for it afterwards, or the other way round?
11. What is the best age for conception of the human female?

What do you think of:

12. Integration?
13. Equality?
14. Birth control?
15. Planned Parenthood?
16. Socialized medicine for America?
17. Equal rights for women?
18. Separate schools for boys and girls?
19. Making divorce easier?
20. Special schools for bright children?
21. Punishing the parents of juvenile delinquents?
22. Changing the law relating to alimony?

23. Congressional investigating committees?
24. Filibusters?
25. Euthanasia?
26. The "clean bomb"?
27. Would you be in favor of a four-hour day for the new parents of a child?
28. Do you read works relating to social problems?
29. Should our immigration laws be changed?
30. Should war be outlawed?

SOCIOLOGY

Answers on page 275

1. Define sociology.
2. What is the family?
3. Distinguish between anthropology and sociology.
4. What is meant by "social"?
5. What is "Social Darwinism"?
6. Define an institution.
7. What sociologist regarded society as akin to an organism?
8. What is the function of ceremonial?
9. What is a civilization?
10. Distinguish between competition and cooperation.
11. Define propaganda.
12. Define "a society."
13. The founder of sociology in America was?
14. Define ethnocentrism.
15. What is a "revolution"?
16. What is meant by "caste"?
17. What is war?
18. Are there any other animals in addition to man that make war?
19. What is a custom?
20. What is "Neo-Malthusianism"?
21. A "class" is defined as?

22. What is an individual?
23. What is ritual?
24. Define sectarianism.
25. Define social distance.
26. Is sociology a science?
27. What do you think of the belief in progess?
28. What is the relation between history and sociology?
29. What would you think of a Department of Human Relations on a city basis?
30. What is the value of sociology?

~~

THE THEATER

Answers on page 278

1. The first plays were?
2. What is the proscenium?
3. Where were the musicians placed in the Elizabethan and Restoration theatre?
4. "To upstage" means?
5. In what play did the word "bloody" create a sensation?
6. Who is Thalia?
7. George S. Kaufman wrote only one play by himself. What is the name of that play?
8. A play written to be read, but not to be performed, is called?
9. Margaret Webster is?
10. Who was Stanislavsky?
11. Who is Guthrie McClintic?
12. Who is John Gielgud?

Name the authors of the following:
13. *The Relapse*
14. *The Inspector General*
15. *Amphitryon*
16. *Ghosts*

17. *Green Pastures*
18. *The Playboy of the Western World*
19. Shelley's best known play is?
20. What was the name of the acting company to which Shakespeare belonged?
21. What is Grand Guignol?
22. What is the Green Room?
23. Who was Rachel?
24. What is the rake?
25. What did George Eliot's husband have to do with the theater?
26. Do you read the theater section of your newspaper?
27. Do you read books on the theater?
28. Do you think that all plays should be passed by a state censor before being presented to the public?
29. Do you believe that there ought to be a national theater?
30. How often do you visit the theater?

~~

WHO SAID IT?

Answers on page 280

1. The proper study of mankind is man.
2. It is said that God is always on the side of the heaviest battalions.
3. The public be damned!
4. The surest way to prevent war is not to fear it.
5. I fear, gentlemen, I am an unconscionable a time a-dying.
6. A thing of beauty is a joy for ever.
7. War is too important a matter to leave to the generals.
8. Hypocrisy is a homage paid by vice to virtue.
9. Let them eat cake.
10. I never read a book before reviewing it; it prejudices a man so.
11. Call no man happy till he dies, he is at best but fortunate.
12. The trouble with people is not that they don't know, but that they know so much that ain't so.

13. The great dust-heap called 'history.'
14. Put your trust in God, but mind to keep your powder dry.
15. Publish and be damned.
16. Fortune, that favors fools.
17. Power tends to corrupt and absolute power corrupts absolutely.
18. A fanatic is a man who redoubles his effort when he has lost sight of his aim.
19. Liberty is not the power of doing what we like, but the right of being able to do what we ought.
20. Almost all our faults are more pardonable than the methods we think up to hide them.
21. Originality is the one thing which unoriginal minds cannot feel the use of.
22. Politeness is fictitious benevolence.
23. Any fool can ask unanswerable questions.
24. Thought makes the greatness of man.
25. The secret of being miserable is to have the leisure to bother about whether you are happy or not.
26. His sins were scarlet but his books were read.
27. I would rather be right than be President.
28. Irrationally held truths may be more harmful than reasoned errors.
29. Words are wise men's counters, they do but reckon with them, but they are the money of fools.
30. No man is a hypocrite in his pleasures.

WORDS

Answers on page 282

1. Define the word "word."
2. Define xenophobia.
3. Define polyglot.
4. Define perfunctory.
5. Define peremptory.

6. Define supererogatory.
7. Define serendipity.
8. Define fatuous.
9. Define unctuous.
10. Define historiographer.
11. Define polymath.
12. Give the names of the authors of these books on words: (a) *Words, Words, Words!* (b) *The Romance of Words,* (c) *Language in Thought and Action,* (d) *The Meaning of Meaning,* (e) *Growth and Structure of the English Language.*
13. From what science is the word *eccentric* derived?
14. The best source book for the origins and first usage of English words is?
15. What is the earliest English dictionary?
16. The standard work on the American language is?
17. What is the meaning of the phrase "a baker's dozen"?
18. Can a single word, apart from a context, have a meaning?
19. What is the origin of the expression "I don't give a tinker's dam"?
20. Is a word a symbol or a sign?
21. Who said "Where an idea is wanting, a word can always be found to take its place"?
22. How do words constitute a language?
23. Can any dictionary keep up with the growth of words?
24. What is meant by a "bastard word"?
25. Who said "Let thy words be few"?
26. Do you have a lively interest in etymology?
27. Do you never let the meaning of an unfamilar word escape you?
28. Do you continue to enlarge your vocabulary?
29. Are you a good speller?
30. Do you take great care in the use of your words?

The Answers

SCORING

Let me say once more that the purpose of the questions is to help you achieve an appraisal of your cultural status, and not to have you sit for an examination for a diploma. Hence, you are not going to be told that if you achieve a certain score you pass, and if you don't you don't. However, as an accommodation to those who would like some sort of rating on the questions, such ratings are provided below.

Since the questions of attitude are worth more than those of knowledge they are doubled in value. Questions of knowledge are assigned a value of 5 points each. Questions of attitude have a value of 10 points each. For our purposes these scales do all that we require of them. Since there are usually 25 questions of knowledge in each category, the achievable possible total knowledge score for most categories is 125 points, and the total possible score on questions of attitude is 50 points, the possible total score for each whole category being 175 points.

The possible grand total score for the 50 categories is 8,770 points, there being four categories composed entirely of factual questions and one category consisting almost entirely of attitude questions. No one is likely to achieve that score. The perfect score for questions on knowledge would be 6,230 points. It is unlikely that anyone will ever achieve that score. The total possible score on questions of attitude is 2,540. It is possible that some will achieve that.

SCORES

For Each Category if Your Total Score Is:	*You Are:*
100 or more	Excellent
85 " "	Good
70 " "	Better than average
55 " "	Average

On Questions of Knowledge if Your Score Is:	*You Are:*
75 or more	Excellent
65 " "	Good
55 " "	Better than average
45 " "	Average

On Questions of Attitude if Your Score Is:	*You Are:*
40 or more	Excellent
30 " "	Good
25 " "	Better than average
20 " "	Average

For achievement on the total scores for all categories the ratings are:

On Questions of Knowledge:		*On Questions of Attitude:*	
3,125	Excellent	2,000	Excellent
3,000	Good	1,950	Good
2,875	Above average	1,900	Above average
2,750	Average	1,850	Average
2,600	Passing	1,800	Passing

"Average" in the above classifications means not that you belong in the same class as the average man, but in the class of the average cultured man. Any score ranking below average suggests a certain weakness in your status as a cultured person.

Agriculture, Botany, and Horticulture

1. Agriculture is the art or science of cultivating food plants and animals and other crops. _____
2. Botany is the science that deals with plants, their life, structure, growth, classification, etc. _____
3. Horticulture is the art or science of growing flowers, fruit and vegetables. _____
4. A truck farm is a farm on which vegetables are grown to be marketed. _____
5. Hydroponics is the art or science or growing plants in solutions containing the necessary minerals, instead of in the soil. _____
6. Plants do possess hormones. _____
7. The largest ranch in the United States is the King Ranch, South Texas, covering nearly a million acres. _____
8. Agronomy is the art and science of crop production and management of soils. _____
9. The earliest known sickles were found in Palestine, in caves on Mount Carmel, in the Wadi-en-Natuf, dating back to about 7000 years ago. _____
10. The date palm has to be artificially fertilized if it is to bear fruit. _____
11. Plant ecology is the science of the relations of plants to their environment and to each other. _____
12. The bark of the tree is analogous to the skin in man. _____
13. A cotyledonous plant is one in which the food of the embryo is mainly stored in the leaves (cotyledons) within the seed coat. A grain of corn contains a single cotyledon, a peanut contains two cotyledons. _____
14. Pomology is the science of fruit cultivation. _____

15. Photosynthesis is the formation of carbohydrates in living plants from water and carbon dioxide by the action of sunlight on the chloroplasts. _____

16. A stamen is a pollen-bearing organ in a flower consisting of a slender stalk (filament) and a pollen sac (anther). _____

17. The pistil is the seed-bearing organ of a flower consisting of the ovary, stigma, and style.

18. Some cultivated grasses are wheat, rye, barley, oats, sugar cane. _____

19. Corn (maize) originated in the Americas. _____

20. The corolla consists of the petals, or inner leaves, of a flower. _____

21. The calyx is the outer whorl of leaves, or sepals, at the base of a flower. _____

22. Indian pipes and pinedrops derive their food from dead or decaying vegetable growth. _____

23. The white potato is believed to have originated in South America. _____

24. True mahogany comes from the West Indies and some parts of Central America—not Africa. _____

25. Silviculture is the art of producing and cultivating a forest. _____

26. Every community ought to have a botanical garden, because of the knowledge it serves to diffuse concerning plants, and the interests it creates and satisfies. _____

27. If you have cultivated plants give yourself full marks. _____

28. If you do take care with matches in the open take full marks. _____

29. The probabilities are the population will outrun the food supply *on a world basis* unless people learn to control the size of their families. _____

30. It is better to have the paper. Some trees have to be cut, and modern methods of silviculture are making up for the errors of earlier days. So we can have both the tree and the paper. _____

Americana

1. The title of Thomas Paine's most famous work is *The Rights of Man*, 1791–92, or, if you prefer, *The Age of Reason*, Part I, 1794, and Part II, 1796. _____

2. The two best works written on America are Alexis de Tocqueville's *Democracy in America*, 2 volumes, 1835 and 1840, and Viscount James Bryce's *The American Commonwealth*, 2 volumes, 1888. _____

3. The American autograph regarded as of highest value is that of Button Gwinnett (1735?–1777), a signer of the Declaration of Independence. _____

4. ASCAP, American Society of Composers, Authors, and Publishers. _____

5. The first Woman's Rights Convention was held at Seneca Falls, N.Y. on 19 July 1848. _____

6. The *Acushnet* was the whaler in which Herman Melville (1819–91) spent 18 months in the years 1841–42. _____

7. New Harmony was a colony founded in 1815 by George Rapp, and in 1825 sold to Robert Owen who turned it into a thoroughgoing communistic society. Owing to internal dissension it ceased to exist as an organized community in 1828.

8. Edward Livingston Youmans (1821–87), American popularizer of science. _____

9. The first American musical composer was Francis Hopkinson (1737–91). _____

10. The *Clermont* was Robert Fulton's (1765–1815) steamboat which, starting on August 17, 1807 steamed up the Hudson from New York to Albany in 32 hours. _____

11. The G.A.R. was The Grand Army of the Republic. _____

12. Scientific activities were late in getting started in America because of the stated policy of the British government which required that its colonies function only as sources of raw materials to be shipped back to England in English ships. Local manufactures were discouraged. This restriction on the

use of tools meant that science and invention were inhibited. Clearly perceiving the evil, Adam Smith wrote in 1776 in *The Wealth of Nations:* "To prohibit a great people from making all that they can of every part of their own produce, or from employing their stock and industry in a way that they judge most advantageous to themselves, is a manifest violation of the most sacred rights of mankind."   _____

13. The most significant provision of the Fourteenth Amendment is the clause "nor shall any state deprive any person of life, liberty, or property, without due process of law." Its importance lies in the fact that it guarantees the individual, and the corporation, civil rights.   _____

14. The Mason-Dixon Line is the boundary between Pennsylvania and Maryland, surveyed by Charles Mason (1730–1787) and Jeremiah Dixon from 1763 to 1767, and regarded as the line of demarcation between the North and the South.   _____

15. The Volstead Act, introduced by Rep. Andrew J. Volstead (1860–1947), was passed by Congress October 28, 1919 to prohibit the manufacture and sale of intoxicating liquors. It was repealed in 1933.   _____

16. The Nineteenth Amendment on August 26, 1920, granted suffrage to women.   _____

17. The first real graduate school in America was at Johns Hopkins University, founded in 1876, which is also the foundation date of the University. Its first graduate degrees were granted in 1878—four Ph.D.'s.   _____

18. The first telephone was invented by Alexander Graham Bell (1847–1922) and perfected on May 10, 1876.   _____

19. The first motor-driven plane flew at Kitty Hawk, N.C., December 17, 1903.   _____

20. Vernon Louis Parrington (1871–1929), educator and literary critic, famous for his *Main Currents in American Thought,* 3 volumes, 1927–30.   _____

21. Ernest Hemingway was called the greatest writer since Shakespeare by John O'Hara, in his review of the former's *Across the River and Into the Trees,* in the *New York Times.*_____

22. If you disagree with John O'Hara's judgment on Hemingway

give yourself full marks, for it is one of the silliest ever made.

23. Sears, Roebuck & Co. bought a million copies of Lew Wallace's (1827–1905) novel *Ben Hur, A Tale of the Christ,* which was first published in 1880.

24. The American responsible for the destruction of 160 tons of books and pictures was Anthony Comstock (1844–1915), organizer of the New York Society for the Suppression of Vice, of which he was secretary till his death. This society was a sad illustration of the truth of the dictum that virtue is so much more dangerous than vice because it is not subject to the constraints of the conscience.

25. The "Big Three" among American universities are Harvard, Yale, and Princeton.

26. Isolationism is both undesirable and impossible. All the nations of this world are in it together, and the sooner this is understood the happier this world will be.

27. Alaska and Hawaii should, of course, be granted Statehood. The only reason this has not been done is that certain elements in the government have feared that they might increase the Democratic vote.

28. As the most important members of the community, they should be paid according to their value.

29. There is too much emphasis on the desire to win, as a rule, when Americans play games. With more emphasis on the sportsmanship and fun of the game and less on being a bad loser, Americans could learn a little more about the meaning of character from their games than they do at present.

30. Americans are often called the most materialistic people in the world because they are thought to be too interested in material things to the detriment of their own spiritual or cultural development. While there may be a modicum of truth in this criticism the fact is that Americans have more material advantages than most other peoples because of the natural wealth of their country, and therefore have more to be material about than the less fortunate countries of the world.

American History

1. America was first discovered by Christopher Columbus (1451?–1506) in 1492. The Vikings Leif Ericson and Thorfinn Karlsefni had each independently discovered America about 1000 A.D., but their knowledge had been merely converted into saga. ⸻

2. The first white settlement in America was at Roanoke Island, N.C., in 1585. ⸻

3. The first Negroes, twenty of them, were landed at Jamestown, Virginia, in 1619, purchased from a Dutch warship.⸻

4. The first book printed in English in America was *The Whole Booke of Psalmes,* Cambridge, Mass., 1640: sometimes referred to as the *Bay Psalm Book.* ⸻

5. The oldest university in America is Harvard University which was founded in 1636. ⸻

6. The Pilgrims arrived at Cape Cod in November 1620.

7. The oldest learned society in America is the American Philosophical Society, founded in 1743. It developed out of the junto formed by Benjamin Franklin (1706–1790) in 1727. Franklin was the first secretary of the society. ⸻

8. The first missionary to the Indians was John Eliot (1604–1690) of Massachusetts in 1646. ⸻

9. King Philip's War was started in 1675 by the Indian chief of the Wampanoag Indians of New England, and ended with the killing of Philip and the practical extermination of Indian tribal life in southern New England. ⸻

10. New York acquired its name in 1664. ⸻

11. John Peter Zenger (1697–1746) German-born American journalist who, in 1735, was tried for libel in New York for publishing in his newspaper, the New York *Weekly Journal,* a libel on the then existing administration. It was in this case that truth was established as a sufficient defense against accusation of libel, and thus was freedom of the press strengthened in America. ⸻

12. The date of the first Continental Congress is September 5, 1774.   _____

13. The dates for the War of Independence are 1775–1783.

14. Articles of Confederation were drawn up in the year (November 15) 1777, and ratified in the year 1781.   _____

15. Cornwallis surrendered at Yorktown October 19, 1781.

16. The Constitution was signed on September 17, 1787, and ratified June 21, 1788.   _____

17. The Bill of Rights, consisting of the first ten amendments to the Constitution, was submitted to Congress September 25, 1789, and put into effect in 1791.   _____

18. The first Congress met in the year (March 4) 1789._____

19. John Brown's raid on the Harper's Ferry U.S. Arsenal was made on October 16, 1859. The purpose of the raid was to obtain a secure base to which slaves and free Negroes could escape, and from which risings could be stirred up, against the institution of slavery.   _____

20. The first reigning European sovereigns to set foot on American soil were King George VI and his Queen. Queen Marie of Romania visited the United States in 1926 while her husband, Ferdinand, still reigned, but he was the ruler and she his consort.   _____

21. The first President of the United States to be inaugurated in Washington was Thomas Jefferson, March 4, 1801.   _____

22. The African Slave Trade was abolished January 1, 1808.   _____

23. The War of 1812 was declared on England on the ground of impressment, violation of the three-mile limit, paper blockade, and orders in council, June 18, 1812.   _____

24. The Dred Scott decision was that of the Supreme Court, in March 1857, denying a former slave of that name the right to his freedom simply in virtue of his having been taken into and living in a State which had outlawed slavery, that Congress had no right to enact a law that deprived persons of their property in the territories of the United States. The

decision was later nullified by the Fourteenth Amendment.

_____

25. The Mexican War (1846–48) was fought to take New Mexico from the Mexicans, and the pretext arranged by Polk was to send American troops into a disputed area, thus precipitating a skirmish which enabled him to say that the Mexicans had "shed American blood on American soil."   _____

26. Compared to most European countries, America is a young country. But there is some truth in Oscar Wilde's jibe that America's claim to youth is one of its oldest myths. Too often the argument of youth is put forward as a defense against the accusation of immaturity.   _____

27. There is only one answer. The way we have treated the American Indian has been disgraceful. It is a story of treachery, exploitation, and lawlessness—and we are doing very little to make amends.   _____

28. Little Rock is a reflection on America. There has obviously been a failure in the education of some Americans in the understanding of the meaning of democracy.   _____

29. If a knowledge of its history is a measure of one's pride in one's country, then Americans don't have much pride in their country, for the average American is woefully ignorant of his country's history.   _____

30. On the whole, Americans appear to be no more capable of learning from history than other peoples. It would appear that no people has a monopoly on boneheads and blunderers.

_____

~~

Anatomy and Physiology

1. The average weight of the normal human male brain is about 1400 grams or 3 pounds.   _____

2. There are 20 milk teeth.   _____

3. There are 32 permanent teeth.   _____

4. The principal blood-forming organ of the body is the red marrow of the bones.   _____

5. The esophagus is behind the trachea.   _____
6. The hardest substance in the body is the enamel of the teeth.
                                                           _____
7. The two coronary arteries are situated on the heart._____
8. The heart has four chambers—two atria and two ventricles.

                                                           _____
9. The aorta is the main artery of the body carrying blood from
   the left ventricle.   _____
10. The pupil of the eye is formed by the central margins of the
    iris. The iris is a muscular diaphragm and the pupil is the
    hole in the middle of that diaphragm.   _____
11. Hair and nails do not continue to grow at any time after
    death. What happens is that the skin contracts with the con-
    sequent exposure of more hair and nail.   _____
12. The metabolic rate is about 5 to 6 per cent higher in the male.
13. The "master gland" of the body is the pituitary gland, so
    called because its secretions dominantly influence the growth
    and development of the organism and the action of all the
    other endocrine glands.   _____
14. An endocrine gland secretes a hormonal substance directly
    into the blood stream and not through a duct.   _____
15. A hormone is a chemical substance formed in one organ, or
    certain cells of one organ, of the body and carried by the blood
    or other body fluid, and having a specific effect on body cells
    far removed from the elaborating organ.   _____
16. Bones are stronger because they are hollow. A cylinder is
    stronger than a solid.   _____
17. Blue eyes are not due to blue pigment but to the smaller
    number of brown pigmented particles in the iris. The larger
    the number of brown pigment particles the browner or darker
    the eye.   _____
18. The Babinski reflex is extension, instead of the normal flexion,
    of the big toe following stroking of the sole of the foot,
    usually associated with disease of the pyramidal tracts of the
    spinal cord.   _____
19. Colostrum is the first milk, a lemony-yellowish fluid which
    comes into the breasts during the last months of pregnancy,
    and very desirable for the newborn to ingest.   _____

20. The gases and other substances contained in tobacco smoke enter the blood stream principally through the mucous membranes of the mouth and pharynx. _____

21. Saliva enters the mouth through ducts under the tongue and in the cheek. _____

22. Shaving has no effect whatever upon the growth of hair.

_____

23. It is inadvisable to cross one's knees for several reasons, the two most important being: (1) pressure on the peroneal nerves may injure them and cause footdrop, and (2) the same pressure will impede the return of the blood in the veins toward the heart and thus cause excessive pressure in the veins with resulting varicosities of these vessels. _____

24. The behavioral trait most frequently associated with the long-lived is placidity. _____

25. Overweight is bad for health because it increases the work that the heart must do in order to service the excess tissues.

26. If you smoke give yourself a zero. If you don't smoke take full marks. _____

27. A civilized and moderate drinker is one who never drinks to excess. _____

28. If you take regular exercise in any form give yourself full marks; if your exercise is irregular, take a zero. _____

29. You should see your dentist at least every six months. If you don't, take a zero. _____

30. You should see your doctor for a general check-up once a year. Take a zero if you don't. _____

～～

Anthropology

1. Anthropology is the science of man as a physical and as a cultural being. It includes his origin and evolution, the way he got to be the way he is today, and what he is today in all the varieties of form and culture in which he exhibits himself.

_____

2. There is only one living species of man: *Homo sapiens.*

———

3. The three major groups of mankind are the Caucasoid, the Mongoloid, and the Negroid.   ———
4. Man has been on the earth about a million years.   ———
5. No one knows. But the probabilities seem to be that if such differences do exist they are of a relatively minor kind.

———

6. The closest known fossil relatives of man are the South African manlike apes, the Australopithecines.   ———
7. The first people who are known to have buried their dead were the Neanderthal men.   ———
8. The father of scientific anthropology in America was Lewis Henry Morgan (1818–1881).   ———
9. The people who when they want to rest take exercises are the Indians and whites who live in the Trans-Andean region.

———

10. Within the normal range of variation, the size of the forehead bears no relation to intelligence whatever.   ———
11. The principal blood groups are A, B, AB, and O. Many other blood factors and subgroups are known.   ———
12. The author of *Primitive Culture* was Edward Burnett Tylor (1832–1917).   ———
13. *The Mind of Primitive Man* was written by Franz Boas (1858–1942).   ———
14. There are quite a number of peoples who have no belief in a supreme god, among them the Australian aborigines and some Eskimos.   ———
15. The only peoples unable to make fire in the twentieth century were the Andaman Islanders and the Congo pygmies. The Andaman Islanders were ignorant of firemaking, but obtained fire by the simple device of never letting their fires go out. The Congo pygmies purchase their fire from their Bantu neighbors.   ———
16. There are no matriarchal societies and there is no record of one ever having existed.   ———
17. A short definition of culture is that it is the way of life of a

people. It is the man-made part of the environment that each people creates for itself. Culture includes all those things, and only those things, that the person has acquired from his social group by conscious learning. Culture represents all the learned behavior that has been socially acquired, and includes the material as well as the immaterial creations of his group, the pots and pans, as well as the laws and religious beliefs.

18. Cultural relativism refers to the fact that the appropriateness of any aspect of a culture must be evaluated in relation to other aspects of that culture. It also refers to the evaluation of any aspect of culture within that culture. It does *not* mean that any aspect of a culture may be *justified* on the relative ground that what is considered right in that culture therefore makes it right for that culture. It also means that any judgment or evaluation of a way of life different from one's own is not valid in terms of one's own.

19. The principal argument of Ruth Benedict's (1887–1948) *Patterns of Culture,* 1936, is that every culture has a distinctive theme around which it patterns itself.

20. The factor principally responsible for the differences in the cultures of the world is the difference in the history of their cultural experience, in what each people has undergone.

21. Several peoples have no chiefs, such as the Australian aborigines and the Eskimo.

22. There are many objections to the use of the word "race," chief among them being that most persons who use the term do not know what they are talking about when they use it. Furthermore, the word is emotionally embarrassed with all sorts of under- and overtones of meanings which do not correspond to the facts. In speaking of the varieties of man it is far better to use the noncommittal term "ethnic group" instead of "race."*

* For a further discussion of this point see Ashley Montagu, *Man's Most Dangerous Myth: The Fallacy of Race,* 3rd edition, Harper & Brothers, New York, 1952. See also Ashley Montagu, *Statement on Race,* Abelard-Schuman, New York, 1952.

23. The languages of nonliterate peoples are usually more complex, and often more highly developed, than those of literate peoples. _____

24. The principle of equality is an ethical principle, *not* a biological one. It is based on the ground that since all human beings are human they have a right to the development of their birthright of humanity and the development of their potentialities to the optimum. _____

25. The most famous *Statement on Race* was issued by UNESCO in 1950 and in 1952. _____

26. Anthropology as the science of man should form the core of every curriculum. _____

27. Race prejudice can be significantly reduced by legislation because law gives the sanction to what is right and makes human beings feel more comfortable in the knowledge that what is required ought to be. _____

28. Recent changes in attitudes traceable to the influence of anthropology are the better understanding of so-called race differences, the emphasis being more intelligently directed to the likenesses which unite, without uniformizing, men, and the more mature consciousness of other peoples. _____

29. Take full marks if you do, zero if you don't. _____

30. The principal use of anthropology is that more than any other discipline it is capable of giving us an insight into the nature of man. _____

~·~

Archaeology

1. The scientific study of the life and culture of ancient peoples or of cultures that no longer exist. _____

2. The oldest known bas-relief is the female figure with bison's horn from the Laussel Cave, in the Dordogne of southwestern France, dating back some 15,000 years or more. _____

3. The oldest known statuettes are the fertility figures of females such as the Venus of Willendorf, Austria, probably of Aurignacian age. _____

4. In the caves of the Dordogne of southwestern France._____

5. Heinrich Schliemann (1822–1890) was the German archaeologist who revived the interest in Greek classical archaeology.

6. The pebble-tools found in various parts of Africa, and notably South Africa sometimes in association with Australopithecine remains.

7. The Rosetta Stone is the tablet of black basalt found in 1799 at Rosetta in Egypt. It bore parallel inscriptions in ancient Egyptian demotic and hieroglyphic characters, and in Greek, and thus made possible the deciphering of ancient Egyptian writing. It is now in the British Museum.

8. The oldest known village site is at Jarmo, northern Iraq, dating back to about 5000 B.C.

9. The earliest known city-state is Ur of the Chaldees in Mesopotamia, dating back to about 4000 B.C.

10. The principal excavators of Tutankhamen's tomb were Howard Carter (1873–1939) and Lord Carnarvon (George E. S. Molyneux, 1866–1923).

11. Radiocarbon dating is a method of determining the age of an object by a count of the carbon-14 remaining in it.

12. Jean François Champollion (1790–1832) was the French Egyptologist who helped to decipher the Egyptian hieroglyphic writing on the Rosetta Stone.

13. The Kensington Stone is a stone inscribed with a runic account of a Norse exploration in 1362, found on a farm near Kensington, Minnesota, in 1898. Whether the stone is genuine or not is still disputed.

14. "The Fertile Crescent" is the name originally given by James Henry Breasted (1865–1935) to the crescent-formed region that fringes the Syrian Desert from the Mediterranean coast of Palestine to the Persian Gulf.

15. The first appearance of pottery is usually associated with the Neolithic, although some Mesolithic examples are known.

16. Sir Leonard Woolley's (1880–   ) name is principally associated with his excavations at Ur.

17. Our knowledge of Cretan civilization is mostly due to the work of Sir John Evans (1851–1941).

18. The Inca ruined city of Machu Picchu was discovered in 1911 by Hiram Bingham (1875–   ).   _____

19. The earliest writing was found at Ur in Mesopotamia dating back to about 4000 B.C.   _____

20. The earliest evidences of raiding are found at several Neolithic village sites in the Near and Middle East.   _____

21. The earliest record of a king occurs among the Gerzeans, who lived somewhat west of the Faiyum in Egypt about 3000 B.C.
     _____

22. Boucher de Crèvecoeur de Perthes (1788–1868) was a pioneering French archaeologist.   _____

23. *What Happened in History* and *Man Makes Himself*, both by V. Gordon Childe (1892–1957), and each obtainable in a 35¢ paperback.   _____

24. The Palaeolithic Period begins at the base of the Pleistocene about a million years ago, and ends with the end of Pleistocene about 25,000 years ago.   _____

25. The Piltdown skull is a fraudulent assembly of human skull fragments together with the lower jaw of an orangutan perpetrated upon the scientific world for some 40 years.*_____

26. Yes. In order to protect valuable ancient remains from damage, loss, or unavailability for study, the state ought to retain possession of most such objects.   _____

27. The most important ones should, and if there are any left over by way of duplicates or representative examples, they could go to other countries.   _____

28. If you've read one or more give yourself full marks.   _____

29. Most people would like to go on an archaeological dig. The principal reason should be "fun."   _____

30. The use of archaeology is that it enables us to establish a sense of continuity with the nonhistoricized past.   _____

* See J. S. Weiner, *The Piltdown Forgery*, Oxford University Press, New York, 1955.

Architecture

1. Architecture is the art or science of constructing buildings.
   _____

2. The Byzantine style in architecture refers broadly to the style of architecture developed at Byzantium after Constantine moved the capital of the Roman Empire to that city in 330 A.D. (now the site of Istanbul). The style is characterized by the richness and color of the decoration combined with the spaciousness of aerial enclosure within the gracious shapes of semicircular apses, domes, and arches. Sancta Sophia at Istanbul and St. Mark's in Venice are good examples of the style.   _____

3. Baroque is the style of architecture characterized by much ornamentation and curved rather than straight lines, in which the architect treated his materials much as a sculptor does. The style flourished in the period 1550–1750.   _____

4. Perpendicular style in architecture is characterized by the perpendicular or vertical lines of its pillars, paneline, and tracery in the final period of English Gothic (late fourteenth to mid-sixteenth century). The finest examples are to be seen in Gloucester and Winchester Cathedrals, and in several of the chapels of Oxford and Cambridge colleges.   _____

5. One of the best-preserved and best-known buildings of antiquity is the Pantheon at Rome.   _____

6. *The Stones of Venice* (3 vols.), 1851–53, was written by John Ruskin (1819–1900).   _____

7. *The Architecture of Humanism,* 1914, was written by Geoffrey Scott (1885–1929).

8. *Sticks and Stones,* 1924, was written by Lewis Mumford (1895-   ).   _____

9. The Geometric style is characterized by decorations developed from straight geometric designs, tracery, ornamented molding, and curvilinear patterns based on shapes in nature. It was a style popular during the latter half of the fourteenth century, during the second period of Gothic architecture in England. Bristol Cathedral is a good example.   _____

10. Banister Fletcher (1833–99), English professor of architecture, was author, with his son Sir Banister F. Fletcher (1866–1953), of *A History of Architecture on the Comparative Method,* originally published in 1896, and in print in a revised edition today.

11. The leaders in the Bauhaus movement, which combined the teaching of the pure arts with the study of crafts, combining architecture and functionalism, science and technology, were Walter Gropius (1883–   ), Marcel Breuer (1902–   ), László Moholy-Nagy (1895–1946), Hannes Meyer, and Miës van der Rohe.

12. By "thrust" is meant the continuous outward pressure as, for example, of an arch against its abutments.

13. The Erechtheum is one of the most beautiful examples of Greek architecture, being the temple in Pentelic marble on the Acropolis at Athens, built between about 420 and 409 B.C. Its design is sometimes attributed to the architect Mnesicles.

14. The triangular part or gable on the top front of Greek, or any other buildings, is known as the pediment.

15. A lintel is the horizontal crosspiece over a door or window, carrying the weight of the structure above it.

16. The Gothic period in architecture lasted from the middle of the twelfth to the middle of the sixteenth century. It is characterized by the use of ribbed vaulting, flying buttresses, pointed arches, steep roofs.

17. The first skyscraper in New York was the Flatiron Building situated at the junction of Broadway and Fifth Avenue at 23rd Street, and erected in 1902. It still is in use.

18. Sir Christopher Wren's (1632–1723) most famous building is St. Paul's Cathedral in London, erected between 1675 and 1710.

19. The Imperial Hotel in Tokyo was designed by Frank Lloyd Wright (1869–   ).

20. The invention of concrete is sometimes attributed to the Romans, but it was certainly not invented, but adopted and widely used by them. The inventing people is not clearly known.

21. An architrave is the lowest part of an entablature, that is to say, the beam resting directly on the tops of the columns.

_____

22. A wood lining or paneling on the walls of a room.   _____

23. An entablature is the horizontal superstructure supported by columns and consisting of architrave, frieze, and cornice.

_____

24. A frieze is a horizontal decorative band between the architrave and the cornice.   _____

25. The most famous living American architect is Frank Lloyd Wright (1869–   ).   _____

26. For one thing it eliminates the necessity of climbing stairs.

_____

27. It is well enough for those who like it—but it has been suggested that it puts those who live on the other side of it in the position of the fish in a transparent bowl.   _____

28. Certainly there should be some regulation of the design and style of buildings in order to secure quality, durability, security, and aesthetic harmony.   _____

29. Utility in architecture should never be sacrificed to beauty—well, hardly ever.   _____

30. The most important quality in an architect is his competence to design a building which is at once efficient and beautiful.

_____

~~

Art

1. Art is the making or doing of things that have form and beauty.   _____

2. The father of Impressionism was Camille Pissarro (1830–1903), who painted the first impressionist pictures. _____

3. The name "Impressionism" originated when the title of a painting by Claude Monet (1840–1926), "Une Impression," exhibited in Paris in 1863 at the Salon des Refusés, was used as a peg for an attack upon the whole school of painters of which Monet was a member, by the critic in _Le Figaro_, who

contemptuously referred to this "Impressionism." Monet's picture bore the title "Sunrise: An Impression."　　　—————

4. The orginator of pointillism was Georges Seurat (1859–91).
　　　—————

5. The "Virgin Among the Rocks" or "Madonna of the Grotto," was painted by Leonardo da Vinci (1452–1519). There are two versions by him of this painting, one in the National Art Gallery in London, the other in the Louvre in Paris. —————

6. The inventor of aerial perspective in painting was Masaccio (Tommaso Guidi), 1401–1428. Paolo Uccello (c. 1396–1475) was, at least, one of the pioneers in the development of linear perspective.　　　—————

7. Benvenuto Cellini (1500–1571), Gian Bologna (c. 1529–1608), and Donatello (1386?–1466). Their works being "Perseus," "The Rape of the Sabines," and "Judith." —————

8. Hubert van Eyck (c. 1366–1426) and Jan van Eyck (c. 1385–1441) have been called the originators of oil painting. They were the first to use a resin or oil medium in naturalistic painting to obtain the greater depth and richness which the medium permits. Antonello de Messina (1430–1479) was the first to introduce the methods of the van Eycks into Italy.　　　—————

9. Tempera is the process of painting in which pigments are mixed usually with egg-yolk to produce a dull finish. —————

10. "La Primavera" was painted by Sandro Botticelli (1444–1510).　　　—————

11. "The Last Supper" was painted by Leonardo da Vinci (1452–1519).　　　—————

12. "La Gioconda" (Mona Lisa) was painted by Leonardo da Vinci.　　　—————

13. "The Blue Boy" was painted by Thomas Gainsborough (1727–1788).　　　—————

14. "The Potato Eaters" was painted by Vincent Van Gogh (1853–1890).　　　—————

15. "A Lady Standing at the Virginals" was painted by Jan Vermeer (1632–1675).　　　—————

16. The sculptor of "David" was Michelangelo (1475–1564).
　　　—————

17. The sculptor of "Night" and "Day" was Michelangelo.
               ————

18. "Hermes with the Infant Dionysus" is by the greatest sculptor of antiquity, the Greek Praxiteles (c. 370–c. 330 B.C.).
               ————

19. "The Thinker" is by François Rodin (1840–1917).   ————
20. "Rima" is by Jacob Epstein (1880–   ).   ————
21. The Baptistery Doors at Florence are by Lorenzo Ghiberti (1378–1455).
               ————
22. Rembrandt's (1606–1669) favorite model was his wife Saskia, and also his housekeeper Hendrickje Stoffels, with whom he lived after his wife's death.
               ————
23. Russia has never produced a first-class painter, unless we turn Marc Chagall (born in Vitebsk, 1887) into a Russian, for his major influences appear to have been French and Jewish.
               ————

24. Pablo Picasso (1881–   ) was the founder of cubism.
               ————

25. Dadaism was a cult in painting, sculpture, and literature (so named because it resembled the meaningless cry of a child), which flourished between the years 1916–22. It was characterized by fantastic, symbolic, and often formless expression of supposedly subconscious matter, and by nihilistic satire, later repudiated by its leading cultist, Tristan Tzara (1896–   ).
               ————

26. It is hoped that you visit an art gallery or an exhibition at least once a year.
               ————
27. Art in education can greatly assist toward the freeing of the individual's thinking, to give him a new angle of vision, as it were.
               ————
28. The more buildings decorated by artists the pleasanter life would be.
               ————
29. It would be delightful if artists were to join in the decoration of a house, and not simply to be represented by framed pictures. Frescoes, for example, would add greatly to the beauty of many a home.
               ————
30. The value of the artist to society lies not only in the beauty

he creates, but in the example of freedom and imagination
which he presents.   _____

~~

Astronomy

1. The science of the stars and other celestial bodies.   _____
2. The diameter of the sun is 865,000 miles.   _____
3. The use of an artificial satellite is largely experimental, and
   to answer many questions about outer space and the possibility
   of human survival in such artificial structures.   _____
4. A star is a sun.   _____
5. The most distant star from the earth visible to the unaided eye
   is Betelgeuse which is some 1,440,000,000,000,000 miles
   away from the earth.   _____
6. The geocentric conception of the universe is sometimes called
   the Ptolemaic.   _____
7. An aphelion is the point farthest from the sun in the orbit
   of a planet or comet.   _____
8. The ecliptic is the sun's apparent annual path or orbit, or that
   of the earth as seen from the sun.   _____
9. A penumbra is the partly lighted area surrounding the complete shadow of a body, as the moon, in full eclipse.   _____
10. The ether is a general term referring to the upper regions of
    space: a term no longer used by contemporary astrophysicists.

11. Only Saturn among the planets possesses a ring or rings.

12. The circumference of the earth is about 24,830 miles at the
    equator.   _____
13. The distance that light travels in one year, approximately
    6,000,000,000,000 years, is a light-year.   _____
14. The planets of the solar system are Mercury, Venus, Earth,
    Mars, Jupiter, Saturn, Uranus, Neptune, and Pluto.   _____
15. A galaxy is a grouping of millions of stars apparently merging
    into a luminous band. Our own galaxy, the Milky Way, is

an example. All the stars visible to us, and the solar system, are part of this galaxy. _____

16. An eclipse is a total or partial darkening of the sun when the moon comes between it and the earth, or of the moon when the earth's shadow is cast upon it. _____

17. William Herschel (1738–1822), English astronomer, discovered the planet Uranus (1781). _____

18. The principal means of studying the heavens is by camera through a telescope. _____

19. Because the moon has no atmosphere, it undergoes extreme variations in temperature such that no type of life of which we know could develop there. _____

20. The distance of the moon from the earth is about 239,000 miles. _____

21. The *Almagest,* the Arabic title of the Arabic translation of the work on astronomy completed by Claudius Ptolemy (second century A.D.) about 150 A.D., the *Great Syntaxis of Astronomy.* _____

22. The most important book in the history of astronomy is Nicolaus Copernicus' (1473–1543) *The Revolutions of the Heavenly Bodies,* 1543. _____

23. Some of the practical uses of astronomy are that it makes navagation at sea and in the air possible, that it makes a calendar possible, which enables us to compute time and predict the seasons. _____

24. The distance of the sun from the earth is about 93 million miles. _____

25. A comet is a heavenly body having a starlike nucleus with a luminous mass around it, and, usually, a long, luminous tail. _____

26. Among other things, it might provide a solution for the population problem. _____

27. Take full marks if you can, and a zero if you can't. _____

28. The fact that the Russians launched an artificial satellite before Americans did constitutes an evidence of the fact long known to many students of Russia, namely, that they have long been exceptionally gifted scientists. Only our military men have been unaware of this. But, then, if you look in the

dictionary under "intelligence" you will find it classified in descending order of merit, as "human intelligence," "animal intelligence," and "military intelligence."   _____

29. A book on astronomy every five years is a good record. _____

30. Most certainly astronomy ought to be well taught in our schools.   _____

~·~

Ballet and Dance

1. Ballet is an intricate group dance using pantomime and conventionalized movements to tell a story.   _____

2. To move gracefully, usually to music, with rhythmical steps, gestures, and figures, is to dance.   _____

3. The Morris dance is an English folk dance, common on May Day, in which fancy costumes are worn: allegedly derived from the Spanish *moresca,* which is, in turn, of Moorish origin.   _____

4. A choral dance is a round dance in which persons dance together rather than as individuals. The rounds may take a great variety of forms.   _____

5. The Castle Walk was a ballroom dance popular in the middle of the second decade of the twentieth century: named for its originators, the dance team of Vernon (1887–1918) and Irene Castle.   _____

6. A choreographer is a person who designs or arranges the movements of a ballet.   _____

7. *La Boutique Fantasque* is a ballet with music by Giacchino Antonio Rossini (1792–1868). It was produced by Sergei Diaghilev (1872–1929) for the first time in London June 5, 1919.*   _____

8. The greatest impresario of the ballet in the twentieth century was Sergei Pavlovich Diaghilev (1872–1929), creator, producer, and choreographer of the Russian Ballet.   _____

9. *The House Party,* also known as *Les Biches,* is a Diaghilev

* For an eye-witness account of the opening night performance see Cyril W. Beaumont, *The Diaghilev Ballet in London,* A. & C. Black, London, 1951, pp. 128sq.

ballet (1924) with music by Francis Poulenc (1899–   ), scenery and costumes by Marie Laurencin (1885–1956), and choreography by Bronislava Nijinska (1890–   ). _____

10. Perhaps the most perfect male ballet solo was danced by Vaslav Nijinsky (1890–1950) in *L'Après-midi d'un Faune.*
   _____

11. The composer of the music for *The Three-Cornered Hat* was Manuel de Falla (1876–1946).   _____

12. The music for *The Fire Bird* was composed by Igor Stravinsky (1882–   ).   _____

13. The music for *Daphnis et Chloé* was written by Maurice Ravel (1875–1937).   _____

14. The most distinguished living English ballet dancer is Margot Fonteyn (1919–   ).

15. A minuet is a slow stately dance for groups of couples. It was introduced as a court dance in France in the seventeenth century. It is a highly stylized courtship dance.   _____

16. The most distinguished English ballet corps is the Sadler's Wells Ballet, known since 1956 as the Royal Ballet. _____

17. Vaslav Nijinsky (1890–1950) was the greatest of all the male Russian ballet dancers.   _____

18. Serge Lifar (1905–   ) is one of the greatest living ballet dancers and choreographers.

19. Isadora Duncan (1878–1927) was a great American dancer and founder of a school of dancing.   _____

20. A pavane or peacock dance is a slow, stuttering, proud court dance, very solemn, of Spanish or Italian origin, performed by couples.   _____

21. Ted Shawn (1891–   ) is a distinguished American dancer. In 1912, with Ruth St. Denis (1877–   ), who became his wife in 1914, he founded the Denishawn School.   _____

22. Moira Shearer (1926–   ) is one of the most distinguished of English ballet dancers.   _____

23. Martha Graham (1893–   ) is an outstanding American dancer.   _____

24. It is natural to dance in the sense that all persons are born with a sense of rhythm and enjoy rhythmical movements.
   _____

25. The outstanding dancer in "The Red Shoes" was Moira Shearer.   _____

26. All children most certainly ought to be taught to dance, so that they might take a proper delight in this art.   _____

27. One should never miss an opportunity to attend a ballet or dance recital. You should go at least once a year!   _____

28. It is good, in many ways and for many reasons, to dance frequently.   _____

29. Of course there ought to be a national ballet.   _____

30. Apart from the fact that dancing is a desirable social accomplishment, it makes for much unity in a family where dancing is frequent, in addition to adding to the grace of one's carriage.   _____

~~

Biography

1. Thomas Hobbes (1588–1679), English philosopher, and author of the famous *Leviathan*, 1651.   _____

2. Thomas Robert Malthus (1766–1834), English economist, author of the famous *An Essay on the Principle of Population*, 1798.   _____

3. Thomas Mott Osborne (1859–1926), American prison reformer, author of *Within Prison Walls*, 1914.   _____

4. Charles Sanders Peirce (1839–1914), American mathematician, philosopher, physician, who developed the idea of pragmatism.   _____

5. Gilbert Murray (1866–1956), British classical scholar and humanist.   _____

6. Henry Thomas Buckle (1821–62), English historian, and author of the panoramic *History of Civilization in England*, 2 vols., 1857 and 1861, left uncompleted by his early death.

_____

7. Thomas Garrigue Masaryk (1850–1937), first president and chief founder of Czechoslovakia.   _____

8. Richard Burbage (1567–1619), English actor and friend of Shakespeare and with the latter in the Lord Chamberlain's

Company. He acted in many of Shakespeare's plays, and the Felton portrait of Shakespeare is believed to be by him.

9. Alfred Adler (1870–1937), Austrian psychiatrist, founder of the school of individual psychology.

10. Walter Bradford Cannon (1871–1945). American physiologist, was professor of physiology at Harvard and author of several important works, among the most famous of which are *Bodily Changes in Pain, Hunger, Fear and Rage,* 1915, and *The Wisdom of the Body,* 1932.

11. Thorstein Veblen (1857–1929), American economist and social scientist, who has had an increasingly wider influence since his death. His most famous book is *The Theory of the Leisure Class,* 1899.

12. Henry Ernest Sigerist (1891–1956), Swiss-American historian of medicine.

13. Harry Stack Sullivan (1892–1949), American psychiatrist, associated with the interpersonal school of psychiatry of which he was a leader.

14. Petr Kropotkin (1842–1921), Russian philosopher, author of the famous *Mutual Aid: A Factor of Evolution,* 1902.

15. Thomas Hunt Morgan (1866–1945), demonstrator of the physical basis of heredity, for which he received the Nobel Prize in physiology and medicine in 1933.

16. John Maynard Keynes (1883–1946), English economist. His most famous book was *Economic Consequences of the Peace,* 1919. He married (1925) Lydia Lopokova (1891–   ), the Russian ballet dancer. Their union was celebrated in the couplet:

> O! what a marriage of beauty and brains,
> The fair Lopokova and John Maynard Keynes!

17. Gaetano Salvemini (1873–1957), Italian historian and anti-Fascist.

18. George Sarton (1884–1956), Belgian-American historian of science, author of the great *Introduction to the History of Science,* 3 vols., 1927–48.

19. Alfred North Whitehead (1861–1947), English mathematician and philosopher, who after teaching a full academic career in England, taught from 1924 to 1937 at Harvard. He is the author of many notable books. _____

20. Havelock Ellis (1859–1939), English psychologist and sexologist, author of the famous seven-volume *Studies in the Psychology of Sex* (1897–1928), and numerous other distinguished works. _____

21. Lionel Trilling (1905–   ), American literary critic, professor of English at Columbia University. _____

22. Paul Tillich (1886–   ), German-American Protestant theologian and philosopher, now teaching at Harvard Divinity School. _____

23. Robert Maynard Hutchins (1899–   ), American educator, formerly President of the University of Chicago, now Director of the Ford Foundation Fund for the Republic. _____

24. Alfred Zimmern (1879–1958), English political scientist, and, among many other valuable books, author of the famous *The Greek Commonwealth,* 1911. _____

25. Lynn Thorndike (1882–   ), American historian, and author of the great work, *A History of Magic and Experimental Science,* 8 vols., 1923–58. _____

26. Percy Williams Bridgman (1882–   ), American physicist, and author of *The Logic of Modern Physics,* 1927; winner of the Nobel prize for physics in 1946. _____

27. Martin Buber (1878–   ), Jewish philosopher and scholar, author of many works, among them *Between Man and Man,* 1947, and *I and Thou,* 1937. _____

28. V. Gordon Childe (1892–1957), British archaeologist, author of the famous works *What Happened in History,* 1942, and *Man Makes Himself,* 1936. _____

29. Niels Bohr (1885–   ), Danish physicist. He received the Nobel Prize in physics in 1922, and the Atoms for Peace Prize of $75,000 in 1957. _____

30. Vladimir Zworykin (1889–   ), American physicist, inventor of the Iconoscope or electric eye, a cathode-ray tube, the Kinescope, both indispensable parts of television equip-

ment, and an electron microscope (1939), among many other inventions.

~~

Biology

1. The science of living matter in all its forms. Biology deals with the history, evolution, origin, structural and functional characteristics of living organisms, whether animal or plant, viral or multicellular.

2. Sex is largely determined by the structure of the chromosomal materials derived from parental organisms. In man when an X-bearing chromosome in the male germ cell unites with an ovum (which always bears an X-chromosome) a female results, when a sperm bearing a Y-chromosome unites with an ovum a male always results.

3. A gene is a hereditary particle contained in a chromosome. It is a giant autocatalytic self-duplicating protein molecule.

4. A chromosome is a rod-shaped body situated in the nucleus of a cell and carrying the genes.

5. There are 23 or 24 chromosomes in the adult human germ cell.

6. Radiation acts upon heredity by producing mutations in the genes.

7. Natural selection is thus defined by Charles Darwin in *On the Origin of Species,* 1859, p. 5: "As many more individuals of each species are born than can possibly survive; and as, consequently, there is a frequently recurring struggle for existence, it follows that any being, if it vary however slightly in any manner profitable to itself, under the complex and sometimes varying conditions of life, will have a better chance of surviving, and thus be *naturally selected.* From the strong principle of inheritance, any selected variety will tend to propagate its new and modified form." A short statement of the principle is *differential fertility,* favoring those possessing the necessary adaptive traits.

8. An atavism, from the Latin *atavus,* meaning an ancestor, refers to the reappearance in a descendant form of a trait which had already been lost in the ancestral form. Such phenomena are, in fact, not known to occur.*　_____

9. Heterosis is the vigor which, as a consequence of the crossing of different varieties of the same species, results in a higher yield, greater resistance, and similar valuable traits.　_____

10. A race is a circumscribed population of a species differing from other populations of the same species in one or more genes.　_____

11. The mule can exhibit neither pride of ancestry nor hope of posterity, being the offspring of a horse *(Equus caballus)* and a donkey *(Equus asinus)*, and, an example of an interspecific cross, it is usually sterile, though exhibiting evidence of hybrid vigor commercially much valued.　_____

12. A mammal is a vertebrate the female member of which gives birth to live young and feeds them from her milk-secreting glands, the mammae, hence the name.　_____

13. It is quite impossible for a union between a white and a white-appearing person of Negroid ancestry to result in any but white-colored offspring, because the white carries only white skin genes, and the white-appearing person of Negroid ancestry has no colored skin genes left. If such a person did have such genes they could not find any to match up with in the other partner. Hence, all stories to the contrary are false.　_____

14. There are no biologically unfavorable effects whatever of human race-crossing. On the contrary, the effects are likely to be beneficial from the biological point of view.　_____

15. Telegony is the erroneous notion that the hereditary characteristics of one sire can be transmitted to or influence the heredity of the offspring of the same female by other sires. The Nazis, for example, alleged that no Aryan woman could ever bear Aryan children once she had had any sexual relations with a non-Aryan!　_____

* See Ashley Montagu, "The Concept of Atavism," in his *Anthropology and Human Nature,* Porter Sargent, Boston, 1957, p. 347.

16. The order of mammals to which man belongs is the Primates.

_____

17. Acquired physical characters are not inheritable.   _____

18. "Darwinian fitness" is another term for "adaptive fitness." It refers to any trait that fits the organism to survive in such a manner that it has naturally selective value.   _____

19. A mutation is a permanent change in the structure of a gene, the permanent change being hereditarily transmissible.

_____

20. The American geneticist Hermann J. Muller (1890–   ), was the first to induce mutations in the fruit fly _Drosophila_. For this achievement he was awarded the Nobel Prize in Medicine and physiology for 1946.   _____

21. An invertebrate is an animal lacking a backbone. The invertebrates include all classes of animals, except fishes, amphibians, reptiles, birds, and mammals.   _____

22. A dolphin is a mammal of the whale family, with a beaklike snout and teeth in the upper jaw. There are also two marine fishes that are known as dolphins.   _____

23. The name of Jean Baptiste Lamarck (1744–1820) is identified with the theory of evolution through the transmission of acquired characters.   _____

24. There is no reason why close cousins should not be permitted to marry if they come from a reasonably healthy stock with no serious hereditary deficiencies or abnormalities. Only when there is a history of such conditions in the families of each would such a marriage be inadvisable. It should be remembered that the Pharaohs married their own sisters for some seven generations, without the slightest untoward effect.

_____

25. A dark-skinned animal kept in a dark room for several years would tend to become depigmented, etiolated, and its skin would appear white, but as soon as it was exposed to the sun the pigment would begin to return.   _____

26. A fossil is any hardened remains or trace of a living form of some former geological period.   _____

27. War is a eugenically disastrous thing because it serves to kill

off a large number of the fit while increasing the population of the relatively less fit. _____

28. Sound eugenics has everything to say for it.* The unsound kind is to be feared. _____

29. Cooperation has the far greater adaptive value for man, because it ensures his survival, whereas competition tends to militate against it.† _____

30. The evolution of man has not come to an end and will never come to an end as long as he endures as a species. _____

Books

1. A book is a self-contained entity consisting of a number of sheets of paper with writing or printing on them, fastened together along one edge, usually between protective covers, distinguished by length and form from a magazine, tract, etc. _____

2. The half title is the title of the book, often abbreviated, usually appearing on the odd page preceding (sometimes following) the title page. _____

3. The colophon is the inscription at the end of a book, giving facts about its production; the colophon may also take the form of an emblematic or ornamental device, the publisher's trademark, put on the last page or title page of a book. _____

4. The signature is (1) the large sheet upon which are printed four, or some multiple of four, pages and which, when folded and bound, forms one section of a book or pamphlet; (2) a letter or number at the bottom of the first page in such a sheet showing in what order the sheet is to be bound. _____

5. A duodecimo is a book the sheets of which have been folded into twelve leaves of approximately 5 by 7½ inches: written 12 *mo* or *12°*. _____

6. A leaf is a sheet of paper with a page on each side. _____

* For an account of a sound eugenic program, see Frederick Osborn, *Preface to Eugenics,* Harper & Brothers, New York, 1940.

† See Ashley Montagu, *Darwin, Competition, and Cooperation,* Abelard-Schuman, 1952; Ashley Montagu, *On Being Human,* Abelard-Schuman, New York, 1950.

7. John Milton (1608–74), in his *Areopagitica,* 1644.   _____

8. The term "bibliography" has a number of meanings, but the question asks what is bibliography, *not* what is *a* bibliography. The answer is that bibliography is the study of the editions, dates, authorship, etc., of books and other writings.   _____

9. Publishers, with a few exceptions, do not print books; the printers they employ do that. Publishers publish books.

   _____

10. Baskerville is the name of a printer's type designed by John Baskerville (1706–75), English printer and type designer.

    _____

11. An edition of a book is the total number of copies printed from the same plates or type and published at about the same time; as de luxe editions, book club editions, paperback editions, and the like.   _____

12. A folio is (1) a large sheet of paper folded once, so that it forms two leaves or four pages of a book; (2) a book usually more than 11 inches in height, made of sheets folded in this way; (3) the number of a page.

13. It is more economical to print in double column in most books and periodicals because one can get more words on a page, and hence the number of pages, etc., is reduced.   _____

14. Usually about 4,000 copies of a book must be sold before the publisher can break even.   _____

15. The most famous production of William Morris's (1834–1896) Kelmscott Press was his *Chaucer.*

16. The most beautiful book produced by Eric Gill (1882–1940) is his *Four Gospels,* published by the Golden Cockerel Press in 1931 and described by the *Times Literary Supplement* as the finest example of the printed book that the twentieth century has produced.   _____

17. The function of the dust jacket is multiple: (1) to draw attention to the book; (2) to describe its contents; (3) to introduce the author; (4) to help preserve the binding. This latter, from the point of view of the book collector, is perhaps its most important function.   _____

18. The first printed book may have been printed in China during the ninth century A.D. No one knows who actually printed

the first book in Europe, but the credit generally goes to
Johann Gutenberg (c. 1398–1468), German printer of Mainz
who produced the 42-line Latin Bible before the year 1456—
the Gutenberg Bible. About 200 copies, in 2 volumes, were
produced, mostly printed on paper but some on vellum.

19. The first type used was made of wood.
20. The author of *The Anatomy of Bibliomania,* 2 vols., 1930–31,
was Holbrook Jackson (1874–1948).
21. Paper, it is believed, was first invented by Ts'ai Lun in China
about 105 A.D.
22. Cloth bindings for books first came into use in the 1820's in
England.
23. *The Magnificent Farce* was written by Alfred Edward Newton
(1863–1940), American book collector.
24. The gold stamp on the front cover of a book is known as the
"brass."
25. In a first edition the original binding is always to be preferred to any other.
26. Everyone should collect books. A home without books is a
home without a soul.
27. If you prefer books it doesn't matter really what form you
prefer them in, unless you are a collector of well-made books
or special editions.
28. You *should* read a book a month, at least.
29. Private-press books are one of the amenities of civilization, the
trumpets that sing publishers into the making of better books
and the delight of bibliophiles.
30. The book clubs are an excellent idea, making many books
available to readers that they might not otherwise have encountered.

Chemistry and Technology

1. Chemistry is the science dealing with the composition and
properties of substances and with the reactions by which sub-

stances are produced from or converted into other substances. _____

2. Technology is the science or study of the practical or industrial arts. _____
3. Water is compounded of two hydrogen atoms and one oxygen atom: H_2O. _____
4. Distilled water is the condensed vapor from water that has been boiled. Distilled water is purer than nondistilled because it is free of the nonvolatile substances which remain in ordinary water. _____
5. Osmosis refers to the passage of fluids through a semipermeable membrane. _____
6. Brass is an alloy of copper and zinc. _____
7. Bronze is an alloy of copper and tin. _____
8. Biochemistry is the branch of science which deals with the chemistry of living things. _____
9. A retort is a container, generally of glass and with a long tube, in which substances are distilled or decomposed by heat. _____
10. The irreducible and ever-present substance in all living matter is carbon. _____
11. Lysis is the process of loosening or dissolution, as at the wall of the ovary immediately prior to ovulation. _____
12. pH is a symbol used to express hydrogen-ion concentration. It stands for "potential of Hydrogen." The pH of a substance is a measure of its acidity or alkalinity. The value of pure water being regarded as neutral, a pH from 0 to 7 indicates acidity, and pH values from 7 to 14 indicate alkalinity. The measure is arrived at by taking the logarithm of the reciprocal of the hydrogen-ion concentration, expressed in gram atoms per liter of a solution. _____
13. Sir William Ramsay (1852–1916), British chemist, discovered helium, and with Lord Rayleigh (1842–1909) he discovered argon. With M. W. Travers (1872–   ), he discovered krypton, neon, and xenon. _____
14. The author of *The Nature of the Chemical Bond,* 1939, is Linus Pauling (1901–   ), American chemist and Nobel prizeman for chemistry in 1954. _____

15. An alembic is a vessel made of glass or copper and formerly used for distilling.   _____

16. Steel is a hard, tough metal composed of iron alloyed with various small percentages of carbon. Steel may be alloyed with other metals, as nickel, chromium, etc., to produce specific properties, as hardness, resistance to rusting, and so on.   _____

17. Plastics occur in nature in the form of resins, proteins, cellulose, etc., and amber-like substances.   _____

18. The great artificial dye industry was made possible by the discovery (1856) of the first aniline dye, mauve, by William Henry Perkin (1838–1907).   _____

19. CO_2 (carbon dioxide) is indispensable for the functioning of the human body.   _____

20. Aluminium is the British form of the word "aluminum." Aluminum is one of the chemical elements, of light weight, easily worked, and resistant to corrosion.   _____

21. Sir Henry Bessemer (1813–98), English inventor of the Bessemer process for the making of steel from cast iron. _____

22. Alfred Nobel (1833–96), Swedish chemist and inventor, patented the mixture of nitroglycerin and gunpowder in 1863, and in 1866 perfected the powder to which he gave the name "dynamite." He established the Nobel Prize awards.

23. Diamonds are made artificially by subjecting a compound containing graphite to great temperatures and pressures equal to those found 240 miles below the earth's surface. The feat was first accomplished by General Electric Corporation scientists and announced in February 1955.   _____

24. Pewter is an alloy of tin with lead, brass, or copper. _____

25. Science is the systematized knowledge derived from observation and study, and from experiment carried on in order to determine the nature or principles of what is being studied. It is theoretically inclined, but with the emphasis on discovering what *is*. Technology is practically inclined, with the emphasis on the practical applications of science; hence, technology may be defined as applied science.   _____

26. All students of technology should receive a basic training in

the humanities in order to keep them human, and as the best insurance against their losing themselves in things. _____

27. A knowledge of chemistry ought to be a part of the basic education of everyone, if only to afford the individual a fuller grasp of and feeling for the world in which he is living. Chemistry is a most exciting subject. _____

28. Of course a person can be considered cultured if he has no knowledge of chemistry. The possession of such knowledge might not add to his cultural status, but it would certainly serve to increase his understanding of the world in which he finds himself, and it would help him to find himself more comfortably in that world. _____

29. In America we are lamentably deficient in technical high schools in which boys and girls could be thoroughly grounded and prepared in all those specialties which a highly developed technological civilization encourages. _____

30. American civilization may not be a dominantly technological civilization, but it very nearly approaches being one. _____

∾∾

Classical Antiquity

1. Tertullian (c. 160–230) first attacked Christianity and then lived to become one of the fathers of the church. _____

2. Marcus Aurelius (121–180 A.D.), Emperor of Rome 161–180, Stoic philosopher and statesman. _____

3. The author of *De Rerum Natura* was Lucretius (96?–55 B.C.), Roman poet and philosopher. _____

4. Socrates' wife was Xanthippe, the prototype of the quarrelsome, nagging wife. In her defense it should, perhaps, be said, that Socrates was probably not an easy man to live with.

_____

5. An amphora was a tall jar with a narrow neck and two handles, one on either side near the top, used by the ancient Greeks and Romans. _____

6. The stoa was a covered walk or portico having a wall on one side and pillars on the other. It was from their habit of meet-

ing in a stoa that the Stoic philosophers derived their name.

7. Zeus was the supreme deity of the ancient Greeks, son of
Cronus and Rhea and husband of Hera. The word Zeus is
related to Sanskrit *dyaus* "the bright sky."*

8. Nausicaa, in Homer's *Odyssey,* was the daughter of King
Alcinous. She discovered the shipwrecked Ulysses and brought
him to her father, from whom Ulysses received safe passage
to Ithaca.

9. *Leucippe and Clitophon* is one of the earliest novels, written
in Greek. Its author was Achilles Tatius, a Greek of Alexandria about the third or fourth century A.D.

10. Parnassus is a mountain in Greece, in ancient times sacred to
Apollo and the Muses, hence, in modern usage, poetry and
the poets collectively, or any center of poetic or artistic activity.

11. Adonis, in Greek mythology, was the young man loved by
Aphrodite because he was so beautiful: alas, he was killed
by a boar. Touched by Aphrodite's grief the gods arranged
to allow him to spend half the year with her, and half in the
underworld.

12. A hetaera (the Greek euphemism for courtesan), being the
feminine form of the Greek word for companion *hetairos,* in
ancient Greece was a courtesan or concubine, usually an educated slave, akin to the geisha girl of Japan.

13. The title of Lucius Apuleius' best-known work is *Metamor-
phoses* or *The Golden Ass,* written in the 2nd century A.D.

14. The Greek philosopher who lived in a tub was Diogenes, the
Cynic (c. 412–323 B.C.).

15. The author of "Heracleitus" was Callimachus (c. 310–240
B.C.?) of Cyrene and Alexandria, *arbiter litterarum* of the
Greek world, poet, natural historian, and ethnographer. Hera-
cleitus was an elegiac poet or writer of epigrams whose work
has not survived. William Cory (1823–92), the translator into
English of Heracleitus, changed his name from Johnson to

* For a supremely magnificent study of Zeus, see A. B. Cook, *Zeus,* 3 vols.,
Cambridge University Press, New York and London, 1914–40.

Cory in 1872. He was a master at Eton College, where he established a phenomenal reputation among his pupils. His *Ionica*, 1858, his first published volume of poems and translations, and his *Letters and Journals*, 1897, are classics. His translation of "Heracleitus" is considered to be the best translation from the Greek into English ever made. Here it is:

Heraclitus

They told me, Heraclitus, they told me you were dead;
They brought me bitter news to hear and bitter tears to shed.
I wept, as I remembered, how often you and I
Had tired the sun with talking and sent him down the sky.
And now that thou art lying, my dear old Carian guest,
A handful of grey ashes, long long ago at rest,
Still are thy pleasant voices, thy nightingales, awake,
For Death, he taketh all away, but them he cannot take.*

----

16. Lucius Annaeus Seneca (4 B.C.?–65 A.D.), Roman Stoic philosopher, statesman, and writer. His tragedies influenced Elizabethan drama; his philosophical writings and aphorisms, generations of readers.   ____
17. The author of *The Nicomachean Ethics* was Aristotle (384–322 B.C.).   ____
18. Aristotle was also the author of *Poetics*.   ____
19. Plato (429?–347 B.C.) was the author of *The Symposium*.

----

20. Homer was the author of *The Odyssey*.   ____
21. *The Frogs* was written by Aristophanes (450?–385? B.C.).

----

22. *Oedipus Rex* was written by Sophocles (496?–406 B.C.).

----

23. Titus Pomponius Atticus (109–32 B.C.), Roman philosopher and patron of letters, was a friend and correspondent of Cicero.   ____
24. Archimedes (287?–212 B.C.), Greek mathematician and

----

* For a lovely edition of Callimachus, see Robert Allason Furness, *Poems of Callimachus*, Jonathan Cape, London, 1931.

physicist, discovered the principles of the lever and of specific gravity.   ———————

25. Malaria is said to have played a role in the decline of Greek civilization, a suggestion greatly to be doubted.   ———————

26. The advantages of a classical education are that it brings one into touch with much of the best that has been thought, said, and done in the world, endows one with a profound understanding of the origins of his own civilization, and contributes to the cultivation of the mind as few other kinds of education are capable of doing.   ———————

27. Certainly every ordinarily well-educated person should have a knowledge of Latin and Greek sufficient to enable him to read in those languages.   ———————

28. Reading a Latin or Greek writer in translation at least twice a year is the minimum for full marks.   ———————

29. The attitude of the Greeks toward women was eccentric and unfortunate, pretty much that of the Nazis with their "kinder, kirche, und kuche."   ———————

30. It is scarcely possible to have a sufficient number of Greek plays produced.   ———————

❦

Culture History

1. The origin of the modern conception of romantic love in the Western world may be said to commence with the development of courtly love at the court of Eleanor of Aquitaine (1122?–1204), queen of Henry II of England, at Poitiers. It was, however, principally through her daughter the Countess Marie of Champagne (1145?–) that the concept of romantic love was developed, and this she caused to be set down in a book written sometime between 1184 and 1186 by her chaplain Andreas Capellanus and entitled *De Arte Honeste Amandi* and translated as *The Art of Courtly Love.** The

* For an excellent English translation of this with an informative introduction, see John J. Parry, *The Art of Courtly Love,* Columbia University Press, New York, 1941.

ideas set out in this work and the stories and events that grew up about the courts of love in Burgundy were embellished and put into song, story, and poetry by the troubadours, who carried them throughout Western Europe. Through the lyric poetry they created eventually spread the notion that every fair lady, however lowly, somewhere had waiting for her the tender, gentle, loving knight of her thus culturally conditioned dreams.*

2. There are several good books on the history of cultural traditions. Here are some of them: Ralph Turner, *The Great Cultural Traditions,* 2 vols., McGraw-Hill, New York, 1941; Crane Brinton, John B. Christopher, and Robert Lee Wolff, *A History of Civilization,* 2 vols., Prentice-Hall, Englewood Cliffs, N. J., 1955; Erich Kahler, *Man The Measure,* George Braziller, New York, 1956; Hermann Schneider, *The History of World Civilization,* 2 vols., Routledge, London, 1931.

3. Charles Darwin's (1809–1882) influence on Western culture has largely been to bring about a correction of many antiquated errors, and to infuse virtually every branch of thought with the idea of change through progressive modification, the idea of evolution. At the same time Darwin's conception of progressive evolution through competition has been overemphasized with virtual complete disregard of his views on cooperation as expressed in his *The Descent of Man,* John Murray, London, 1871. The misinterpretation and misapplication of Darwin's views has, in many respects, been very damaging.†

4. The cultural traditions are mainly of English origin. ———

5. The first printed English book was *The Recuyell of the Historyes of Troye,* translated and printed by William Caxton

* For further treatments of this fascinating subject see Denis de Rougemont, *Love in the Western World,* Anchor Books, New York, 1957; Donald Day, *The Evolution of Love,* The Dial Press, New York, 1954.

† For further reading on this subject see George Nasmyth, *Social Progress and Darwinian Theory,* G. P. Putnam's Sons, New York, 1916; Jacques Barzun, *Darwin, Marx, Wagner,* 2nd ed., Anchor Books, New York, 1957; Richard Hofstadter, *Social Darwinism in American Thought, 1860-1950,* University of Pennsylvania Press, Philadelphia, 1944; Ashley Montagu, *Darwin, Competition, and Cooperation,* Abelard-Schuman, New York, 1952.

(c. 1422–1491) at Bruges, 1474–1475. The work runs to more than 700 pages. _____

6. The argument of William Godwin's (1756–1836) *Enquiry Concerning Political Justice,* 1793, was that "the characters of men originate in their external circumstances." Our conventional schools, he felt, were the slaughterhouses of the mind, but the most important influence upon the human mind was political. Since politics are "the proper vehicle of a liberal morality," it must be the primary concern of men to realize justice for all, and this can be achieved by educating men to reason.* _____

7. The Royal Society was founded in 1662. _____

8. The *Académie des Sciences* was founded in 1666. _____

9. Lyric poetry in the Western world was largely the creation of the troubadours. _____

10. The Marquis de Condorcet (1743–94), French mathematician, philosopher, and political leader. He made important contributions to the mathematical theory of probability. He took part in the French Revolution, but was thrown into prison for opposing the extremes of the Jacobins. In prison he wrote *Esquisse d'un tableau historique des progrès de l'esprit humain.* He died in prison, and the work was posthumously published in 1801–04. _____

11. The Philosophes was the name given to the French philosophers of the second half of the eighteenth century who belonged to what is sometimes called the "Romantic Movement" and at other times the "Age of Enlightenment." _____

12. The idea of equality received its first major impetus from the American War of Independence, and its second major impetus from the proclaimed principles of the French Revolution. _____

13. The Industrial Revolution began in England about 1750.† _____

14. The greatest obstacle to social reform in the centuries pre-

_____

* For one of the most brilliant discussions of this book and its influence, see H. N. Brailsford, *Shelley, Godwin, and Their Circle,* Henry Holt, New York, 1913.

† See Arnold Toynbee, *Lectures on The Industrial Revolution in England,* London, 1884; reprinted Beacon Press, Boston, 1957.

ceding the nineteenth was the existence of a class with vested interests.

15. The checks on population increase first stated by Thomas Robert Malthus (1766–1834) were war, poverty, epidemics, and vice. See his *An Essay on the Principle of Population*, London, 1798.

16. Puritanism, as a movement to purify the Church of England of elaborate ceremony and form, is translated into everyday conduct as extreme strictness in matters of morals and religion. As someone has remarked, "If you're enjoying anything, it can't possibly be any good for you."*

17. The Julian calendar was introduced by Julius Caesar in 46 B.C. The ordinary year had 365 days and every fourth year (leap year) had 366 days. The Gregorian calendar, which is the one we use today, was introduced by Pope Gregory XIII in 1582. This provides for an ordinary year of 365 days and a leap year of 366 days exclusive of century years which are leap years only if exactly divisible by 400. Up to 1582 the legal year began on March 25, and it was only with the adoption of the Gregorian calendar that the year commenced with January 1. Since up to 1752 the English, as Voltaire put it, preferred to disagree with the sun rather than agree with the Pope, England found itself eleven days behind the Continent in its reckoning, a fact which has caused some confusion to many who happen to deal with the events of this period.

18. The argument of Rousseau's *Émile*, 1762, is the original goodness of human nature, from which it follows that all education must be based upon an understanding of that nature, upon a knowledge of the psychology of the child based on observation and experiment. The object of education is not primarily vocational, to produce a magistrate, a soldier, or a priest, but a man.†

* See William Haller, *The Rise of Puritanism*, Harper Torchbooks, New York, 1957; Perry Miller, *The New England Mind: The Seventeenth Century*, Macmillan, New York, 1939.

† An admirable book on Rousseau giving a clear account of his views, among other things, on education, is F. C. Green, *Jean-Jacques Rousseau: A Study of His Life And Writings*, Cambridge University Press, New York and London, 1955.

19. The first country to abolish the slave trade was England, which outlawed the trade in slaves in the year 1807.   _____

20. Denis Diderot (1713–1784), French philosopher and encyclopedist, one of the universal geniuses of his era, an editor of the great *Encyclopédie,* the most remarkable work of its time, one of the leading Fathers of the Age of Enlightenment to whom we are all indebted.*   _____

21. Incunabula—the word means "cradle"—are the early printed books, specifically those printed before 1500.   _____

22. *The Subjection of Women* was written by John Stuart Mill (1806–1873) in 1869.   _____

23. "Racism" is a modern development. In former times groups might be discriminated against on the grounds of religion, nationality, and the like, but seldom or never on biological grounds. "Racism" is a nineteenth-century invention.†   _____

24. Seven Dynastic Egyptian kings married their own sisters and bore descendants in every instance of marked distinction.

_____

25. Both sides were too dogmatic in the conflict between science and religion in the nineteenth century. The religionists and theologians could not see the scientists' point of view; the scientists could see the religionists' and theologians' point of view only too clearly, but erred in not being sufficiently sympathetic to the weaker side. When one considers the number of great men who have been scientists during the last century, and attempts to call to mind the number of theologians who have been great men, the conclusion is rather appalling.

_____

26. Among the leading nineteenth-century antagonists of revealed religion were Thomas Henry Huxley (1825–1895), Herbert Spencer (1820–1903), Ernst Heinrich Haeckel (1834–1919), and Robert Ingersoll (1833–1899).   _____

27. The value of a cultural tradition, among other things, lies in

* See Jonathan Kemp, *Diderot, Interpreter of Nature,* Lawrence & Wishart, London, 1937; Lester G. Crocker, *The Embattled Philosopher: A Life of Denis Diderot,* Michigan State University Press, Lansing, 1954.

† See Ashley Montagu, *Man's Most Dangerous Myth: The Fallacy of Race,* 3rd ed., Harper & Brothers, New York, 1952; T. J. Haarhoff, *The Stranger at the Gate,* Blackwell, Oxford, 1948.

the fact that it provides its members with roots and affords them something to which to be loyal.   _____

28. One book a year is the minimum to qualify for full marks.

_____

29. The purpose of teaching cultural history in our schools should be principally to afford the student an opportunity to understand that in all the great variety of cultural traditions there is a unity which binds all men together.   _____

30. By, presumably, acquiring a deeper understanding of the history of man.   _____

~~

Economics

1. Economics is the science that deals with the production, distribution, and consumption of wealth, and with the various related problems of labor, finance, taxation, and the like.

_____

2. Gresham's law, named after the founder of the English Royal Exchange and of Gresham College in London, Sir Thomas Gresham (1519–79), who explained the principle to Queen Elizabeth in 1558, namely, that when two or more kinds of money of equal denomination but unequal intrinsic value are in circulation at the same time, the one of greater value will tend to be hoarded or exported. In general usage this has come to be popularly interpreted as the principle that bad money will drive good money out of circulation.   _____

3. The economic interpretation of history has it that political authority is formed by those who own the means of production, and by this means determine the structures and functions of society.*   _____

4. Thomas Carlyle (1795–1881) first described economics as "the dismal science" in his essay "The Nigger Question" in 1849, reprinted in his *Miscellaneous Essays,* 1872, VII, 84.

_____

* See Edward Heimann, *History of Economic Doctrines,* Oxford University Press, New York, 1945.

5. Economic rivalry has been the principal cause of war. Innate factors are in no way connected with the causes of war.*

_____

6. Marginal utility is the minimum degree of utility, below which activity is not profitable enough to be continued._____

7. No, it is not true that "competition is the life-blood of a nation." The life-blood of anything, and especially of nations, is not competition but cooperation—and America is one of the best examples of this fact. It is often stated that America has achieved its present greatness because of competition. I suggest that it has done so in spite of competition.†   _____

8. *An Inquiry into the Nature and Causes of The Wealth of Nations,* 1776, is by Adam Smith (1723–90), Scottish economist.   _____

9. *The Great Transformation,* 1944, is by Karl Polanyi (1886–   ).   _____

10. *An Essay on the Principle of Population,* 1798, is by Thomas Robert Malthus (1766–1834).   _____

11. *A Dissertation on the Poor Laws,* 1786, is by Joseph Townsend (1739–1816).‡   _____

12. *The Economic Consequences of the Peace,* 1919, is by John Maynard Keynes (1883–1946).   _____

13. *Principles of Political Economy,* 1848, is by John Stuart Mill (1806–73).   _____

14. Money may be defined as any material, usually coin and paper, stamped by government authority, and used as a medium of exchange and a measure of value.   _____

15. Henry George (1839–97), American political economist, ad-

_____

* See Jesse D. Clarkson and Thomas C. Cochran (editors), *War As A Social Institution,* Columbia University Press, New York, 1941; John U. Nef, *War and Human Progress,* Harvard University Press, Cambridge, 1951; L. L. Bernard, *The Causes of War,* Henry Holt, New York, 1944; Hadley Cantril (editor), *Tensions That Cause War,* University of Illinois Press, Urbana, 1950.

† See Marquis W. Childs and Douglass Cater, *Ethics in a Business Society,* Harper & Brothers, New York, 1954; Thomas C. Cochran and William Miller, *The Age of Enterprise,* Macmillan, New York, 1942; Max Lerner, *America As A Civilization,* Simon & Schuster, New York, 1957.

‡ This is a most important work in the history of the evolution of ideas. It powerfully influenced the thought of Malthus, who in turn influenced that of Darwin. See Ashley Montagu, *Darwin, Competition, and Cooperation,* Abelard-Schuman, New York, 1952.

vocate of the single tax, and author of the inspired *Progress and Poverty,* 1877–79. _____

16. William Stanley Jevons (1835–82), English economist and logician, author of *The Principles of Science,* 1874, and *Theory of Political Economy,* 1871. _____

17. David Ricardo (1772–1823), English economist, and author of *Principles of Economics and Taxation,* 1817. _____

18. Vilfredo Pareto (1848–1923), Italian economist and sociologist, author of *Mind and Society,* 4 vols., 1935, a work originally published in Italian in 1916. _____

19. Trade is the process of buying or selling, or the exchange of commodities, thus commerce. _____

20. Barter is trade by exchanging goods or services without the use of money. _____

21. Inflation is an increase in the amount of currency in circulation, resulting in a relatively sharp and sudden fall in its value and a rise in prices: it may be caused by an increase in the volume of paper money issued or of gold mined, or by a relative increase in expenditures, as when the supply of goods fails to meet the demand. _____

22. The gold standard is the monetary standard solely in terms of gold, in which the basic currency unit is made equal to and redeemable by a specified quantity of gold. _____

23. The World Bank is the International Bank for Reconstruction and Development, affiliated with the United Nations and with headquarters at Washington, D.C., formally organized in 1945. The function of the World Bank is to facilitate productive investment, encourage foreign trade, make loans to member nations, and help in the discharge of burdensome international debts. _____

24. The Federal Reserve System is the centralized banking system of the United States, consisting of twelve Federal Reserve banks, each acting as the central bank for its district, and over 10,000 affiliated banks. It was established by the Federal Reserve Act of 1913 to develop a currency that would fluctuate with business demands, and regulate the member banks of each district. _____

25. It was Thomas Robert Malthus (1766–1834) who greatly

influenced Darwin. "I happened to read for amusement 'Malthus on Population,' and being well prepared to appreciate the struggle for existence which everywhere goes on from long-continued observation of the habits of animals and plants, it at once struck me that under these circumstances favourable variations would tend to be preserved, and unfavourable ones to be destroyed. The result of this would be the formation of new species. Here then I had at last got a theory by which to work."*   _____

26. Once every ten years would do for a full score.   _____
27. Economics *should* be a moral science, and most certainly should be concerned with *human* values.†   _____
28. Economics should be in the service of man, and not man in the service of economics.   _____
29. Necessity is the mother of invention the greater part of the time.   _____
30. Economic planning would greatly assist every society and every segment thereof.   _____

✎✎

In General

 1. Stefan George (1868–1933) distinguished German poet, leader of the revolt against realism in German literature, editor of the influential *Blätter für die Kunst,* and the author of many volumes of poetry and translations of the French and English poets as well as of Dante. His most notable disciple was Rainer Maria Rilke (1875–1926).   _____
 2. Peter Abelard (1079–1142), French scholastic philosopher, teacher, and theologian. His autobiographical *Historia calamitatum,* and his celebrated romance with the beautiful and learned Heloise (died 1164) have formed the subject of many books, perhaps the most beautiful of which is George Moore's, *Héloïse and Abélard,* 1921.   _____

* Charles Darwin, "Autobiography," in *The Life and Letters of Charles Darwin* (edited by Francis Darwin), John Murray, London, 1888, vol. i, p. 83.

† See Walter A. Weisskopf, *The Psychology of Economics,* University of Chicago Press, Chicago, 1955; Karl Polanyi, *The Great Transformation,* Rinehart, New York, 1944.

3. A thespian is an actor, especially a tragedian. Thespis was a Greek sixth-century B.C. poet, traditionally the originator of tragedy. _____

4. Henry Brooks Adams (1838–1918), American historian and writer, author of the monumental *History of the United States of America,* 9 vols., 1889–91. His most famous book was *The Education of Henry Adams,* privately printed in 1906, and published in 1918. _____

5. The Admirable Crichton was James Crichton (1560?–82?), a Scottish savant and athlete, a good Catholic, and an excellent swordsman. Brilliantly clever and an accomplished linguist, he is said to have disputed with the scholars of Paris in twelve languages. He was killed in a brawl at Mantua. The epithet "Admirable" originated in John Johnston's *Heroes Scots* (1603) and made widely known by Sir Thomas Urquhart (1611–60) in his narrative of Crichton's career contained in his *Ekskubalauron,* 1652. *The Admirable Crichton* is also the title of a delightful play by Sir James Barrie (1860–1937), and frequently made into a movie. _____

6. John Knox (1505–72), fierce Scottish theologian and preacher for the reformed Protestant religion, writer of numerous tracts and epistles. His criticism from abroad of the rule of Mary Tudor in England and of Mary of Lorraine in Scotland, culminated in his *First Blast of the Trumpet against the Monstrous Regiment of Women,* 1558, of which George Saintsbury (1845–1933) remarked that the title was the best part._____

7. Fridtjof Nansen (1861–1930), Norwegian arctic explorer, naturalist, writer, and statesman. He received the Nobel peace prize for 1922. _____

8. The nautch is an Indian dance, usually performed by professional dancing girls (of low caste). _____

9. Sun Yat-sen (1866–1925), Chinese political leader, organized the revolution against the Manchus and founded the Kuomintang (1911). He was the first President of China (1911), was called "the Father of the Revolution."

10. Domenico (or Kyriakos) Theotokopoulos (c. 1541–1614) was the real name of El Greco, who was born in Candia, Crete, and painted in Spain. _____

11. Xenophobia (from Greek *xenos*, stranger, and *phobos*, fear) is a fear of and hatred of strangers or foreigners. _____

12. *Ralph Roister Doister,* 1566, the title of an English play by Nicholas Udall (1505–56), produced c. 1553. _____

13. "The fourth estate" is a term applied to the press. Its origin is obscure. It has been attributed by Thomas Carlyle to Edmund Burke (1729–97). "Burke said there were Three Estates in Parliament; but, in the Reporters' Gallery yonder, there sat a *Fourth Estate* more important far than they all." *Heroes and Hero Worship,* 1841, *v.* The attribution has thus far not been traced in the works of Burke. The term has also been attributed to Lord Henry Peter Brougham (1778–1868), and also to Thomas Babington Macaulay (1800–59) about 1828. But a correspondent in *Notes and Queries,* First Series, vol. 11, p. 452, states that he heard Brougham use it in the House of Commons in 1823 or 1824, and that at that time it was regarded as original. It is interesting that Carlyle himself used the term in 1837, when he wrote "A Fourth Estate, of Able Editors, springs up," in *The French Revolution,* vol. 1, vi, v. _____

14. A collage is the assemblage of bits of flat objects, as newspaper, cloth, pressed flowers, etc., pasted together in incongruous relationship for their symbolic or suggestive effect. It is often used in abstract painting. _____

15. The Japanese code of chivalry is Bushido. It was the code of conduct prescribed for samurai, the knights of feudal Japan, emphasizing loyalty, courage, plain living, and the preference of suicide to dishonor. _____

16. Jo Mielziner (1901–   ), American stage designer. He was for a short time an actor. Since 1924 he has devoted himself entirely to scenic design and has been responsible for many fine productions. _____

17. Quetzalcoatl was the plumed serpent god and legendary ruler of the Toltec of Mexico. He is credited with having brought civilization and ethics to the Toltec. _____

18. Christian is the hero of John Bunyan's (1628–88) *Pilgrim's Progress,* 1678. _____

19. Terrazzo is flooring of small chips of marble set in cement and polished.

20. Stendahl's real name was Marie Henri Beyle (1783–1842).

21. The great inspiration of Dante's life was Beatrice Portinari (1266–90), the Florentine beauty believed to have been the Beatrice of the *Divina Commedia* (begun c.1307) and *La vita nuova*, 1292. Dante Alighieri (1265–1321) was not yet nine when he first saw Beatrice in 1273 or 1274. Dante never exchanged more than a dozen words with Beatrice, and it is doubtful whether he caught a glimpse of her as many times.

22. A morganatic marriage is one in which a man of high rank marries a woman of inferior social status with the stipulation that, although the children, if any, will be legitimate, neither they nor the wife may lay claim to his rank or property.

23. The ides of March corresponds to the 15th day of March in our calendar, the fatal day of Julius Caesar. The ides in the ancient Roman calendar were the fifteenth day of March, May, July, or October, or the thirteenth of the other months.

24. Simon Bolivar (1783–1830), Venezuelan general and revolutionist, helped free Venezuela, Colombia, and Peru from Spain. He is called *the Liberator,* and is sometimes compared to George Washington. He was president of Colombia and Peru, and organized a new republic named Bolivia.

25. H. L. Mencken (1880–1956) said that "Every man is his own hell." But John Milton before him had said, "The mind is its own hell."

26. Paul Gustave Doré (1833–83), French illustrator and painter, known for his highly imaginative, weird, and fantastic illustrations. He is perhaps the world's best-known illustrator. Perhaps his most famous illustrations are those he did for the *Divina Commedia* and *Don Quixote.*

27. "The dogs of St. Ernulphus": this is *very* obscure. I don't expect anyone to answer this one, but someone, of course, will, and that is the only justification for asking the question. I first came upon the expression as a youth, when reading T. H.

Huxley's (1825–1895) *Man's Place in Nature*, 1863. I found him writing that "If there is a young man of the present generation, who has taken as much trouble as I did to assure himself that they are truths, let him come out with them, without troubling his head about the barking of the dogs of St. Ernulphus." Huxley probably learned of St. Ernulphus and his dogs from that mickle wight Laurence Sterne (1713–68), who, in *Tristram Shandy* (8 vols., 1760–67), refers to Ernulphus, and quotes the Bishop's awful curse—of which Uncle Toby remarked: "I declare . . . my heart would not let me curse the devil himself with so much bitterness"—almost in full. Ernulphus or Arnulf (1040–1124) was a French Benedictine, appointed prior of Canterbury by Anselm, was subsequently Abbot of Peterborough (1107–14), and Bishop of Rochester (1114–24). It is to an extract from his *Textus Roffensis* that he owes the invidious distinction given him in *Tristram Shandy*. The "dogs" of St. Ernulphus are his words. "Let dogs delight to bite and bark, it is their nature to."   _____

28. "Nature abhors a vacuum" is Baruch Spinoza's (1632–77) remark, and occurs in his *Ethics* (*Ethica Ordine Geometrico Demonstrata*), Part 1, Proposition XV, note.   _____

29. François Marie Arouet Voltaire (1694–1778) wrote "Let us cultivate our garden" in *Candide,* 1759, Chapter 30.   _____

30. The words, "I disapprove of what you say, but I will defend to the death your right to say it," are usually attributed to Voltaire. In fact he never uttered them, though there is no doubt that he fully subscribed to them. The statement appears to have originated in S. G. Tallentyre (E. Beatrice Hall), *The Friends of Voltaire,* 1907, where it was employed as a paraphrase of Voltaire's words in the *Essay on Tolerance:* "Think for yourselves and let others enjoy the privilege to do so too."   _____

Geography and Meteorology

1. Geography is the descriptive science dealing with the surface of the earth, its division into continents and countries, and the

climate, plants, animals, natural resources, inhabitants, and in-
dustries of the various divisions. _____

2. The Great Divide is the popular name for the Rocky Mountains, the system of mountains in western North America,
extending from New Mexico to Alaska. In fact it is the Continental Divide running from Northern Canada to the Andes.

3. A pole of cold, a place of extreme cold, such as Verkhoyansk
in the taiga forest of northeastern Siberia, more than 250 miles
inland, where the average July temperature is about 60° while
in January, the coldest month, the average is nearly 60 degrees
below zero! Verkhoyansk was a town to which many Russians
were exiled by the Czars, chiefly for political offenses. An
extraordinary book on Verkhoyansk by a political exile is
Vladimir Zenzinov's *The Road to Oblivion,* Robert M. Mc-
Bride, New York, 1931. In January 1913, Zenzinov states, he
recorded a temperature of 95.4° below zero (p. 219)._____

4. The diameter of the earth at the equator is 7,926.68 miles. Its
diameter through the north and south poles is 7,899.98 miles.
This leaves a difference of some 27 miles. The slight flattening
at the poles is due to the rotation of the earth on its axis, a fact
which tends to shift the materials of which the earth is composed toward the equator. _____

5. Graham Land or Graham Coast is the British name given to
Palmer Peninsula in Antarctica. Graham Land is officially
attached to the Falkland Islands. _____

6. Arnhem Land is an area of some 31,200 square miles, on a wide
peninsula west of the Gulf of Carpentaria on the north coast of
Northern Territory, Australia. _____

7. Precipitation is the process of condensing vapor and causing
it to fall as rain, snow, sleet, etc. It is also the amount of rain,
snow, etc., which falls. _____

8. The Admiralty Islands are a group of small islands in the Bismarck Archipelago, in the western Pacific Ocean. They are
part of North-East New Guinea, part of the Australian man-
date, Territory of New Guinea. _____

9. Phrygia is the name of an ancient coastal country in West
Central Asia Minor; the region is now part of Turkey._____

10. Innisfail is the poetical name for Ireland.   _____

11. Longitude is the angular distance of a place east or west of a given meridian, usually that of Greenwich, England.   _____

12. The largest desert in the world is the Sahara of North Africa occupying an area of 3,500,000 square miles, and extending from the Atlantic Ocean to the Nile and from the Mediterranean to the Sudan.

13. Meteorology is the science of weather and climate; also the science of the atmosphere and atmospheric phenomena.   _____

14. Friedrich Ratzel (1844–1904), German geographer, pioneer in developing the study of anthropogeography. He emphasized the factor of environment as influencing and even determining human cultures. His main works are *Anthropogeographie*, 2 vols., 1881–92, and *Völkeskunde*, 3 vols., 1885–88, translated as *The History of Mankind*, 2 vols., 1896–98.   _____

15. The southernmost populated island is New Zealand, with Tasmania a close second.   _____

16. A savannah is a more or less treeless plain or relatively flat, open region; a grassland characterized by scattered trees.   _____

17. A sirocco is a hot, steady, oppressive wind blowing from the Libyan deserts across the Mediterranean into southern Europe, where it is sometimes accompanied by rain; any hot, oppressive wind, especially one blowing toward a center of low barometric pressure.   _____

18. An isobar is a line on a map connecting points on the earth's surface having equal barometric pressure over a given period or at a given time.   _____

19. A tornado is the result of violent movements of air caused by the intense heating of the ground by the sun, accompanied by opposing winds of greatly differing temperatures. From the resulting heavy cumulonimbus cloud a dark funnel-shaped cloud develops. Moving at great speed the funnel rises, falls and twists about, and wherever it strikes in its path it causes great destruction.   _____

20. A cumulus cloud is a thick cloud formation with a horizontal base and rounded masses piled up on each other.   _____

21. The Caspian Sea, Lake Superior, Victoria Nyanza, the Aral Sea, Lake Michigan, and Lake Huron are some of the world's largest lakes. _____

22. Sir Halford John Mackinder (1861–1947), English geographer who first proposed the general theory of geopolitics, the study of the relation of politics to geography. In an article entitled "The Pivot of History," published in *The Geographical Journal* (London), 1904, Mackinder proposed the notion that the great land mass of Europe, Asia, and Africa might be considered as the world island, while the heart land, which might most logically appear to control this mass, lay in the center and included Germany and Russia. These ideas greatly influenced the Germans, for Mackinder stated that whoever rules the heart land rules the world island, and whoever rules the world island commands the world. In Germany the chief exponent of this viewpoint was General Karl Haushofer (1869–1946), a close adviser of Hitler.* In the general confusion it seems to have escaped attention that the most devoted subscribers (and the most successful) to the principles of geopolitics are the leaders of the Soviet Union. _____

23. Topography is the science of drawing on maps and charts or otherwise representing the surface features of a region, including hills, valleys, rivers, lakes, canals, bridges, roads, cities, etc.; also, these surface features. _____

24. The Tropic of Cancer is the northern circle of the celestial sphere, 23°27′ north of the equator. The Tropic of Capricorn is precisely the same number of degrees south of the equator.

25. The Irrawaddy is the great river in eastern Asia flowing southward through central Burma into the Bay of Bengal. It is 1350 miles long. _____

26. Man is the only creature on the face of the earth adapted to life in all climates, *not* genetically but in virtue of the fact that he possesses the intelligence that enables him to do so.

27. The weather most certainly influences moods. It took Dr.

* See Griffith Taylor (editor), *Geography in the Twentieth Century*, Philosophical Library, New York, 1951.

Johnson half a lifetime to come to that conclusion. Most people arrive at it sooner, "in sad or singing weather."* _____

28. Meteorology tells us what we could not otherwise know of the nature of the earth's atmosphere and helps us to predict the weather. _____

29. Whether there is any relation between the explosion of atomic bombs and the weather remains an open question. _____

30. The teaching of geography and meteorology could be greatly improved, especially by making their principal referent *man*.

—————

Geology

1. Geology is the science dealing with the structure of the earth's crust and the formation and development of its various layers; it includes the study of individual rock types and early forms of life found as fossils in rocks. _____

2. A fault is a break in rock strata or veins that causes a section to become dislocated along the line of fracture. _____

3. A stalactite is an icicle-shaped deposit of carbonate of lime hanging from the roof or sides of a cave. A stalagmite is a cone-shaped deposit of carbonate of lime extending vertically upward from the floor of a cave. For speleologists this one is easy; for all others, difficult without the mnemonic which helps one to distinguish the one from the other, namely, the image of the little *mite* standing on the ground looking up at the *tights* which are hanging on the line. _____

4. The Paleocene is an epoch of the Tertiary period of the Cenozoic era of earth history. It is the beginning epoch of the Tertiary and sees the commencing radiation of the mammals. It starts about 75 million years ago and lasts some 17 million years. _____

5. Sandstone is a common sedimentary rock ranging in color from yellow to red or brown, and consisting of sand grains, usually

* See Clarence A. Mills, *Living with the Weather,* The Caxton Press, Cincinnati, 1934.

quartz, cemented together by silica, lime, etc.; much used for building. _____

6. Feldspar is any of several crystalline minerals made up mainly of aluminum silicates, usually glassy and moderately hard, found in igneous rocks. _____

7. Alfred Lothar Wegener (1880–1930), German geologist, meteorologist, and arctic explorer: originator of the theory of continental drift, set out in his book *Die Entstehung der Kontinente und Ozeane,* published in 1915 and in English in 1924 as *The Origin of Continents and Oceans.* _____

8. The age of the earth is estimated to be 3 to 4 billion years. _____

9. A glacier is a large mass of ice and snow that forms in areas where the rate of snowfall constantly exceeds the rate at which the snow melts; it moves slowly down a mountain slope or valley until it melts or breaks away. _____

10. Petroleum is thought to be of organic origin, supposedly the organic remainder of innumerable plants and animals of past ages, especially of such microscopic forms as mollusks, seaweed, peat, and the like. _____

11. The oldest rocks are known as igneous rocks. _____

12. A volcanic eruption is caused by the pressure of explosive gases either in the reservoirs of magma (molten rock) below the earth's surface or within the volcano itself. _____

13. A terminal moraine is a mass of rocks, gravel, sand, etc., carried or deposited by a glacier at its lower end. _____

14. Alluvium is sand, clay, etc., deposited by flowing water, especially along a river bed. _____

15. Geology is of the greatest help to the archaeologist in checking on the approximate dates of the strata in which he digs, and sometimes the archaeologist is able to help the geologist date his deposits by the known age of the archaeological materials found in them. _____

16. A petrologist is a scientist trained in the study of the composition, structure, and origin of rocks. _____

17. Crater Lake is a lake in the crater of an extinct volcano in Crater Lake National Park (area, 251 sq. mi.) in southwestern Oregon. Crater Lake has an area of about 30 square miles. It

is not to be confused with Crater Mound in central Arizona, a huge circular depression believed to have been produced by a giant meteorite.   _____

18. Geology helps the anthropologist date the succession of animals of especial interest to him, including the human animal.

_____

19. Pierre Simon, Marquis de Laplace (1749–1827), French astronomer and mathematician. His name is most prominently associated with the nebular hypothesis set out in his *Exposition du Système du Monde,* 1796.   _____

20. The famous *Principles of Geology,* 3 vols., 1830–33, was written by Sir Charles Lyell (1797–1875).   _____

21. A paleontologist is a student of the life of past geologic time.

_____

22. A diamond consists mainly of nearly pure carbon in crystalline form: it is one of the hardest substances known and has great brilliance.   _____

23. Pumice stone is the light, porous, spongy, volcanic rock that was once lava.   _____

24. Talus, a sloping pile of rock fragments at the foot of a cliff or mountain.   _____

25. A meteorite is a mass of metal or stone that has fallen upon the earth from outer space; a fallen meteor.   _____

26. An elementary knowledge of geology should be part of the equipment of everyone. We live on and by the earth, we should, at the very least, have some acquaintance with it in its manifold geologic forms.   _____

27. Evidences of past glaciation are lateral and terminal moraines, dissociated rocks, glacial incisions, former glacier beds, and the like.   _____

28. Radiocarbon dating is being much compromised these days by atom bomb explosions; nevertheless, the dates yielded by this method are still pretty accurate.   _____

29. Seismology, the study of earthquakes, tremors, and related matters, is of the greatest assistance in the prediction of earthquakes, and thus in warning the populations of the areas likely to be affected.   _____

30. The uses of geology are briefly that they enable us to exploit

the resources of the earth, to mine its mineral ores, obtain its gases, use its heat, and reveal to us something of the history of our planet.   ———

~᠈

European History

1. History is that branch of knowledge which deals systematically with the past, with what has happened in the life or development of a people.   ———
2. Magna Charta or Magna Carta is the great charter that King John of England was forced by the English barons to grant at Runnymede June 15, 1215. It guaranteed certain civil and political liberties to the English people.   ———
3. The Peace of Westphalia, 1648, marked the general settlement and termination of the Thirty Years' War. Spain and the Holy Roman Empire on the one hand and Sweden and France were the principal participants in the negotiations. The Peace brought an end to the era of religious warfare, and signalized the first general attempt at toleration.   ———
4. The Wars of the Roses, 1455–1485, the name given to the intermittent armed conflicts between the House of Lancaster (whose emblem was a red rose) and the House of York (whose emblem was a white rose). The end of this thirty-year conflict witnessed the end of feudalism in England._____
5. The Crimean War (1854–56) was a fiasco because of the gross incompetence of practically all the leaders involved.* Nevertheless, it did put an end to the dominant role which Russia had played in southeastern Europe.   ———
6. Justinian I (483–565) Byzantine emperor (527–65), known for the codification of the Roman Law by his jurists, the Justinian Code.   ———
7. The German general who turned the tide at the Battle of Waterloo and thus helped defeat Napoleon was Gebhard Leberecht von Blücher (1742–1819).   ———
8. The Heights of Quebec were taken by the English general

* See Cecil Woodham-Smith, *The Reason Why*, McGraw-Hill, New York, 1951.

James Wolfe (1727–59) September 13, 1759, and thus ended France's possession of any part of North America, with the exception of two islands off the Newfoundland coast. Wolfe was fatally wounded during the battle. _____

9. The *ancien régime* was the old order in France before the social and political changes introduced by the French Revolution of 1789. _____

10. It was Frederick II (1194–1250) of Germany and Sicily who was known as *Stupor Mundi* (the wonder of the world), because of his remarkable talents. _____

11. Charles I (1600–49) was beheaded January 30, 1649. _____

12. The dates of the French Revolution are 1789–99. _____

13. The Boston Tea Party date is December 16, 1773. _____

14. The date of the Franco-Prussian War is 1870–71. _____

15. The circumnavigation of the globe is generally credited to Ferdinand Magellan (1480?–1521), but Magellan died before the last stage of the circumnavigation, which was actually completed by one of his admirals, Juan Sebastian del Cano (died in 1526), the voyage having taken from 1519 to 1522.

16. Fra Salimbene d'Adamo (1221–89?), Italian Franciscan monk and chronicler. In 1284 he completed in Latin a chronicle dealing with the period 1167–1287, constituting one of the most valuable autobiographical accounts of the period in existence. As Henry Osborn Taylor wrote, "It was to be his lot to paint for posterity a picture of his world such as no man had painted before."* It is astonishing that to this day a complete edition in English of his *Chronica* does not exist. _____

17. The Second Empire was the period of the reign of Napoleon III from 1852 to 1870 in France. _____

18. Voltaire (1694–1778) defined history as "little else than a picture of human crimes and misfortunes," in his *L'Ingénu*, 1767, Chapter 10.

19. There are, of course, many reference works on modern history; the following are a representative sample: John Emerich

---

* Henry Osborn Taylor, *The Mediæval Mind*, Macmillan, London and New York, 1927, 2 vols. Chapter 22, "The World of Salimbene," gives a good account of this remarkable man's book. See also G. G. Coulton, *From St. Francis to Dante*, London, 1907, and T. L. K. Olyphant, in *Translations of the Historical Society*, London, vol. 1, 1872, pp. 449-478.

Dalberg-Acton, Lord Acton (1834–1902), planner and editor, *Cambridge Modern History,* 12 vols., index, and atlas, Cambridge University Press, Cambridge, 1912; Sir George Clark (editor), *The New Cambridge Modern History,* 14 vols., Cambridge University Press, London and New York, 1957– (in process of being issued). _____

20. Elizabeth I (1533–1603), Queen of England, was the daughter of Henry VIII (1491–1547) and Anne Boleyn (1507–36). _____

21. Edward VII (1841–1910), King of England, was called "Edward the Peacemaker." _____

22. The last king to invoke, unsuccessfully, the doctrine of the divine right of kings was Charles I (1600–49) of England.

23. Several works critical of Arnold Toynbee's (1889–   ) *A Study of History* are the following: Ashley Montagu (editor), *Toynbee And History,* Porter Sargent, Boston, 1956; Maurice Samuel, *The Professor and the Fossil,* A. A. Knopf, New York, 1956; Pieter Geyl, *et al., The Pattern of the Past,* Beacon Press, Boston, 1949; Pieter Geyl, *Use and Abuse of History,* Yale University Press, New Haven, 1955; Pieter Geyl, *Debates With Historians,* Philosophical Library, New York, 1955.

24. You should have many. If not, see the above works. _____

25. Every man tends to see according to the kingdom that is within him; hence, the historian's principle task must be to check his prejudices and to view the evidences of the past and attempt to describe and interpret them as dispassionately as possible, and always to check on his sources. The historian's constant endeavor should be to reduce the truth in La Rochefoucauld's comment that "History never embraces more than a small part of reality." _____

26. The most important trait of the historian should be objectivity, which means that he will take no man's word for anything, but check everything for himself.* _____

27. The teaching of history could be improved by adding the

* See Jacques Barzun and Henry F. Graff, *The Modern Researcher,* Harcourt, Brace & Co., New York, 1957, for a discussion of the methods of the historian, a book that can be read with advantage by everyone.

anthropological and sociological as well as psychological dimensions to the analysis and presentation of the facts of history.

28. The reading of historical works is an excellent supplement or substitute for the reading of fiction.   _____

29. The principal use of history is to teach the lesson that those who do not learn from experience are condemned to repeat the errors of their forerunners. We learn that man does not learn from history, and that the errors of the past that we are called upon to chronicle are equaled only by those which we ourselves commit. Hence, we may learn that we need to be both charitable and understanding in viewing and judging the follies and the errors of our ancestors.   _____

30. Is history true? Carlyle defined history as "a distillation of rumour," and so, indeed, has much of what passes for history been. Mr. Henry Ford is on record as having defined history as "bunk." D'Israeli advised against the reading of history, but suggested that biography was more profitable. God, it has been said, cannot alter history but historians can. History often takes the form of a mythology deliberately created by the victors. See George Orwell's *Nineteen Eighty-Four* for an exposition of the method. So, to the question, "Is history true?" we must reply that all history must be treated as an open question subject to further investigation and verification. Until then all historical statements that have not been investigated and verified should be put in the category of "It is said that . . ."   _____

~>

History of Ideas

1. An idea is a thought, a mental image, a notion, a conception.   _____

2. The idea of the benzene ring first occurred (1865) in the mind of Friedrich August von Kekulé (1829–96), German organic chemist. He is said to have developed the idea of the benzene ring while ruminating on top of a London bus, conceiving of the benzene atoms as a ring of monkeys each with

the other's tail in its mouth, together comprising the benzene molecule which, he showed, was probably made up of six atoms of carbon and six of hydrogen.   _____

3. The idea of the unity of mankind is clearly expressed in the Old Testament in many passages, such as "Thou shalt love thy neighbor as thyself" (Leviticus 19:18), "The stranger that sojourneth with you shall be unto you as the homeborn among you, and thou shalt love him as thyself" (Exodus 11:34), and in *The Analects of Confucius,* in such passages as "Men's natures are alike; it is their habits that carry them far apart." Confucius was born c. 551 and died in 479 B.C.   _____

4. Aristotle (384–322 B.C.) thought that the intelligence was situated in the heart.   _____

5. William Paley (1743–1805), English theologian, wrote several influential books, the most celebrated of which are *View of the Evidences of Christianity,* 1794, and *Natural Theology, or, Evidences of the Existence and Attributes of the Deity,* 1802.   _____

6. The first person to give an accurate account of the circulation of the blood was William Harvey (1578–1657), English physician, in his book *De Motu Cordis,* 1628.   _____

7. Democritus (460–362 B.C.), Greek philosopher of Abdera, was the first exponent of the atomic theory.   _____

8. The originator of Social Darwinism was Herbert Spencer (1820-1903) English philosopher, who was a knowledgeable evolutionist and great supporter of Darwin.*   _____

9. T. H. Huxley (1825–95) never reversed himself on the subject of the cosmic process as a "cosmic struggle for existence," though in his 1893 Romanes Lecture, "Evolution and Ethics," he strongly emphasized the necessity of the development of an ethics which opposed "the cosmic process."†   _____

10. The idea of the unconscious occurs in many writers before Sigmund Freud (1856–1939), but it was Freud who developed that idea.   _____

* See George Nasmyth, *Social Progress and the Darwinian Theory,* G. P. Putnam's Sons, New York, 1916; Richard Hofstadter, *Social Darwinism in American Thought,* Beacon Press, Boston, 1955.

† See T. H. & Julian Huxley, *Touchstone for Ethics,* Harper & Bros., New York, 1947.

11. The author of *Protestant Ethic and the Spirit of Capitalism*, 1920, is Max Weber (1864–1920), German sociologist.

12. *The Great Chain of Being*, 1936, is by Arthur O. Lovejoy (1873–   ), American philosopher and historian of ideas.

13. *Gemeinschaft und Gesellschaft*, 1887, in English translation *Community and Society*, 1957, is by Ferdinand Tönnies (1855–1936), German sociologist and political scientist.

14. *The Eighteenth Century Background*, 1940, is by Basil Willey (1897–   ), professor of English literature at Cambridge University.

15. *The Mediaeval Mind*, 2 vols., 1911; 4th ed., 1927, is by Henry Osborn Taylor (1856–1941), American scholar and historian.

16. *Religion and the Rise of Capitalism*, 1926, is by Richard Henry Tawney (1880–   ), English economist.

17. *Dialogue on the Two Great World Systems*, 1632, is by Galileo (1564–1642), Italian astronomer, mathematician, and philosopher.

18. *A History of the Warfare of Science with Theology in Christendom*, 1896, is by Andrew Dickson White (1832–1918), American educator and diplomat, first president of Cornell University.

19. *De Revolutionibus Orbium Coelestium*, 1543, is by Nicolaus Copernicus (1473–1543), Polish astronomer.

20. *De Humani Corporis Fabrica*, in 7 books, 1543, is by Andreas Vesalius (1514–64), Flemish-Italian anatomist.

21. *Ideen zur Philosophie der Geschichte der Menschheit*, 4 vols., 1784–91, is by Johann Gottfried von Herder (1744–1803), German philosopher, poet, and critic.

22. Freud developed the idea of the death instinct first in his book *Beyond the Pleasure Principle*, 1920.

23. *The Journal of the History of Ideas*, New York; *Diogenes*, Chicago; *Victorian Studies*, Bloomington, Indiana; *The American Scholar*, Richmond, Va.

24. The Jews are credited with being the first people to develop the idea of monotheism.

25. There is no scientific basis whatever for astrological ideas.

_____

26. If you read books on the history of ideas, take full marks.

_____

27. The belief in the idea of progress is the wine of the present poured out as a libation to the future. Of course, progress occurs, but it does not do so automatically as was at one time widely believed. Things do not go "onward and upward" of themselves.*   _____

28. We are inclined to pay too much attention to the fact-grubber and not enough to the man of imagination and ideas. Speculation and conjecture is much discouraged in American scientific writing; in Europe it is much encouraged. We need more rather than less speculation and conjecture as a habit of mind to be trained in our future thinkers.   _____

29. The steady worker and the man of imagination are not incompatible, but in the history of science the greatest honors go to the men of imagination: Galileo, Copernicus, Newton, Einstein, Niels Bohr.   _____

30. Because ideas influence the lives of men and of nations, because they are the life blood of art, science, philosophy, and technology, the study of the history of ideas helps us to understand the evolution of human society more completely than would otherwise be possible.   _____

History of Science

1. The symbol for zero was independently invented by the Hindus, by the Maya Indians of Central America, and probably by the Babylonians.   _____

2. The two most important source books for the history of science are George Sarton, _Introduction to the History of Science,_ 3 vols., Carnegie Institution of Washington, Washington,

* See J. B. Bury, _The Idea of Progress,_ Dover Publications, New York, 1955; F. J. Teggert (editor), _The Idea of Progress: A Collection of Readings,_ University of California Press, Berkeley, 1949.

D. C., 1927–48, and Lynn Thorndike, *A History of Magic and Experimental Science,* 8 vols., Columbia University Press, New York, 1929–58.

3. The discoverer of the electron was Sir Joseph John Thomson (1856–1940), English physicist. He was awarded the Nobel prize for physics in 1906.

4. The two books that are generally regarded as ushering in the Renaissance of science are Nicolaus Copernicus' (1473–1543) *De Revolutionibus Orbium Coelestium,* published May 25, 1543, and Vesalius' *De Humani Corporis Fabrica,* June 1, 1543. Observe that these two books were published within six days of each other!

5. Roger Bacon (1214?–1294) was a Franciscan Monk, English scholastic philosopher, and scientist, called "the Admirable Doctor."

6. William Gilbert (1540–1603), English physician and experimental scientist, the introducer of the inductive and experimental method into England. His great book, *De Magnete,* 1600, English translation, *The Loadstone,* 1892.

7. Phlogiston was the hypothecated substance that Johann Joachim Becher (1635–82) and Georg Ernst Stahl (1660–1734), German chemists, advanced and advocated as the substance that was given off in burning. All substances, they held, that burn contain phlogiston, which is necessary to combustion. Joseph Priestley, the discoverer of oxygen, adhered to his belief in phlogiston throughout his life. It remained for Antoine Laurent Lavoisier (1743–94) to uncover the true nature of combustion.

8. The discoverer of Halley's comet was Edmund Halley (1656–1742), English astronomer and mathematician. He first observed the comet in 1682, recognized it as the one observed in 1531 and 1607, and predicted its return in periodic cycles. This was the comet seen in 1066, and is shown in the Bayeux tapestry.

9. Joseph Priestley's (1733–1804), English theologian and chemist, most notable discovery (1774) was oxygen, which he called *dephlogisticated air.* Priestley was unaware of the nature of his discovery. It was Lavoisier who first named the

gas oxygen, and it was he who discovered that it was a component of the atmosphere. _____

10. *On the Origin of Species by Natural Selection* by Charles Darwin (1809–82) was published November 24, 1859, by John Murray at London, in an edition of 1250 copies._____

11. Konrad von Gesner (1516–65) was the most famous naturalist of his time. His great work, in 5 volumes, *Historia Animalium*, 1551–87, is said to mark the beginning of modern zoology. _____

12. Gregor Johann Mendel's (1822–84) original memoir was published in 1865 and noticed by no one. The principles there enunciated and demonstrated were almost approached in the work of August Weismann (1834–1914), German biologist, in 1883. Mendel's memoir was independently discovered by the Dutch botanist Hugo de Vries (1848–1935) in March, 1900, by Carl Correns (1864–1933), German botanist, a month later, and by Erich Tschermak (1871–   ), Viennese botanist, a few weeks later. _____

13. James Clerk Maxwell (1831–79), Scottish physicist, whose work in electricity and magnetism was and will continue to be of immense importance. Without his fundamental studies physics would have made much slower progress than it has. Television, for example, would have been impossible without the special equations which he developed. _____

14. Johannes Peter Müller (1801–58), German physiologist and anatomist, whose monumental work on physiology, *Handbuch der Physiolgie des Menschen,* 1833–40, systematized the subject and made a science out of physiology. _____

15. The term vitamine was coined by Casimir Funk (1884–   ), Polish-American biochemist, in 1912 while working in London. Funk erred in classifying vitamines as amines, and the *e* was later dropped. _____

16. Josiah Willard Gibbs (1839–1903) American mathematical physicist, great and fundamental contributor to thermodynamics, whose paper published in two parts (1876, 1878) in *Transactions of the Connecticut Academy of Science,* "On the Equilibrium of Heterogeneous Substances," has been referred to as "one of the mightiest works of genius the human

mind has ever produced" (Donnan). Gibbs devised the Phase
Rule, a statement $(P+F=C-Z)$ of the equilibrium or relationship between the number of phases (P) and components
(C) in a system and the degrees of freedom (F) possible
under given conditions. ⸻

17. Sir Isaac Newton's (1642–1727) most important book was
Philosophiae naturalis principia mathematica, 1687. ⸻

18. The discoverer of radioactivity was Antoine Henri Becquerel
(1852–1908), French physicist. Becquerel discovered radioactivity in uranium in 1896. Pierre Curie (1859–1906) and
his wife Marie Curie (1867–1934), French chemists and
physicists, made further discoveries in radioactivity and shared
the Nobel prize in physics with Becquerel in 1903. ⸻

19. Anton van Leeuwenhoek (1632–1723), Dutch protozoolo-
gist and maker of microscopes. He assembled some 247 microscopes and 419 lenses, and made some that magnified objects
270 times. He was the first to see red blood cells, protozoa,
and bacteria. ⸻

20. Karl Pearson (1857–1936), English scientist and mathematician, author of the famous *Grammar of Science,* 1899;
original edition, 1892. ⸻

21. The infinitesimal calculus, which includes the differential and
integral calculus, was invented by Isaac Newton and by Gottfried Wilhelm von Leibnitz (1646–1716), German mathematician and philosopher, quite independently: by Leibnitz
in 1675–76, and by Newton several years earlier. Leibnitz
published in 1684, and Newton in 1693. Leibnitz's notation
is still in use. ⸻

22. The first telescope was made by a Dutch optician, Hans Lip-
pershey, in 1608, but was really developed by Galileo, who
made his first telescope in 1609. ⸻

23. "Pauca sed matura" was the motto of Karl Friedrich Gauss
(1777–1855), German mathematician and astronomer, who
was, among other things, the propounder of the method of
least squares, and after whom the *gauss* is named, the unit
of electricity used in measuring magnetic induction or magnetic intensity, equal to one line of magnetic force per square
centimeter. ⸻

24. Periodicals devoted to the history of science are *Isis,* Cambridge, Massachusetts, and *Annals of the History of Science,* London.

25. Évariste Galois (1811–32), French mathematician, began making original contributions to mathematical theory at 17, and his pioneering work in establishing the theory of groups in algebraic substitutions still provides an inexhaustible mine for mathematicians to exploit. His republican sympathies landed him in prison on two occasions, and at the age of 22 he was killed in a duel with a political opponent.

26. The history of science is a branch principally of the humanities, but should also be a branch of the sciences.

27. Science is an important part of the history of culture, the scientific revolution being at least as important as the industrial revolution; hence, it should form a necessary part of the teaching of culture history.*

28. All universities should teach the history of science. Every university ought to have a department of the history of science, and it ought to be one of the busiest in the university. Very few universities teach the subject and only a few have departments in the subject.

29. The history of science should be taught by men who are interested in the subject whether or not they have been trained in the sciences, and the subject should be taught as a part of cultural history.

30. The uses of the history of science are numerous, among a few of its uses being the important lesson that the history of science could well be written in terms of the history of fruitful errors. The principal use is the contribution made to our completer understanding of the history of man's development.

* See Herbert Butterfield, *The Origins of Modern Science,* Macmillan, New York, 1957; I. B. Cohen, *Science, Servant of Man,* Little, Brown & Co., Boston, 1948; R. N. Anshen (editor), *Science and Man,* Harcourt, Brace & Co., New York, 1942; Bertrand Russell, *The Scientific Outlook,* Norton, New York, 1931; J. B. Conant, *On Understanding Science,* New American Library, New York, 1955.

Language

1. Language is a system of conventional, arbitrary verbal symbols by which the members of a social group communicate ideas, cooperate, and interact, and through which learning and the continuity of a given way of life and change is achieved.

    ___

2. Since grammar constitutes the formal rules which govern the usage of words it is quite impossible for any language to exist without a grammar.   ___

3. An infix is an element consisting of one or more sounds or syllables placed within the body of a word to modify its meaning: it corresponds in function to a suffix or prefix. Quite common in American Indian languages and in Arabic, it is practically unknown in English. Recent English examples are "abso-bloomin'-lutely" and "im-bloody-possible."   ___

4. Phoneme: a class or family of closely related speech sounds (*phones*) regarded as a single sound and represented in phonetic transcription by the same symbol, as the sounds of *r* in *bring, red,* and *round.* The discernible phonetic differences between such sounds are due to the modifying influence of the adjacent sounds.   ___

5. Speech is the expression or communication of thoughts and feelings by means of uttered words, vocal sounds, and gestures; it is the uttered form of language. The following question should make the relation clear: "What language do you speak?" Language is here the *system* of vocal symbols; speech is the active utterance of them. Speech, in short, is the vocal form of the system of symbols we call language.

    ___

6. Linguistics is the science of language.   ___

7. Mood convection is the means by which animals communicate. Animals do not possess language, only man does. But animals are capable of communicating, mainly emotional states, to each other by mood convection.*   ___

* See the chapter, "The Language of Animals," in Konrad Lorenz, *King Solomon's Ring,* Crowell, New York, 1952.

8. Semantics is the branch of linguistics concerned with the nature, structure, and, especially, the development and changes of the meanings of speech forms. Also, in a second meaning, the scientific study of the relations between signs, or symbols, and what they mean or denote, and of behavior in its psychological and sociological aspects as it is influenced by signs.

9. A word is a formal unit of speech, a sound or series of sounds having a definite meaning and used as a unit of language. Words may consist of a single morpheme or of combinations of morphemes.

10. *The Meaning of Meaning* is a famous book by Charles Kay Ogden (1889–1956) and Ivor A. Richards (1893–   ) subtitled "A Study of the Influence of Language upon Thought and of the Science of Symbolism," with two admirable and important essays supplementing the work by Bronislaw Malinowski (1884–1942) and F. G. Crookshank, published in 1923, and continuously influential to the present day.

11. Here are some good books on language: Otto Jespersen, *Language: Its Nature, Development, and Origin,* Allen & Unwin, London, 1922; Otto Jespersen, *Growth and Structure of the English Language,* 1st ed., 1905; Anchor Books, New York, 1957; Alan H. Gardner, *The Theory of Speech and Language,* Oxford University Press, New York, 1932; Grace de Laguna, *Speech,* Yale University Press, New Haven, 1927; Edward Sapir, *Language,* Harcourt, Brace & Co., New York, 1921; S. I. Hayakawa, *Language in Thought and Action,* Harcourt, Brace & Co., New York, 1949; Wilbur M. Urban, *Language and Reality,* Macmillan, New York, 1949; Leonard Bloomfield, *Language,* Henry Holt, New York, 1933; H. L. Mencken, *The American Language,* 3 vols., A. A. Knopf, New York, 1936–48.

12. The best English is spoken at Cambridge, and possibly the worst English, in so far as pronunciation is concerned, is spoken at Oxford. This is the type of pronunciation that has given rise to the vaudeville conception of the Englishman "with the hot potato in his mouth." This is the author's

opinion, but it is shared by many others. I don't think that
an "official" judgment exists on the matter.   ———

13. The subjunctive is that mood of a verb expressing condition,
desire, hypothesis, contingency, possibility, supposition, etc.,
rather than actual fact. Example, "He would go if he could."

            ———

14. The glottal stop is a speech sound produced by a momentary
complete closure of the glottis: it is commonly heard, often
as a variant for medial *t* (in *water, bottle,* etc., as *wa'er, bo'le,*
etc.), in many Scottish and British dialects.   ———

15. Communication as the transmission of a meaning may be
achieved without any form of language, as by mood convection. Language consists of a *system of symbols,* whereas
communication may be achieved without system or symbols.

            ———

16. Slang is language before it becomes respectable; more strictly,
colloquial language that is outside of conventional or standard
usage and comprises both coined words *(blurb, whoopee)*
and those with new or extended meanings *(square, sap).*
Slang develops from the attempt to find fresh and vigorous,
colorful, pungent, or humorous expression, and generally
either passes into disuse or comes to have a more formal status.

            ———

17. English belongs in the family of Indo-European languages,
in the Germanic subfamily, and in the western Low Germanic
group.   ———

18. Hungarian belongs to the Ugric group of the Finno-Ugric
family of languages.   ———

19. A morpheme is any word or part of a word, as an affix or
combining form, that conveys meaning, that cannot be further
divided into smaller elements conveying meaning, and usually
occurs in various contexts with relatively stable meaning.

            ———

20. Semitic refers to a family of languages and is incorrectly used
of any race.   ———

21. The following are some theories of the origin of language:
    (*a*) The *bow-wow* theory: that language is imitative of
sounds, such as the barking of dogs, etc.

(*b*) The *pooh-pooh* theory: that language is derived from instinctive ejaculations evoked by pain or other intense feelings or sensations.

(*c*) The *dingdong* theory: namely, that there is a mystic harmony between sound and sense, that to every impression within there is an appropriate vocal expression without—"everything which is struck rings. Each substance has its peculiar ring."

(*d*) The *yo-he-ho* theory: that words first came into being as a result of the expressions following upon strong muscular effort.

All these theories have been abandoned by serious students of language.

Other theories are:

(*e*) The *gestural* theory: that language came into being when men began to imitate with their tongues the gestures they made with their bodies. There are few serious subscribers to this theory.

(*f*) The *tarara-boom-de-ay* theory: that language originated in the collective half-musical expressions of early man when his principal vocal exercise was a meaningless humming or singing. Suppose that they have together succeeded in bringing down a great mammoth, they will strike up a chant of triumph, say something like "tarara-boom-de-ay." The sounds of the chant might easily come to mean, "We have brought him down. We have conquered the enemy. Hooray! Let us give thanks." And so on from there. This theory has been suggested by Jespersen. It is strangely true that what cannot be spoken can often be sung. _____

22. I have tried them all and I find Interlingua by far the best international language thus far devised. Any ordinarily educated person can read it with 90 per cent comprehension virtually immediately, and understand it when spoken to an equal degree, which is more than can be said for any other international language with which I am acquainted. *Science News Letter,* Washington, D. C., frequently prints a column or two in Interlingua. _____

23. The best English in America is spoken in Massachusetts, New

England. Mencken says this is a popular error. Mencken was wrong more than once and I think him so on this point.

_____

24. Dialect is the form or variety of a spoken language peculiar to a region, community, or social group: in this sense dialects are regarded as being mutually intelligible while languages are mutually unintelligible.   _____

25. American English is vastly more colorful and inventive than English English, as is abundantly demonstrated by the frequency with which the English adopt Americanisms.   _____

26. You should speak at least one other language in addition to English.   _____

27. You should read at least three languages in addition to English, namely, French, German, and one other.   _____

28. Of course there should be an international language. Such a language would be one of the most powerful instruments for peace and understanding in the world.   _____

29. In learning a foreign language for the purpose of speaking and reading it the first thing to do is to concentrate on speaking and reading it. The last thing one should do is to learn its grammar, for the grammar of a language is its philosophy, and that can best be understood at the end rather than at the beginning of the learning enterprise. If one is learning the language for scholarly purposes, most certainly start with the grammar.   _____

30. In _Pygmalion_ (1912), now made even more widely familiar through _My Fair Lady,_ George Bernard Shaw (1856–1950) makes Professor Higgins say: "The English have no respect for their language, and will not teach their children to speak it. . . . It is impossible for an Englishman to open his mouth, without making some other Englishman despise him." Americans, however, are quite safe. They can open their mouths as widely as they like, the same ruin of a language emerges from far too many of them. If it is true, as Dr. Johnson said, that language is the dress of thought the conclusion is only too painfully obvious. So, then, if you take especial care about the manner in which you dress your thought you may go to the head of the class.   _____

The Law and Liberty

1. Law refers to all the rules of conduct established and enforced by the authority, legislation, or custom of a given community or other group. _____

2. *Ignorantia legis neminem excusat* means "Ignorance of the law excuses no one." _____

3. *Amicus curiae* means a friend of the court, an adviser with no personal interest in the case; specifically, one who assists the court. _____

4. The attorney for the defense in the Sacco-Vanzetti case (1921–27) was Arthur Garfield Hays (1881–1954), American lawyer. _____

5. There are nine judges, or, more specifically, justices, of the Supreme Court of the United States. _____

6. The relation between law and liberty or freedom is that law is the principal means by which liberty and freedom is secured to the individual. _____

7. *Corpus delicti* (literally, the body of the crime), the facts constituting or proving a crime; the *corpus delicti* in a murder case is not the body of the victim, but the fact that death has occurred and that it is the result of murder. _____

8. Statutory law refers to the legislative enactments of any lawmaking body, as distinguished from the common law which is based on the custom, usage, and the decisions of law courts. _____

9. The earliest preserved code of law is the Code of Hammurabi. Hammurabi (c. 1955–1913 B.C.) was the great humanitarian king of Babylon. _____

10. The attorney for the defense in the "Monkey Trial" was Clarence Darrow (1857–1938), American lawyer. _____

11. *Habeas corpus* is a writ or order requiring that a prisoner be brought before a court at a stated time and place to decide the legality of his detention or imprisonment: the right of *habeas corpus* is a safeguard against illegal detention or imprisonment. _____

12. Jurisprudence is the science or philosophy of law. _____

13. The author of *Ancient Law,* 1861, was Sir Henry Maine (1822–88), English jurist and historian.   _____

14. The great contribution of the Greeks to the theory of law was that the law is made by men and not by gods, and can, therefore, be changed by men.*   _____

15. There are far too many things wrong with the law of libel to mention them all here, but they can all be summed up in the statement that they do not sufficiently protect the libeled.

_____

16. The *jus gentium* was the system of law developed by the Romans designed to apply to all the conquered peoples within the Roman Empire, as distinct from the Law of the Twelve Tables which applied only to Roman citizens.   _____

17. The best definition of liberty I know is by Lord Acton (1834–1902), English historian: "Liberty is not the power of doing what we like, but the right of being able to do what we ought."   _____

18. In England a barrister is a qualified member of the legal profession who presents and pleads cases in court; he is a member of the bar; whereas a solicitor, though a qualified lawyer, is not a member of the bar and may not plead cases in superior courts. He generally prepares the brief for the barrister. A person cannot be both a barrister and a solicitor at the same time. Should a barrister desire to become a solicitor, he must apply for disbarment, and then go through the regular training of the solicitor.   _____

19. The basic freedoms secured to every American are set out in the Constitution of the United States.   _____

20. The greatest safeguard of freedom in the United States is the Supreme Court. Edward Gibbon (1737–94) does not seem to have been quite sound when he remarked that "The principles of a free constitution are irrecoverably lost when the legislative power is nominated by the executive." *History of the Decline and Fall of the Roman Empire,* Chapter 3.

_____

21. The statute of limitations is a law which provides a legal

* See Plato, *Laws.*

limit of time in which an action may be taken in certain cases.

_____

22. It was illegal to intern persons of Japanese ancestry during World War II; nevertheless it was done by the government of the United States.*   _____

23. Elijah Lovejoy (1802–37), American abolitionist, editor of the Presbyterian weekly *Observer*, in the pages of which he advocated abolition. Mobs destroyed three of his presses, and on November 7, 1837, while guarding another of his presses, he was killed by the mob, at Alton, Illinois. He was America's first martyr to a free press, and his martyrdom greatly served to advance the cause of the abolitionists in the North.   _____

24. Capital punishment is indefensible on any ground whatever. When a man commits a wrong, let us say, by murder, justice is not done by taking the life of the murderer. For if the murderer is wrong for having committed murder, how can society be right by killing the murderer? Terrible crimes do not call for terrible punishments, but for understanding and the action appropriately indicated.†   _____

25. In the First Amendment to the Constitution it is provided that "Congress shall make no law . . . abridging the freedom of the press." But even this amendment does not secure the people against the infringements of federal and state governments upon the right of the people to learn the truth. Furthermore, various pressure groups and advertisers can prevent news from being printed by threatening a boycott. At the present time there is no available means by which the people can be protected in their right to know the truth.   _____

26. Every thinking person ought to be in some organization protecting civil liberties.   _____

27. Laws with which we do not agree we should work through the existing legal framework to see changed, but while they are laws we should observe them.   _____

28. Freedom is not free, it has to be worked for, and earned to be maintained.   _____

* See Dorothy S. Thomas and Richard S. Nishimito, *The Spoilage*, University of California Press, Berkeley, 1946.

† Arthur Koestler, *A Treatise on Hanging*, Macmillan, New York, 1957.

29. Congress should certainly not have the right to investigate anyone's political beliefs, any more than it should have the right to investigate his religious beliefs. In Russia such things are done. They should not be done here. In a war it is necessary to be careful that we do not fall into the error of imitating the vices of the enemy.   ———

30. Yes, legislation *can* bring about changes in public opinion and attitudes. The FEPC, and the Fair Employment Practices Act, is a good example of the manner in which "race" attitudes have been influenced in many parts of the East by appropriate legislation.   ———

The Facts of Life

1. The average duration of pregnancy is 267 days.   ———
2. The average duration of menstruation is about 4 days. ———
3. The average interval between first menstruation (menarche) and the menopause is about 35 years.   ———
4. Average duration of adolescence* in the female is about 9½ years, i.e., from about 13½ years to about 23 years of age.
    ———
5. Average duration of adolescence* in the male is about 12 years, i.e., from about 15 years to 27 years of age.   ———
6. The average age of puberty in the female is 13½ years.
    ———
7. The average age of puberty in the male is 15 years. ———
8. The average female is *not* usually capable of procreation at puberty. On the average, three years elapse after puberty (menarche) before the female becomes capable of procreation.†
9. Epidemics of flu do occur in cycles. There are two types of

* Adolescence is here taken to mean the period from the arrival of puberty to the age at which growth of the bones ceases.

† See Ashley Montagu, *The Reproductive Development of the Female,* Julian Press, New York, 1957.

flu, Type A and Type B. Type A has a cycle of two or three years, and Type B about twice as long.* _____

10. Babies whose mothers have been drug addicts during pregnancy will be born as drug addicts, and will have to be treated much the same as addicts for their morphinism or whatever similar condition they exhibit.† _____

11. The average expectation of the life of the white female in the United States as of the end of 1957 was 73.4 years. _____

12. The average expectation of life of the white male in the United States as of the end of 1957 was 67.3 years. _____

13. Females live longer than males, virtually throughout the whole of animated nature, because they are the biologically more valuable part of the species capital. All the males on the earth could die at this moment, but the species would still go on. But if all the females were to die—the conclusion is or should be obvious. The female must be preserved during the gestation period at the very least, the male need not be preserved for any time after he has produced conception.‡

_____

14. More men are killed in home accidents than women. The death rate from such accidents for men is about 50 per cent higher than for women. _____

15. The factors most influencing the rate of growth in children are mainly nutritional. _____

16. Cancer is a disease characterized by uncontrolled cell reproduction; the uncontrolled cancer cells invade healthy tissues and destroy their functions, thus causing eventual death.

_____

17. Cancer kills principally by invading the healthy tissues and depriving them of their nutrition, also by destroying the healthy tissue, and often by migrating to other parts of the

---

* See Louis I. Dublin, *The Facts of Life*, Macmillan, New York, 1951, p. 168.

† See Ashley Montagu, "Constitutional and Prenatal Factors in Infant and Child Health," in his book *Anthropology and Human Nature*, Porter Sargent, Boston, 1957.

‡ See Ashley Montagu, *The Natural Superiority of Women*, Macmillan, New York, 1953; Amram Scheinfeld, *Women and Men*, Harcourt, Brace & Co., New York, 1944.

body and producing the same effects at the same time.

18. Hemophilia cannot be eliminated because the normal hereditary particle, the gene, mutates to the abnormal one responsible for hemophilia, in 1 out of every 100,000 persons per generation.

19. The skin color of the offspring of mulattoes may vary from white to black including all intermediate possibile combinations of black and white.

20. Physiological age, as contrasted to chronological age which is measured by the clock, refers to the developmental level of the individual. A child of 10 years by the clock may be physiologically or developmentally much older or much younger.

21. The average rate of respiration in the adult at rest is 18 per minute.

22. The principal factors in influencing blood pressure are the force of the heart beat, the elasticity of the vessel walls, volume and viscosity of the blood, etc. Hypertension or abnormal blood pressure may be produced by functional disturbances in the kidney, liver, the blood vessels themselves, or in the portal system of veins by obstruction. Glandular disorders may also produce increase in blood pressure. Stress, strain, and nervous excitement are significant influences in producing high or low blood pressure.

23. At each beat the heart pumps about 7½ ounces of blood (about 2,600 gallons a day).

24. The average human body contains between 3½ to 5½ quarts of blood, or between 5 to 7 per cent of total body weight.

25. The growth of children varies with the seasons, tending to be slow during the winter, more rapid during the spring, and most rapid during the summer.

26. Children should begin to be instructed in the facts of life as soon as they are capable of understanding them—usually before the age of seven.

27. A book on social biology ought to be read at least once every three years.

28. The cultured man should be fairly well grounded in the facts of life, and should be able to make a score of 70 per cent on a series of questions such as these. _____

29. Artificial insemination is often the best solution to the problems besetting a married couple who might otherwise remain childless, and is therefore to be recommended. _____

30. Most certainly social biology should be a school subject. The subject should form an indispensable part of the school curriculum, because of its great value in preparing the individual for the better understanding of himself and of his fellow man. _____

~~

Literary Curiosities

1. Harold Skimpole, the plausible but selfish character of Charles Dickens's (1812–1870) *Bleak House* (1852–53) was a skit on Leigh Hunt (1784–1859), at least as regards "the light externals of character," namely, a certain vagueness and alleged irresponsibility. The skit is unfair, and Hunt was much displeased. _____

2. The original of Percy Bysshe Shelley's (1792–1822) Adonais is John Keats (1795–1821) in *Adonais: An Elegy on the Death of John Keats,* 1821. _____

3. Buck Mulligan is the character in James Joyce's (1882–1941) *Ulysses* for which the original was provided by Oliver St. John Gogarty (1878–1957), Irish author and surgeon.

_____

4. Alroy Kear is the character in Somerset Maugham's (1874–) *Cakes and Ale,* 1930, modeled on that of the English novelist Hugh Walpole (1884–1941). _____

5. Scythrop, in Thomas Love Peacock's (1785–1866) *Nightmare Abbey,* 1818, is modeled on the frame of his friend Percy Bysshe Shelley. _____

6. Mr. Boythorn is Walter Savage Landor (1775–1864) in Dickens's *Bleak House.* _____

7. Gustave Flaubert (1821–80), the French novelist, often spent days and sometimes weeks on finding the exact word. _____

8. Alexandre Dumas père (1802–70), well over 200 novels. Eden Phillpotts (1862–   ), over 300 novels. John Creasey (1908–   ), over 400. Georges Simenon (1903–   ), nearly 500.

9. Merrill Moore (1903–57), American psychiatrist, wrote over 100,000 sonnets.

10. Alexandre Dumas (1802–70) employed a large number of helpers to whom he would give the ideas for his books, and when they had roughed out the general idea he would then put it into final shape.

11. *Curiosities of Literature*, 6 vols., 1791–1824, was written by Isaac D'Israeli (1766–1848), father of Benjamin Disraeli.

12. The world's best-seller is the *Holy Bible*.

13. George Eliot's real name was Marian or Mary Ann Evans (1819–80).

14. It was Havelock Ellis (1859–1939), English scientist and writer, who was called "the most civilized Englishman alive" by H. L. Mencken.

15. George Sand's real name was Amandine Aurore Lucie Dupin, Baronne Dudevant (1804–76).

16. The best all-round English weekly is a choice between *The Listener, The New Statesman,* and *The Spectator.*

17. Currer Bell's real name was Charlotte Brontë (1816–55).

18. The distinguished American painter who was also a brilliant controversial essayist was James McNeill Whistler (1834–1903).

19. Saki's real name was Hector Hugh Munro (1870–1916), English writer.

20. The American Nobel laureate in literature who never went to college is Ernest Hemingway (1898–   ).

21. William Shakespeare (1564–1616) left practically no writing behind in his own hand. Nor did John Donne (1573–1631).

22. Remy de Gourmont (1858–1915), French writer, and Sinclair Lewis (1885–1951), American novelist, both suffered from serious skin disorders of the face.

23. Edward Gibbon (1737–94) never married because he suffered from a hydrocele of the testes, an easily repairable disorder even in his own day. _____

24. The largest library in the world is the British Museum Library, which at the present time has over 5 million books. _____

25. The author of the novel *Sibyl*, 1844, was Benjamin Disraeli (1804–81). _____

26. It is to be hoped that you return all borrowed books. _____

27. A "Little Magazine" is the name usually applied to an avant-garde literary journal, the function of which is to bring new talents to notice and new ideas and methods into the public forum.* _____

28. It would be difficult to come upon a better measure of a man's mind than the manner in which he writes. _____

29. The people must be allowed to provide its own censorship. A cultivated taste is the best of all censors. _____

30. Anyone who deprives himself of the pleasures of dictionary-tasting is a person to be commiserated with. _____

English and American Literature

1. Literature refers to that class of writing which is distinguished either for beauty of form or expression, especially imaginative prose, poetry, and the like, and regarded as of permanent value. _____

2. *Pamela: or Virtue Rewarded,* 1740, by Samuel Richardson (1689–1761), English printer and writer, is generally regarded as the earliest novel of character in the English language. Richardson's combined output of novels, *Clarissa Harlowe,* 7 vols., 1747–48, and *Sir Charles Grandison,* 1753, had a powerful influence upon writers both in England and abroad. _____

3. Cham is an obsolete form of the word *Khan.* Tobias Smollett (1721–71) referred to Dr. Samuel Johnson (1709–84) as "that great Cham of literature," and the name stuck. _____

* See Frederick J. Hoffman, Charles Allen, and Carolyn F. Ulrich, *The Little Magazine,* Princeton University Press, Princeton, N.J., 1947.

4. The longest American novel is James Farrell's (1904–   )
   Danny O'Neill, complete in five volumes: *A World I Never
   Made,* 1936, *No Star Is Lost,* 1938, *Father and Son,* 1940,
   My Days of Anger, 1943, and *The Face of Time,* 1953.

5. Leopold Bloom is a character in James Joyce's (1882–1941)
   Ulysses, Paris, 1922.

6. Iambic pentameter was first used in English verse by Geoffrey
   Chaucer (1340?–1400) in *The Canterbury Tales.* He called
   his 7-line stanza *rhyme royal,* in pentameter couplets, later it
   was called *heroic couplets.*

7. Frederick Jackson Turner (1861–1932), American historian,
   in 1893 addressed the American Historical Association on
   "The Significance of the Frontier in American History," a
   work which subsequently had a considerable influence upon
   American historical thought. This address was incorporated
   in Turner's *The Frontier in American History,* 1920. _____

8. It was Edgar Allan Poe (1809–49) who wrote the final lines
   ". . . the play is the tragedy, 'Man,'/And its hero, the Conqueror Worm," in "The Conqueror Worm," 1845. _____

9. John Fiske (1842–1901), American philosopher and historian, the chief popularizer of science and philosophy in
   the age of Victoria in America. _____

10. *The Hind and the Panther,* 1687, is a poem by John Dryden
    (1631–1700). _____

11. *The Shoemaker's Holiday,* 1600, is by Thomas Dekker
    (1572?–1632), English dramatist and noble spirit. _____

12. Jonathan Swift (1667–1745) was the author of the prose
    satire *The Battle of the Books,* 1704. _____

13. *Euphues, the Anatomy of Wit* (1578–79) is the first part of a
    two-part prose romance by John Lyly (1554?–1606), the first
    English writer of high comedy in prose. _____

14. *A New Way To Pay Old Debts,* 1632, is a play by Philip
    Massinger (1583–1640), English dramatist. _____

15. *A History of the Earth and Animated Nature,* 4 vols., 1774,
    was written by Oliver Goldsmith (1728–74). _____

16. *Epithalamion,* 1595, is the poem by Edmund Spenser (1552?–
    99). _____

17. *The Titan*, 1914, is a novel by Theodore Dreiser (1871–1945). _____

18. *The Turn of the Screw*, 1898, is the title of a tale of the supernatural by Henry James (1843–1916). _____

19. "Benito Cereno," 1856, is a story by Herman Melville (1819–91), first published in *Piazza Tales*, 1856. _____

20. *Manhattan Transfer*, 1925, is a novel by John Dos Passos (1896–   ). _____

21. *The American Jitters*, 1932, is the title of a book by Edmund Wilson (1895–   ). _____

22. *Light in August*, 1932, is a novel by William Faulkner.

23. *The Flowering of New England, 1815–1865*, 1936, is a critical exposition of that period in American literature, by Van Wyck Brooks (1886–   ). _____

24. *The American*, 1877, is by Henry James. _____

25. *The Degradation of the Democratic Dogma*, 1920, is by Brooks Adams (1848–1927), American historian. _____

26. To qualify you should read at least one work of literary criticism a year. _____

27. You should subscribe to at least two literary journals per annum. _____

28. A literary critic does not have to be competent in the medium he criticizes, any more than a preacher must practice what he preaches. _____

29. "Poetry" wrote Wordsworth, "is the breath and finer spirit of all knowledge; it is the impassioned expression which is in the countenance of all science." In which case it must be, and is, indispensable to the cultured man. _____

30. There are *no* areas of human experience which should not be written about. _____

~~

Literature in General

1. *L'Histoire de Gil Blas de Santillane*, 1715–35, picaresque romance by the French novelist and dramatist Alain René Lesage (1668–1747). _____

2. *The Cloister and the Hearth,* 1861, a novel by Charles Reade (1814–84), English novelist.   _____

3. *La Comédie Humaine,* the great collection of romances, 47 vols., so-called by one of the greatest of novelists, Honoré de Balzac (1799–1850).   _____

4. *Là-Bas,* 1891, is a novel by the French writer Joris Karl Huysmans (1848–1907).   _____

5. *Les Fleurs du Mal,* 1857, title of a volume of poems by Charles Pierre Baudelaire (1821–67), French poet and critic.   _____

6. *The Wind in the Willows,* 1908, a book for children, also enjoyed by many adults, by the English writer Kenneth Grahame (1859–1932).   _____

7. *Il Principe (The Prince),* 1513, a treatise on statecraft by the Florentine statesman and philosopher Niccolò di Bernardo dei Machiavelli (1469–1527).   _____

8. *The Art of Courtly Love,* 1185, by Andreas the Chaplain (Andreas Capellanus), chaplain to the royal court of Troyes, written at the instigation of the Countess Marie of Champagne (1145?–?).   _____

9. *A Wreath of Cloud,* 11th century, a novel, the third part of *The Tale of Genji,* by the Lady Murasaki (978?–1030?), Japanese lady of the court and writer.   _____

10. *Candide,* 1759, is by Voltaire (1694–1778).   _____

11. *Ambrosio, or The Monk,* 1796, a romance by the English writer Matthew Gregory Lewis (1775–1818).   _____

12. *The Shepheardes Calendar,* 1579, is a long poem by Edmund Spenser (1552?–99).   _____

13. *The Castle of Otranto,* 1764, a supernatural romance by Horace Walpole (1717–97).   _____

14. *Orlando,* 1928, a novel by Virginia Woolf (1882–1941).
_____

15. *John Brown's Body,* 1928, a drama in verse dealing with the Civil War, by Stephen Vincent Benét (1898–1943).
_____

16. *The River,* 1937, a prose poem written by Pare Lorentz (1905–   ), as the spoken text to accompany his beautiful film of the same name.   _____

17. *Imaginary Conversations,* 5 vols., 1824, 1828, 1829, 1853, by Walter Savage Landor (1775–1864). _____

18. *Conversations with a Cat,* 1931, a book of essays by Hilaire Belloc (1870–1953). _____

19. *archy and mehitabel,* 1927, a book by Don Marquis (1878–1937), American writer. _____

20. *Don Juan,* 1819–24, a satirical epic in *ottava rima* by George Gordon, Lord Byron (1788–1824). _____

21. *Le Père Goriot,* 1835, a novel by Balzac. _____

22. *Madame Bovary,* 1856, a novel by Gustave Flaubert (1821–80). _____

23. *War and Peace,* 1865–69, a novel by Leo Tolstoy (1828–1910). _____

24. *The Sorrows of Young Werther,* 1774, is a romance by Johann Wolfgang von Goethe (1749–1832). _____

25. *Paradise Lost,* 1667, an epic poem in ten books, by John Milton (1608–74). _____

26. It is possible to read too much. Aubrey tells us that Hobbes had read much, but his contemplation was much more than his reading. He was wont to say that if he had read as much as other men, he should have known no more than other men. Reading can become a form of indolence and a substitute for the necessity of thinking. Then there are the ignorantly read, with loads of lumber in their heads. As William Penn (1644–1718) put it, "Much reading is an oppression of the mind, and extinguishes the natural candle, which is the reason of so many senseless scholars in the world." It is necessary to know what not to read as well as what is important to read. The principal purpose of reading should be as a stimulus to thought, and only secondarily as an accretion to one's knowledge—and thinking need not be incompatible with reading for pleasure. The cultured man is necessarily a well-read man, but he knows the difference between a book that is to be tasted and one that is to be chewed and digested. _____

27. A work of literature is to be distinguished from a mere piece of writing, however competent. Most of us write; few of us create literature. If you read at least four works of literature a year you qualify. _____

28. As a rule it is not a good idea to meet the authors whose works one admires, unless one believes in the reality principle and desires to have one's illusions shattered. _____

29. Programs on literature on TV and radio have proved their value time and again; the difficulty is obtaining sponsors for them. _____

30. Foreign literary reviews or journals keep one abreast of what is going on in the rest of the world; hence, they should be seen. _____

~·~

Manners

1. It was Emerson who defined manners as the happy way of doing things. And that is what manners are: the graces of being, of conduct. The dictionary says: the polite ways of social behavior. _____

2. There are never any occasions when good manners are con-traindicated. _____

3. It is always necessary to be considerate. _____

4. Those who pour oil upon troubled waters are most likely to be helpful in a storm. _____

5. Where excessive and unnecessary pain may be brought to anyone or their very lives or health endangered by telling them the truth, it is permissible to withhold it. _____

6. It was Louis XVIII (1755–1824) who said that punctuality is the politeness of kings. Since very few men are ever kings, punctuality seems to be among the rarest of virtues. The punctual spend much of their lives waiting for the unpunctual, hence punctuality becomes the thief of time. Being punctilious about punctuality can be overdone, and human frailty being what it is, and most people having so little sense of time, the good-mannered man will allow for these weaknesses and be tolerant of them, though by no means encouraging them. You should be punctual within reason, turning up at the stated time yourself, but do not be angry when others don't. _____

7. Courtesy in driving is, among other things, adaptively of the highest survival value. _____

8. The proper word is napkin (in English).   _____

9. Private communications of any sort which are intended by their writer to be seen only by the addressee and whosoever the addressee designates, unless otherwise specified, should not be read by others—until, and if, they become documents of literary or historic interest, and are in the open domain.

     _____

10. Children are persons in their own right and should be respected as such.   _____

11. It is well to have a proper sense of one's worth, but not an exaggerated one. But whatever that self-estimate is, there are occasions when the justice of the situation demands our voluntarily taking ourselves down a peg.   _____

12. By "A gentleman refrains . . ." Dr. Johnson meant that a gentleman never puts anyone in an embarrassing position.

     _____

13. Ralph Waldo Emerson (1803–82) in *The Conduct of Life,* 1860.   _____

14. The counsel of perfection is that you should never lose your temper, for no man has ever acted in temper and been glad of it afterward; but if you must lose your temper, put it down as a fault which you recognize in yourself and seek to remedy.

     _____

15. It is a mark of the generous mind to let others fumble—but not too often.   _____

16. The man who makes way for others is the man who is perfectly capable of making his own way.   _____

17. There is a simple distinction between a woman and a lady. The term *woman* is the generic one, the term *lady* is the particular one. Every lady is a woman, but not every woman is a lady. The Colonel's Lady and Judy O'Grady may be sisters under the skin, but it is what is outside the skin that makes the difference. And what is that difference? It used to be breeding, but the equivalent of good breeding will do, namely, refinement of manner and grace—however acquired . . . the woman lacking in grace and refinement is a woman, she is not a lady.   _____

18. Those who listen learn. "It is the province of knowledge to

speak and it is the privilege of wisdom to listen": Oliver
Wendell Holmes (1809–94). ⸻

19. Blank contradictions are exchanged among rude people by
crude people only. ⸻

20. In medieval times bores used to be shot as a form of sport.
We have grown more civilized. But no one should suffer a
bore gladly. The age of chivalry is past, and bores have succeeded bogeymen. ⸻

21. Renunciation is the sincerest form of compassion. ⸻

22. A gift is a manifestation of grace and in part a present of
yourself. ⸻

23. Games should be played for fun, to bring out the best in the
other so that they may reciprocally bring out the best in you,
and whoever wins you are glad that the best man did so.

⸻

24. It was Dr. Johnson who defined politeness as fictitious benevolence. ⸻

25. Graciousness is the beneficence of manners. We trust you are
or will become beneficent in your manner. ⸻

26. As a rule it is an iniquity to drop in on anyone without first
inquiring whether it will be convenient or agreeable.⸻

27. A person may be judged by his manners—only in so far as
his manners are concerned. ⸻

28. The cooperative approach is in all matters the more advisable.

⸻

29. In general it is a good idea to adhere to the form required.

⸻

30. However repugnant the views of others may be, their right to
hold those views must at all costs be defended, unless, of
course, those views are in any way damaging to the persons
and property of others. ⸻

❦

Marriage

1. Marriage is the legal union of a man with a woman entered
into with the assumption of permanency. ⸻

2. The soundest basis for marriage is character. _____

3. The engagement period should last between three and twelve months. _____

4. The arguments against premarital relations with the betrothed are that: (1) it is not a good idea to begin a relationship by rejecting the mores of one's society; premarital laxity may mean marital infidelity; (2) unsatisfying premarital sexual intercourse with the betrothed may put an end to the relationship which might otherwise never have foundered—the discovery of the satisfactions of sex should be part of the marital, *not* the premarital experience. _____

5. Yes, it is a good idea to wait a year or two before having children, for the simple reason that there is a certain amount of adjusting to go through before one is ready for children. _____

6. A wife should not work who has small children at home. Children need their mothers, particularly during the first six years of their lives.* _____

7. Most certainly a husband should help his wife with domestic chores. There should be no question of it. _____

8. What a husband and wife should do about visiting their friends separately on an occasional evening must be determined by the conditions of their own particular situation. In general, there should be not the least objection. _____

9. Of course husband and wife may have separate friends. _____

10. Married couples at any age should not, if possible, live in the same house as their in-laws. _____

11. The female ought to be older than the male at marriage for the reason that if the married couple are to live out their years together, it is more likely that they will do so upon this than upon the usual arrangement. _____

12. The married live longer than the unmarried. _____

13. The best age at marriage for the female is about 21 to 23 years. _____

14. Husband and wife ought to occupy the same bed, a double bed,

* See Ashley Montagu, *The Direction of Human Development,* Harper & Brothers, New York, 1955.

for the reason that it serves to bind them more closely together, and this is reflected in their family life.* _____

15. Endogamy is the custom of marrying only within one's own tribe or social group. _____

16. Approximately 1 out of every 3 marriages ends in divorce in the United States. _____

17. The usual age at marriage for both males and females ought to be modified in the light of the facts that neither males nor females are physiologically or psychologically ready for marriage until they have reached their twenties.† _____

18. The objection to the marriage of Edward VIII to Mrs. Wallis Simpson was not on the ground that the marriage would be a morganatic one, but because Mrs. Simpson was a divorced woman. _____

19. There are no societies in which marriage does not exist.

_____

20. Sequential polygamy, in which one may have numerous wives or husbands, one at a time, is a form of marriage fairly often practiced in certain parts of the United States, principally Hollywood. _____

21. The form of marriage in which a woman may have two or more husbands at the same time is known as polyandry.

_____

22. Marriage between Catholics may be dissolved by Pauline Privilege by the Congregation of the Holy Office of Rome or by an act of the Pope. _____

23. The most amusing exchange on marriage, possibly in the whole of literature, is to be found in Book III of François Rabelais' (1494?–1553) *Gargantua and Pantagruel*, 1532–34. Chapters 35 and 36 are the funniest.‡ _____

24. The most famous and the best of all histories of marriage is Edward Westermarck's, *The History of Human Marriage*, 3 vols., Macmillan, New York, 1921; 1st ed., 1891. See also

* See Ashley Montagu, "Some Factors in Family Cohesion," *Psychiatry*, vol. 7, 1944, pp. 349-352.

† See Ashley Montagu, *The Reproductive Development of the Female*, Julian Press, New York, 1957.

‡ See the American translation by Samuel Putnam, *All the Extant Works of François Rabelais*, Covici-Friede, New York, 1929, vol. 1, pp. 463-468.

the same author's *Three Essays on Sex and Marriage,* Macmillan, New York, 1934, and his *The Future of Marriage in Western Civilization,* Macmillan, New York, 1936. Also see Robert Briffault, *The Mothers,* 3 vols., Macmillan, New York, 1927; Robert Briffault and Bronislaw Malinowski, *Marriage: Past and Present,* Porter Sargent, Boston, 1956. _____

25. Polygyny is the form of marriage in which a man may have two or more wives at the same time. _____

26. The most important single factor making for success in marriage is the willingness to adjust. _____

27. Marriage counseling serves a most valuable purpose in helping married couples solve their problems. _____

28. The divorce rates are high in the United States because, among other reasons, the individual is able to obtain a divorce more easily in this country than in most others, and because most individuals marry for the wrong reasons, making physical attraction the primary instead of a quaternary basis for marriage. When the physical attraction palls the marriage often does, too. _____

29. If you are married you may take the full score. If not—unless the circumstances are extenuating ones—you may go to the corner of the room. _____

30. It is quite impossible that the institution of marriage could ever be abolished. _____

~~

Medicine

1. Medicine is the science and art of diagnosing, treating, curing, and preventing disease, relieving pain, and improving and preserving health. _____

2. Hippocrates (c.460–377 B.C.), Greek physician, is known as the Father of Medicine. _____

3. Suśruta (fl. c.600 B.C.), great Indian physician. _____

4. Vaccination was first proved beneficial in the prevention of smallpox by the English physician Edward Jenner (1749–1823). _____

5. Galen (c.130–c.200), Roman physician, anatomist, and physiologist.   _____

6. Reduction in the incidence of poliomyelitis is principally due to the work of Jonas Salk (1914–   ), American physician and bacteriologist.   _____

7. Pellagra is a chronic disease caused by a deficiency of nicotinic acid or niacin (a part of the vitamin-B complex) in the diet, characterized by gastrointestinal disturbances, skin eruptions, and nervous disorders. It is principally due to the poor socio-economic conditions which result in an impoverished diet. With the improvement in socioeconomic conditions the disease generally disappears.   _____

8. Philippus Aureolus Paracelsus (1493–1541) whose real name was Theophrastus Bombastus von Hohenheim, Swiss physician and alchemist, an extraordinarily interesting character with ideas much in advance of his time. He is the hero of Browning's *Paracelsus,* 1835.   _____

9. ACTH are the initials standing for *a*dreno*c*ortico*t*ropic *h*ormone, that is to say, the hormone of the anterior portion of the pituitary gland which acts upon the cortex of the adrenal gland to stimulate it to secrete its hormones.   _____

10. A medical eye specialist is called an ophthalmologist. He is an M.D. An optician is not an M.D., but one who is capable of measuring optical defects and prescribing corrective glasses for them.   _____

11. The normal oral (mouth) temperature of a human being is 98.6° with a normal range of 97.0° to 99.1°. The rectal temperature is normally 1 degree higher than the oral._____

12. Diathesis is the constitutional state of the body predisposing it to disease.   _____

13. More or less cyclic enlargement of the tonsils does not indicate that they should be removed. Tonsils are removed altogether too frequently. When they are enlarged, that is when they are doing their major work. Only when they become seriously disordered is their removal indicated, and this is very rarely.

          _____

14. Constitution is generally taken to mean something that one acquired in his biological endowment. This is not correct.

Constitution is not a static but a dynamic condition. Constitution is the sum total of the structural, functional, and psychological characters of the organism. It is in large measure an integral of genetic potentialities influenced in varying degrees by internal and external environmental factors. It is not a *given,* but a *process,* and as such is amenable to external influences. _____

15. Masturbation is not capable of leading to insanity, but brooding upon the myths associated with it sometimes has done so. It has been estimated that over 90 per cent of persons have masturbated. There are no known ill effects, except in those cases where the habit has been practiced to excess. _____

16. Penicillin is a bacteriostatic, not a bacteriocide. It acts by inhibiting the growth and multiplication of bacteria, thus affording the normal blood cells of the body the opportunity to destroy the harmful bacteria. _____

17. A boil should never be squeezed, particularly in the dangerous area extending from the level of the mouth to the hairline, because the infecting organisms are thus caused to spread, and in the facial region may very readily enter the veins leading to the cavernous sinus in the head, where a fatal thrombosis may develop. _____

18. A coronary thrombosis is a blood clot in one or both of the coronary arteries which are the main blood supply of the heart, which may reduce or entirely cut off the supply of blood to the heart. _____

19. During the first three months of pregnancy German measles contracted by the mother is capable of seriously damaging the development of some 20 per cent or more of fetuses._____

20. The first antibiotic, penicillin, was discovered by Sir Alexander Fleming (1881–1955), British bacteriologist. He received the Nobel prize for medicine in 1945 (with E. B. Chain and H. Florey). _____

21. A peptic ulcer is an ulcer of the stomach or duodenum. _____

22. There is no cure for the normal form of baldness in men. This appears to be entirely genetic. _____

23. A metastasis is the shifting of disease from one part or organ

of the body to another unrelated to it, through the blood or lymph vessels, as by the transfer of pathogenic organisms or the cells of a malignant tumor.

24. The principal acid secreted by the stomach glands is hydrochloric acid.

25. Vitamins are complex organic compounds found variously in natural foods, and essential, in small amounts, for the normal functioning of the animal organism.

26. The health of the people is the principal interest of the people, and therefore should also be the interest of the state and the community. The health of the people should not be in the charge of any private monopoly.

27. Of course babies should be born at home. Where else? Having a baby is a domestic affair, not a disease or a disorder. The birth of a baby is something in which the whole family should participate—*at home,* where it is a happier, safer, and healthier experience for everyone concerned.

28. The giving of contraceptive advice should be limited to those possessing the proper knowledge, and this would include physicians.

29. Midwives are a crying necessity. Soon there will not be enough obstetricians available to take care of the oncoming wave of newborn babies. Midwives could do all and more than is necessary to take care of this problem of which most people seem to be unaware.

30. Medical insurance is a highly sensible form of protection against unanticipated heavy expenses.

Movies, Radio, and Television

1. Though Fritz Lang was assigned to direct *The Cabinet of Dr. Caligari,* it was Robert Wiene who actually directed the film and destroyed the original intention of the authors of the script, Hans Janowitz and Carl Mayer, which was to expose the madness inherent in authority.

2. The director and producer of *Grand Illusion* was Erich von Stroheim (1885–1957).

3. The star of the movie *M* was Peter Lorre (1904–   ).

_____

4. The star of *The Last Laugh* was Emil Jannings (1887–1950).

_____

5. *The Birth of a Nation* was criticized on the ground that it dealt unfairly with the Negro.   _____

6. The Hays Code is the moving-picture-industry moral code drawn up by William Harrison Hays (1879–1954)._____

7. The star of *The Blue Angel* was Marlene Dietrich (1904–   ), or, if you like, Emil Jannings.   _____

8. The young female star of *Mädchen in Uniform* was Dorothea Wieck.   _____

9. The best psychological history of the German film is Siegfried Krackauer's *From Caligari to Hitler,* Princeton University Press, Princeton, 1947.   _____

10. The producer and director of *Nanook of the North* was Robert Joseph Flaherty (1884–1951), American explorer and moving-picture producer.   _____

11. The star of *The Circus* was Charles S. Chaplin (1889–   ).

_____

12. The first man to make moving pictures was Eadweard Muybridge (1830–1904), English photographer, who took moving pictures of horses and other animals in motion during the 1870s.   _____

13. The first sound moving picture was *The Jazz Singer* (1927) featuring Al Jolson (1888–1950).   _____

14. *Invasion From Mars,* an adaptation of *The War of the Worlds* by H. G. Wells, broadcast over the radio by Orson Welles (1915–   ), caused thousands of people to believe that the earth had been invaded by Martians.*   _____

15. The first commercial television broadcasts in the United States were begun April 30, 1939.   _____

16. The FCC is the Federal Communications Commission, executive agency of the U. S. government charged with the regulation of broadcasting.   _____

17. A teleprompter is an electronic device that, unseen by the

* See Hadley Cantril, *The Invasion From Mars,* Princeton University Press, Princeton, 1940.

audience, unrolls a prepared speech, script, etc., line by line, as a prompting aid to a speaker or actor. _____

18. The first person to win over $100,000 on a quiz show was Charles Van Doren. _____

19. Early radio sets were called wireless crystal sets. _____

20. NBC are the initials of the National Broadcasting Company; CBS are the initials of the Columbia Broadcasting System, and BBC are the initials of the British Broadcasting Company.

_____

21. "Omnibus" is a network television show broadcast on Sundays. _____

_____

22. In 1958 there were nearly 50 million television sets in the United States. _____

23. The initials AM stand for amplitude modulation. FM stands for frequency modulation. _____

24. Edwin Howard Armstrong (1890–1954), American engineer and radio inventor, invented the regenerative circuit (1912), the superheterodyne circuit (1918), and frequency modulation (1933). _____

25. If TV ceased to exist as a form of entertainment, it might leave you with more time for more profitable expenditures of time.

_____

26. Television seems to have had very little effect upon the content and character of movies, except to bring about the translation of several shows designed originally for television to the movie screen. _____

27. TV has not ousted radio because there are still a large number of persons who can *listen* but are not in a position to drop their work and *look*. _____

28. Most certainly the violence, the crudities, and the murder of the English language could be dispensed with much to the benefit of TV and everyone else concerned. _____

29. Television subscription would be a good thing in that the subscribers could have a say in the programs they wanted.

_____

30. The general level of TV and radio programs could be greatly elevated with advantage. _____

Music

1. Music is the art and science of combining vocal or instrumental sounds or tones in varying melody, harmony, rhythm, and timbre, especially so as to form structurally complete and emotionally expressive compositions.   _____
2. Ludwig van Beethoven's (1770–1827) Ninth Symphony differs from his others in that it is the only one that includes a choral finale.   _____
3. Niccolò Paganini (1782–1840), Italian violinist and composer.   _____
4. Henry Purcell (1659–1695), English composer.   _____
5. Some of the German-American Kurt Weill's (1900–1950) compositions are: *The Protagonist*, 1926, *The Royal Palace*, 1926, *The Rise and Fall of the City of Mahagonny*, 1929, *The Threepenny Opera*, 1928, and *Lost In the Stars*, 1949.

6. Formerly, a musical composition with the several distinct movements of an orchestral suite, but played by a small group, of solo instruments with a larger orchestral ensemble, a concerto is a composition for one, or two or three, solo instruments and an orchestra: it is based on the sonata form and usually has three movements.   _____
7. A fugue is a musical form or composition in which a theme is taken up and developed by the various instruments or voices in succession according to the strict laws of counterpoint.

8. An oratorio is a long dramatic musical composition, usually on a religious theme, consisting of arias, recitatives, duets, trios, choruses, etc., sung to orchestral accompaniment; it is presented without stage action, scenery, or costumes._____
9. The most famous test for measuring musical talent was developed by Carl Emil Seashore (1866–1949), American psychologist.*   _____
10. Andrés Segovia (1894–   ), Spanish guitarist.   _____

* C. E. Seashore, *The Psychology of Music*, 1938.

11. The English can't play jazz because they lack that culturally indefinable quality known as "oomph." _____

12. A lute is an old stringed instrument related to the guitar, with a body shaped like half of a pear, and six to thirteen strings stretched along the fretted neck, which is often bent to form a sharp angle. _____

13. Terpsichore, in Greek mythology, the Muse of dancing. _____

14. A cadenza is an elaborate, often improvised, musical passage played by an unaccompanied instrument in a concerto, usually toward the end of the first movement. Also, any brilliant flourish put into an aria or a solo passage. _____

15. A berceuse is a lullaby.

16. The Guarnieri family were a family of distinguished violin-makers of Cremona, Italy, who flourished from the middle of the seventeenth into the early eighteenth century. _____

17. The musical *Oklahoma* (1943) is based on the play *Green Grow the Lilacs* (1931) by Lynn Riggs (1899–   ).

18. *My Fair Lady* (1957) is based on George Bernard Shaw's (1856–1950) play "Pygmalion" (1912). The title is from the old English catch, "London Bridge is falling down,/My fair lady." _____

19. Chamber music is music suitable for performance in a room or a small hall, as trios, quartets, and quintets. _____

20. There were altogether six Bachs of the same family who were composers: Johann Sebastian (1685–1750), and his sons Wilhelm Friedmann (1710–84), Karl Philipp Emanuel (1714–88), Johann Christoph Friedrich (1732–95), Johann Christian (1735–82). Johann Christoph (1642–1703) was the son of Heinrich Bach (1615–92). The family of Johann Sebastian Bach were actively musical for seven generations, of which his was the fifth; of some sixty Bachs known by name and profession all but seven were musicians. _____

21. Hector Berlioz (1803–69), French composer, was the composer of the two-part opera, *The Trojans* (1858)._____

22. *Le Coq d'Or* or *The Golden Cockerel* (produced post-

humously) was composed by Rimski-Korsakov (1848–1908).

23. *La Danse Macabre* (1874) was composed by Charles Camille Saint Saëns (1835–1921).   _____

24. *Tea For Two* is by Vincent Youmans (1898–1946)._____

25. *St. Louis Blues* (1914) is by William Christopher Handy (1873–1958).   _____

26. If you read one book a year on music, take full marks.

27. The ability to read music should be a minimal accomplishment.   _____

28. The ability to play a musical instrument is a desirable accomplishment.   _____

29. It is to be expected that you attend musical events as often as you are able.   _____

30. All children, regardless of musical talent, should receive a musical education.   _____

~~

Numbers, Weights, and Measures

1. Number is the sum of any collection of things or individuals; a measure of a discrete quantity. It also denotes the place of a thing or individual in an order. And it is the symbol of the sum, or measure, or place.   _____

2. Weight is a measure of the force with which bodies are pulled toward the center of the earth by gravity. It is heaviness as a quality of things.   _____

3. Measure, the extent, dimensions, capacity, etc., of anything, especially as determined by a standard.   _____

4. Area, the total surface of anything, as measured in square units.   _____

5. There are 5280 feet in a mile.   _____

6. According to tradition the yard (36 inches, or 3 feet) was established by taking the distance from the tip of the nose to the end of the thumb when the arm and hand were outstretched.   _____

7. There are 2000 pounds in a ton in the United States (2400 in Great Britain).   _____

8. Horsepower is the unit for measuring the power of engines or motors, equal to a rate of 33,000 foot-pounds per minute (the force required to raise 33,000 pounds at the rate of one foot per minute).   _____

9. A calorie is the heat needed to raise the temperature of one gram of water 1 degree centigrade: called the *small calorie*. The *large* or *great calorie* is the amount of heat required to raise the temperature of one kilogram of water 1 degree centigrade: used as the unit for measuring the energy produced by food when oxidized in the body.   _____

10. There are 25.4 millimeters in an inch.   _____

11. There are 2.11 liquid pints in a liter.   _____

12. There are 39.37 inches in a meter.   _____

13. Specific gravity is the ratio of the weight or mass of a given volume of a substance to that of an equal volume of another substance (water for liquids and solids, air or hydrogen for gases) used as a standard.   _____

14. Volume of a rectangular solid, such as a box, is determined by multiplying the length by the width by the depth; the volume of a sphere is determined by the formula $v = \pi D^3$ (where D is the diameter). Liquids are measured by glass devices having a special scale.   _____

15. There are 4840 square yards in an acre.   _____

16. There are 6 feet in a fathom.   _____

17. There are 16 drams in an avoirdupois ounce, 8 drams in an apothecaries fluid ounce.   _____

18. There are 480 grains in a troy ounce, 437.5 grains in an avoirdupois ounce.   _____

19. A pica is a size of type: ⅙th of an inch or 12 points._____

20. A ream is 480 sheets of paper, or in printers' use, 518 or often 500.   _____

21. The median is the statistical term referring to the point on the scale of a frequency distribution below and above which just 50 per cent of the observations occur.   _____

22. The mean, or arithmetic mean, is the sum of the measures,

items, magnitudes, or scores in a statistical series divided by
their number or frequency.   ———

23. A value is any particular quantitative determination.———

24. The letters XL mean 40.   ———

25. The letters $\overline{XL}$ mean 40,000.   ———

26. Mathematics or at least an exposure to mathematics is an
essential part of the education of the well-equipped man.

                                                              ———

27. All methods of measurement should be uniform throughout
the world.   ———

28. Statistics never tell the cause of anything; all they do is to
reveal whether or not a statistical association exists. This in
turn may lead to the closer tracking down of the cause.———

29. Giant mechanical brains have already replaced the thought of
some human beings, but it is unlikely that they will altogether
replace human thought even at their most developed. The
danger is not so much that we will create machines that think
like human beings, but that we may create human beings that
think like machines.   ———

30. The metric system ought to be universally adopted.   ———

~~

Opera

1. An opera is a play having all or most of its text set to music,
with arias, recitatives, choruses, duets, trios, etc., sung to
orchestral accompaniment, usually characterized by elaborate
costuming, scenery, and choreography.   ———

2. *Eurydice,* 1600, by Jacopo Peri (1561–1633), Florentine
musician, and the poet Ottavio Rinuccini (1562–1621), is
generally regarded as the first opera.   ———

3. The subjects of the first operas were myths and legends.

4. *Opéra comique* is not comic opera but opera in which the
spoken voice is the defining characteristic.   ———

5. The great reformer of opera was Christoph Willibald Gluck (1714–87), German composer, who returned opera to its dramatic and poetic qualities. _____

6. *Opera seria* is serious opera as distinguished from *opera buffa*. _____

7. The word *Ruddigore*, title of a comic opera by Gilbert and Sullivan, is a play on the words "bloody gore." _____

8. An intermezzo is a short, light, dramatic, musical, or ballet entertainment between the acts of a play or opera. In *music*, (*a*) a short movement connecting the main parts of a composition; (*b*) any of certain short instrumental pieces similar to this. _____

9. Grand opera is opera on a serious theme in which the whole text is set to music. _____

10. The title of Friedrich Nietzsche's (1844–1900) book in which he jettisoned Wagner is *Der Fall Wagner*, 1888; *The Case Wagner*, English translation, 1910. _____

11. The composer of *Pelléas et Mélisande*, 1902, is Claude Debussy (1862–1918). _____

12. *Peter Grimes*, 1945, was composed by Benjamin Britten (1913–   ), English composer. _____

13. *The Consul*, 1950, was composed by Gian-Carlo Menotti (1911–   ), American composer. _____

14. The composer of *Die Zauberflöte*, 1791, is Wolfgang Amadeus Mozart (1756–91). _____

15. The composer of *The Beggar's Opera*, 1728, is John Gay (1685–1732), English poet. _____

16. *The Threepenny Opera*, 1928, was composed by Kurt Weill (1900–50). _____

17. *Hänsel und Gretel*, 1893, is by Engelbert Humperdinck (1854–1921), German composer. _____

18. The composer of *Dido and Aeneas*, c.1689, is Henry Purcell (c.1659–95), English composer. _____

19. *Porgy and Bess*, 1935, was composed by George Gershwin (1898–1937), American composer. _____

20. The composer of *Oberon*, 1826, is Carl Maria von Weber (1786–1826), German composer. _____

21. An operetta is a short, amusing, musical play. _____

22. Richard Wagner's (1813–83) "Wedding March" occurs in his opera *Lohengrin* (1848).   _____

23. An *opéra bouffe* is a comic opera, designed on a trivial scale, lighter than *opéra comique*.   _____

24. A good biography of Sir William Schwenck Gilbert (1836–1911) of Gilbert and Sullivan is Hesketh Pearson's *Gilbert: His Life and Strife*, Harper & Brothers, New York, 1957.

                    _____

25. People who don't like opera generally fall into the class who like the music but not the fat ladies playing the roles of delicate damsels. This is perfectly understandable and forgivable.

26. Of course there ought to be a National Opera House._____

27. And there ought to be a State Opera House in every state.

                    _____

28. The staggering total of over 42,000 operas are known to have been composed!   _____

29. It is to be hoped that you enjoy comic opera.   _____

30. If you attend opera as well as may be, it is well enough.

                    _____

~·~

Parent-Child Relationships

1. To a very large extent parents determine the fate of their children by forming their personalities and outlook, hence, the critical position in which parents stand in relation to their children and to the world.*   _____

2. Parents cannot be too loving, for of genuine love it is impossible to give too much. It is the counterfeit kind which is smothering and damaging.†   _____

3. Frustration is defined as the thwarting of an expected satisfaction. As such the piling up of frustrations is to be avoided, but a certain amount of frustration is not only unavoidable but necessary, for the child must learn to postpone immediate

* See Ashley Montagu, *The Direction of Human Development*, Harper & Bros., New York, 1955.

† See David Levy, *Maternal Overprotection*, Columbia University Press, New York, 1943.

satisfactions for long-term ends, a very necessary discipline. Children who are adequately loved take such frustrations well.

4. Parents should seek to help their children realize their potentialities for being warm loving human beings before all else, and secondarily to acquire all the graces of mind and the techniques of knowledge to help them achieve their best selves.

5. The best way to lay the foundations in childhood for the development of a cultured person is to endow him with cultured parents and a cultured environment.   ———

6. Children should not be permitted to call their parents, or any adult, by their first names. This is not being stuffy, but insisting upon the recognition of roles and statuses. A parent is not a pal of his children. He is or should be a parent first and foremost, and that is the role in which he should appear to his children. This is not incompatible with being the best friend of one's child, but that is only one of the functions of being a parent.   ———

7. Sibling rivalry is not inevitable; it is avoidable by forestalling its development and by paying particular attention to the child who is in danger of developing such a complex.   ———

8. Children should not always be given reasons for the parent's demands. Young children under four won't usually require them, older children may develop the habit of asking for reasons as a form of attention-getting, in which case there is something wrong with the attention the child is receiving or rather not receiving. The child who has confidence and trust in his parents will not usually require reasons. When he does, the appropriateness of the situation will determine whether or not a reason should be given.   ———

9. The Electra complex refers to the unconscious tendency of a daughter to be attached to her father and hostile to her mother.

10. Kibbutz is the name of the Israeli farming village in which all the property, with few minor exceptions, is collectively owned, and in which the living arrangements are to a large degree collective, including the rearing of children.*   ———

* See Melford E. Spiro, *Kibbutz: Venture in Utopia,* Harvard University Press, Cambridge, 1956; Esther Tauber, *Molding Society to Man,* Bloch Publishing Company, New York, 1955.

11. It would be possible to abolish the human family and set up other forms of existence for children and adults in social groups. Plato planned such a society in *The Republic,* Book V, 461. The Kibbutz represents another plan this way. The Soviet Russians flirted with the idea in their early days but soon abandoned it.   _____

12. Adoptive parents can in every way be just as good as biological parents.   _____

13. An adopted child should in every way be legally treated as if he were the biological issue of his adoptive parents. The law is tending to adopt this view.   _____

14. Candy consumption should certainly be regulated by parents, and certain kinds—those which cling to the teeth—should be altogether interdicted.   _____

15. It is quite true that the child is father to the man, but this does not mean that the man cannot do anything about the child in himself.*   _____

16. Potential parents most certainly ought to be tested for the most important of all the roles a human being is called upon to play, one that is critical to human society.   _____

17. Parents should be pals to their children when their children have reached the age of being capable of being pals themselves. Until then parents should be parents. Their children want them to be parents. They do not want them to be pals.

18. The Oedipus complex is the unconscious desire of a child to be attached to the parent of the opposite sex and hostile toward the other parent; the term is usually restricted to the son's attachment.   _____

19. Parents should allow their children to select their own occupations, though advice should always be offered, even though it may be declined.   _____

20. Parents are certainly not the best judges of their children; they are far too involved with them to be so.   _____

21. Children learn more by example than they do by precept— and so does everyone else.   _____

22. Parent-child organizations should be encouraged in every

* See W. Allison Davis and Robert J. Havighurst, *Father of the Man,* Houghton, Mifflin Company, Boston, 1947.

way, particularly those concerned with the instruction and preparation of prospective parents.   _____

23. Grandparents should play the role of grandparents and not of parents.   _____

24. Fathers are for the most part too much away from the home to make adequate parents.   _____

25. The Parent-Teacher Association is a most important organization which should receive the support of all parents, potential as well as actual.   _____

26. Parents and teachers should cooperate to complement each other in the task of assisting the child to develop its potentialities.   _____

27. Parents who disagree on discipline should take their problem to a detached person whose judgment they respect and agree to abide by his decision.   _____

28. Those who have voluntarily foregone the benison of children are going to miss full marks.   _____

29. It was Jeremy Bentham (1748–1832) who said that "All punishment is mischief: all punishment is itself evil." Corporal punishment is simply not permissible.   _____

30. The best encyclopaedia on parent-child relationships is *Childcraft*, Marshall Field Enterprises, Chicago, Illinois, 1957.

_____

~~

Philosophy

1. Philosophy is the study of the processes governing thought and conduct. Originally it meant the love of wisdom or knowledge; now most generally it is understood to be the study or theory or investigation of the principles or laws that regulate the universe and underlie all knowledge and reality. Included in the study are aesthetics, ethics, logic, metaphysics, etc.

_____

2. George Edward Moore's (1873–   ) *Principia Ethica*, 1903, is his most influential book.   _____

3. Bertrand Russell (1872–   ) and Alfred North Whitehead (1861–1947), English philosophers and mathematicians,

collaborated on the famous *Principia Mathematica,* 3 vols.,
1910–13.   _____

4. Empiricism is the theory that sensory experience is the only
source of knowledge.   _____

5. "The categorical imperative" is the conception of the German
philosopher Immanuel Kant (1724–1804) that ethical judgments are essentially matters of faith based on arbitrary but
necessary moral law, expressible in the two forms of the categorical imperative: (1) "Act as if the maxim from which
you act were to become through your will a universal law
of nature," and (2) "So act as to treat humanity, whether
in your own person or that of another, in every case as an end
in itself, never as a means."   _____

6. The Stoics constituted a school of philosophy founded by the
Greek Zeno about 308 B.C.: so called because Zeno (of 4th
and 3rd centuries B.C.) taught under a colonnade, the *Stoa
Poikile* or "Painted Portico," at Athens.   _____

7. The main subject discussed in Plato's (427?–347 B.C.) *Symposium* (c.384) is the nature of love.   _____

8. Logical positivism is a contemporary form of British empiricism. Logical positivists conceive of philosophy principally
in terms of logical analysis, more particularly, as a clarification
of the language we all speak in everyday life. Rejecting all
metaphysics, they maintain the tautology of logical and mathematical truths and subscribe to the Humean view on causality
and induction. As a general philosophical movement it is
concerned with the unification of the sciences, especially by an
analysis of the language of science and the consequent development of a vocabulary applicable to all the sciences._____

9. Existentialism is a literary-philosophic cult of nihilism and
pessimism, popularized in France after World War II chiefly
by Jean-Paul Sartre (1905–   ): it holds that each man
exists as an individual in a purposeless universe, and that he
must oppose his hostile environment through the exercise of
his free will.   _____

10. Idealism is any of a number of theories which hold that the
objects of perception are actually ideas of the perceiving mind
and that it is impossible to know whether reality exists apart

from the mind: celebrated in the limerick (in British Broadcasting Company pronunciation):

> A philosopher, one Bishop Berkeley,
> Remarked, metaphysically, somewhat darkly,
> That what we don't see
> Cannot possibly be,
> And the rest's altogether unlarkly.   ———

11. Pragmatism is the system or method of philosophy in which
the validity or truth of a proposition is tested by its practical
results.   ———

12. Charles Sanders Peirce (1839–1914), American mathematician, physicist, and philosopher, one of the most original
thinkers and greatest logicians of his time. His most representative essays are to be found in the volume, edited by M. R.
Cohen, *Chance, Love, and Logic,* 1923. See also his collected
papers in 6 volumes, 1931–35, and Justus Buchler's *Charles
Peirce's Empiricism,* 1939.   ———

13. Metaphysics is the branch of philosophy that deals with first
principles and seeks to explain the nature of being or reality
(*ontology*) and of the origin and structure of the world
(*cosmology*). It is closely associated with a theory of knowledge (*epistemology*).   ———

14. A value judgment is one that affirms that a certain state or
condition *ought* to be. It is usually maintained that the world
of what ought to be and the world of fact are mutually ir-
reconcilable, and that the chasm which separates them cannot
be bridged.   ———

15. Ethics is moral philosophy, or the study of those principles
which lead to the good life.   ———

16. Aristotle (384–322 B.C.) was the pupil of Plato.   ———

17. The naturalistic fallacy is identified with G. E. Moore and
his great book, *Principia Ethica,* 1903, in which Moore developed the notion that "good" is indefinable because it is simple
and has no definable parts which would constitute it a whole.
Too many philosophers, says Moore, have thought that when
they named the properties of the "good" they were actually
defining it, that these properties were in fact the same with

goodness. This is the naturalistic fallacy, the fallacy committed when one identifies an ethical property such as intrinsic goodness with any natural or empirical property. Again, take yellow, for example. To define it you can describe the physical light waves which must stimulate the retina and the brain before you can perceive yellow. But it is clear that the light waves are not the same as yellow. *They* are not what we perceive. They are what correspond in space to what we perceive in our minds as yellow. Moore, however, erred in identifying "good" as a property exclusively. It isn't a property in his sense of the term nor is it a value judgment as his critics would have it, but a combination of both. For a development of this viewpoint see Philip Blair Rice, *On The Knowledge of Good and Evil*, Random House, New York, 1946, and Ashley Montagu, *The Direction of Human Development*, Harper & Bros., New York, 1955. ————

18. Some existentialist philosophers are Sören Kierkegaard (1813–55), Friedrich Nietzsche (1844–1900), Karl Jaspers (1883–), and Sartre.* ————

19. The *Tractatus Logico-Philosophicus*, 1922, the keybook of logical positivism, is by Ludwig Wittgenstein (1889–1951), Polish-English philosopher. ————

20. *Die Welt als Wille und Vorstellung*, 1818, is by the German philosopher Arthur Schopenhauer (1788–1860). ————

21. *Die Philosophie des Als Ob*, 1911 (English translation, *The Philosophy of 'As If'*, 1924) is by the German philosopher Hans Vaihinger (1852–1933). ————

22. *The Critique of Pure Reason*, 1781, is by the German philosopher Immanuel Kant. ————

23. *Either/Or*, 1843, is by the Danish philosopher Sören Kierkegaard. ————

24. Occam's razor is a doctrine which states that "entities must not be unnecessarily multiplied." It originates with William of Occam or Ockham (1300?–49), the "Invincible Doctor," English scholastic philosopher. ————

25. Ernst Cassirer's (1874–1945) most important work is his

* See Walter Kaufmann, *Existentialism From Dostoyevsky to Sartre*, Meridian Books, New York, 1956.

Philosophie der symbolischen Formen, 1923 and later (translated as *Philosophy of Symbolic Forms,* 1953–57).   _____

26. There are few exercises calculated to sharpen the wits more than the reading of philosophical works.   _____

27. The will is that which stimulates the person to purposeful activity is an assumption. The motivations of human beings to activity are usually complex, and no one is capable of acting spontaneously free of the influence of all his past experiences. In this sense there is no such thing as free will. But in the sense that the person is free to come to his own decisions, however influenced he may be by his past experience, the individual may be said to possess freedom of the will.   _____

28. Knowledge does not necessarily lead to wisdom, but it is a help.   _____

29. The usefulness of the philosophy of science is that it constitutes a constructive criticism of what the scientist is doing.

    _____

30. The uses of philosophy lie in the critical insights it provides into those things with which science cannot deal. But when science is able to take a problem out of the hands of philosophers and provide the verifiable answer, seven hosannas are offered up in Heaven.   _____

~~

Physics

1. Physics is the science dealing with the properties, changes, interaction, etc., of matter and energy.   _____

2. Light travels at the rate of 186,284 miles per second._____

3. Heat is a form of energy whose effect is produced by the accelerated vibration of molecules. Heat must be distinguished from temperature. The temperature of a body is a measure of the average kinetic energy of its individual molecules. Heat is the measure of the total kinetic energy of all the molecules of the body.   _____

4. The boiling point of water at sea level is 212° F, or 100° C.

    _____

5. To convert Fahrenheit into centigrade subtract 32 from the Fahrenheit reading and multiply the remainder by $\frac{5}{9}$. Also $\frac{9}{5} C° + 32 = F°$. _____

6. The melting point of ice is achieved when the surrounding temperature rises to more than 32° F. _____

7. The particles of the nucleus of the atom are the proton and the neutron. _____

8. The periodic table presents an arrangement of the chemical elements according to their atomic numbers, to exhibit the periodic law, according to which the physical and chemical properties of the chemical elements recur periodically when the elements are arranged in increasing order of their atomic numbers. _____

9. The first law of thermodynamics states that there is an equivalence between work and heat, and that one cannot get more work done by a system than the equivalent amount of energy or heat that has been put into the system. _____

10. The second law of thermodynamics states that within any envelope in which the temperature and the pressure remain constant no work is done, or to put it in another way, heat cannot of itself pass from a colder to a hotter body. _____

11. Newton's three laws of motion are:
    (1) Inertia: Every body persists in a state of rest or of uniform motion in a straight line unless compelled by force to change that state.
    (2) Acceleration: The acceleration of a body is proportional to the force causing it.
    (3) Interaction: For every action (or force) there is an equal and opposite reaction. _____

12. Mass is the quantity of matter in a body as measured by the inertia, or resistance to acceleration shown by the body. Mass must be distinguished from the weight of a body, weight being the acceleration experienced by a body due to the gravitational attraction of some sheer mass. On earth we measure weight by referring to the acceleration a body undergoes due to the force exerted on it by the gravitational attraction of the earth. Its mass is its weight divided by the acceleration due to gravity. _____

13. $E = mc^2$, where E stands for Energy contained in a body at rest, m is its mass, and c represents the velocity of light. This equation of Albert Einstein's (1879–1955) expresses the mass-energy law, namely, that mass may be changed into energy or energy into mass, according to a simple rate of exchange, represented by the equation $E = mc^2$, where the energy measured in ergs if the mass m is measured in grams, and c is the velocity of light, namely, 30,000,000,000 centimeters a second. It is interesting that, more than 250 years ago, that other great genius Sir Isaac Newton (1642–1727), said "The changing of Bodies into Light, and Light into Bodies, is very Comfortable to the Course of Nature, which seems delighted with Transmutations."   _____

14. A molecule is the smallest particle of an element or compound that can exist in the free state and still retain the characteristics of the element or compound. The molecules of elements consist of one atom or two or more similar atoms, those of compounds consist of two or more different atoms. Atoms combine to form molecules; they are the smallest particles of an element that combine with similar particles of other elements to produce compounds.   _____

15. A centripetal force is one that moves toward a center; a centrifugal force is one that moves away from a center.   _____

16. Gravity is the force that tends to draw all bodies in the earth's sphere toward the center of the earth. Gravitation is the force by which every mass or particle of matter attracts and is attracted by every other mass or particle of matter.   _____

17. The oceans could be turned into a mass of fire that would burn for three or four months by starting a chain-reaction in the fission of the hydrogen atoms of which they contain the greatest number.   _____

18. The principle of indeterminacy, or uncertainty principle, first formulated by Werner Heisenberg (1901–   ), German physicist and winner of the Nobel prize for physics in 1932, states that it is impossible to determine simultaneously the exact measure of certain physical variables such as velocity and position, or that the exact determination of the one necessarily causes a change in the measurement of the other. This is ex-

tended to mean that there are limits to the precision with which it is possible to predict the position and distribution of the quanta of energy in any universe, and to our ability to assign numerical values to such properties as position, velocity, and energy, and that this imprecision is not due to the inadequacies of our instruments or measurements, but is inherent in the nature of things. The principle is perhaps more accurately called the *principle of limited measurability*. It may be that with the increase in our knowledge the principle of indeterminacy may have to be retired; at the present time, however, it is quite valid. _____

19. The Michelson-Morley experiment (1887) was the work of two American physicists, Albert Abraham Michelson (1852–1931), and Edward Williams Morley (1838–1923), who together made the first accurate experimental determination of the speed of light, and found that the absolute motion of the earth through the ether is not measurable. _____

20. A cloud chamber is an instrument used in atomic and other physical studies, consisting of a closed chamber supersaturated with water vapor for revealing the presence of moving charged particles by their ionization of the vapor. _____

21. Pressure is the thrust distributed over a surface or the force exerted against an opposing body: expressed in weight per unit of area. _____

22. The Leaning Tower of Pisa is famous for many things: one is that it is 180 feet high and leans more than 14 feet out of the perpendicular; another is that Galileo (1564–1642), who was both student and teacher at Pisa, is said to have used the tower for the purpose of experimentally determining the rate of falling bodies. There is, in fact, no evidence that he did so. _____

23. When water is frozen it occupies more space than when it is in the liquid state; hence, the explanation of bursting water-pipes in the winter! _____

24. A volt is that unit of electromotive force or potential difference which will cause a current of one ampere to flow through a conductor whose resistance is one ohm. _____

25. Amp. is the abbreviation for ampere, the standard unit for measuring the strength of electric current; the amount of current sent by one volt through a resistance of one ohm. _____

26. Physicists, as well as all scientists, would greatly benefit by a fundamental training in the humanities. It would make or tend to make them more complete men. _____

27. It would not at all be a bad idea to declare a moratorium on all military weapons and all violent means of settling disputes, but until that is done it would be foolish to declare a moratorium on work in nuclear physics. It is war that must be outlawed; not nuclear physics. _____

28. Atom bombs should be outlawed and all atom testing should be forbidden at once by mutual agreement by all the nations of the world. _____

29. The dangers of the fallout are summed up in the words that any radiation is likely to produce genetic change, and genetic change induced by radiation is likely to be harmful to those yet unborn. _____

30. To protest against the testing of atom bombs is the least that a man can do. _____

Politics and Government

1. Politics is the art of government, sometimes called a science, but more than dubiously so. _____

2. Communism is the theory or system of the ownership of all means of production (and distribution) by the community or society, with all members of the community or society sharing in the work and in the products; specifically, such a system as practiced in the Soviet Union since 1917, and later in China, Poland, Czechoslovakia, and other communist countries, theoretically based on the doctrines of Marx, Engels, Lenin, Stalin, and latterly Khrushchev. It is characterized by state planning and control of the economy, ruthless suppression of all opposition political parties and all deviation within the

Party, and the suppression of individual liberties under a dictatorship. A state which puts economics before human beings. _____

3. Democracy is government by the people, either directly or through elected representatives: the best hope of man because it permits and encourages the maximum order of freedom and the freest form of order. _____

4. Republicanism is the form of government in which the supreme power rests in all the citizens entitled to vote (the electorate) and is exercised by representatives elected, directly or indirectly, by them and responsible to them. On the face of it it is no different from democracy than Tweedledum is from Tweedledee, but Democrats and Republicans are very different things, the one characterized by the fact that they mean well, the other by the fact that they don't mean well enough. _____

5. The first English Labour Government was elected in November 1924. _____

6. Franklin Delano Roosevelt (1882–1945) was first elected President of the United States in 1932. _____

7. The Electoral College is an assembly elected by the voters to perform the formal duty of electing the President and the Vice-President of the United States. The electors of each State, equal in number to its members in Congress, are expected to cast their votes for the candidates elected by the popular vote in their state. _____

8. A ward-heeler is a hanger-on of a ward committee or politician, usually a ward worker who solicits votes for his party and performs various small tasks for his political bosses: a term of contempt. _____

9. Turkey has for long been known as "The Sick Man of Europe." _____

10. Aristotle (384–322 B.C.) is the author of *Politics*, in 8 books, 330 B.C. _____

11. Arnold Toynbee (1852–83) is the author of *The Industrial Revolution*, 1884. _____

12. Walter Bagehot (1826–77) is the author of *Physics and Politics*, 1869. _____

13. *Behemoth,* 1942, is by Franz Neumann (1900–54).—————

14. David Lloyd George (1863–1945), British statesman, Prime Minister of England, 1916–22. He was created first Earl of Dwyfor in 1945.   —————

15. The Monroe Doctrine was essentially stated by President James Monroe (1758–1831) in a message to Congress, on December 2, 1823, that the United States would regard as an unfriendly act any attempt by a European nation to interfere in the affairs of the American countries or increase its possessions on the American continents, and that the United States would not interfere in European affairs. Isolationism was the child of the Monroe Doctrine.   —————

16. The Weimar Republic, the German Republic which lasted from 1919 to 1933: so-called because its constitutional assembly met at Weimar in 1919.   —————

17. Pan-Germanism, the nineteenth-century German militarist-nationalist doctrine aiming at the unification under German rule of all German-speaking peoples, and all those linked by German "blood," a doctrine fervently embraced by the Nazis, and, indeed, a doctrine which led inevitably to the rule of the Nazis.   —————

18. *Human Nature in Politics,* 1908, was written by the English political scientist and sociologist Graham Wallas (1858–1932).   —————

19. The Potsdam Agreement, made at Potsdam (Berlin) in Germany, by Truman, Churchill (later Attlee), and Stalin, July-August 1945, transferred the chief authority in Germany to the American, Russian, British, and French military commanders.   —————

20. It is not possible for a naturalized citizen to become Secretary of State of the United States.   —————

21. The House of Representatives is the lower branch of the legislature of the United States.   —————

22. It was Aristotle who defined man as a political animal in *Politics.*   —————

23. Thomas Hobbes (1588–1679) was an English philosopher, "The Sage of Malmesbury" (where he was born), his most famous work being *Leviathan, or the Matter, Forme and*

Power of a Commonwealth Ecclesiastical and Civil, 1651.

24. "For forms of government let fools contest;/Whate'er is best administered is best": was written by Alexander Pope (1688–1744) in *An Essay on Man,* (1733) Ep. iii, 1, 303.

25. *The Spirit of the Laws,* 1748, was written by Charles Louis de Secondat de Montesquieu (1689–1755).

26. Politics is life; hence, everyone should participate in government whether directly, or, as most must, indirectly.

27. It is to be expected that you vote regularly in all elections relating to government.

28. One should vote for the man, regardless of party affiliation.

29. The opprobrium which attaches to the word *politician* in the United States has been well-earned by a succession of nasty pieces of work such as Tom Watson, Bilbo, Rankin, McCarthy, and the like. But clearly not all politicians are of this stripe, either upon the local or the national level. Fortunately for the United States the majority are very different.

30. Our attitude to the Russians should be such that we inspire them with a feeling that we can be trusted, rather than to inspire them with the continuing feeling that we mean to meet belligerency with further belligerency. Certainly physical force is not physical force when it is used to repel physical force, but it is far better to avoid force by the more efficient means of reconciliation—if such is, indeed, still possible.

~~

Psychology

1. Psychology is the science dealing with the mind and mental processes.

2. A one-word synonym for mind is "psyche."

3. Behaviorism is a term coined in 1912 by John Broadus Watson (1878–   ), American psychologist, as the name for the theory that all human behavior can be explained in physi-

ological terms as response to stimuli affecting the nervous system.   _____

4. The unconscious is that part of the mind in which function the thoughts, impulses, desires, feelings, etc., of which the person is not conscious but which influence his behavior.

   _____

5. The mind is chiefly in the head because the mind is chiefly in the brain, and the brain is in the head. The brain is in the head because in all animals, in their daily lives, it is the first part of the organism to come into contact with the world of experience.   _____

6. Psychoanalysis, a method developed by Sigmund Freud (1856–1939) of treating neuroses, is based on the theory that such disorders are the result of the rejection by the conscious mind of factors that then persist in the unconscious as dynamic repressions. These cause conflicts which may be resolved by discovering and analyzing the repressions through the use of such techniques as free association, dream analysis, etc.   _____

7. Behavior is any act of the organism.   _____

8. Intelligence consists in behavior best calculated to solve the problem presented; the ability to learn from experience.

   _____

9. Alfred Adler's (1870–1937) psychology is known as "individual psychology."   _____

10. "Displacement" is the transference of an emotion to a logically inappropriate object.   _____

11. By "libido" Freud meant the whole of the available energy of the love instinct or Eros.   _____

12. "Repression" is the process whereby ideas and impulses painful to the conscious mind or unacceptable to the "self-image" are forced into the unconscious where they remain.   _____

13. "Cathexis," the concentration of psychic energy on some particular person, thing, or idea; the projection of feelings and meanings upon persons, things, or ideas.   _____

14. It was William James (1842–1910) who defined mind as "a stream of consciousness."   _____

15. The Weber-Fechner law which states that in observing the

difference between two magnitudes, what we perceive is the ratio of the difference to the magnitudes compared, or, for a given difference to remain constant, the proportion of the stimuli to one another must remain constant. The experienced difference in magnitude or intensity between two stimuli varies as the ratio of the stimuli. For example, in the shadow experiment, Fechner showed that where two shadows from a rod, cast alongside one another by two lights, fall on a screen, they may be altered in intensity by altering the two lights from the screen. _____

16. "Insanity" is a legal and not a medical term. It is defined as the condition of a person in which he is incapable of governing his own affairs. _____

17. The opposite of love is indifference—*not* hatred. _____

18. The Moro reflex, first described by the German pediatrician Ernest Moro (1874–   ) in 1918, consists of the response, in infants up to about 4 months of age, to a sudden jarring, withdrawal of support, sudden loud noise, and the like stimuli. Essentially the response consists of an extension of the arms followed by their bowing, the legs making much the same kind of movement. Actually the arms are extended, spread, and then drawn toward the midline of the body with the fingers spread and half bent. The legs are extended, and the toes spread and bent. _____

19. It is normally quite impossible to overwork the mind so that it breaks down. Most people don't get anywhere near approaching a 9 per cent use of the work their minds are capable of doing. _____

20. Instinct, with respect to man, is a term that has fallen into disrepute, and the contemporary practice is to assume that man has no instincts, and that virtually everything that he does as a human being which is not reflex he has to learn from other human beings. He has needs or drives or urges, such as the basic needs for oxygen, food, liquid, etc., but these are not instincts. _____

21. A sensation is the immediate reaction to external stimulation of a sense organ. A perception is a sensation invested with recognition and meaning. _____

22. A reflex is an involuntary and invariable response, such as a sneeze, resulting when a stimulus is carried by a sensory nerve to a nerve center and the response is reflected along a motor nerve to some muscle or gland. An instinct is an unlearned complex adaptive response accompanied by a specific emotional excitement. _____

23. The best biography of Freud is Ernest Jones' *The Life and Work of Sigmund Freud,* 3 vols., New York, Basic Books, 1953–57. _____

24. A neurosis is a mental disorder characterized by a wide symptomatology which may take various forms, such as combinations of anxieties, compulsions, obsessions, phobias, and motor or sensory manifestations, such as tics, without apparent organic or structural injury or change. It results in only partial disorganization of the personality and is less serious both in form and prognosis than a psychosis. _____

25. A psychosis is any mental disorder in which the personality is very seriously disorganized. Psychoses are of two sorts: (*a*) functional, characterized by lack of apparent organic cause, and principally of a schizophrenic or manic-depressive type, and (*b*) organic, characterized by pathological organic conditions, such as general paresis, brain tumor, alcoholism, etc.

_____

26. The death instinct or destructive instinct of Freud, according to him comprises the impulses aiming at destruction, the final aim being to reduce living things to an inorganic state. Even Freud's biographer, Ernest Jones, cannot subscribe to this theory, and most serious students feel that it was one of Freud's most profitless speculations.* _____

27. Whatever one may think of psychoanalysis it must be admitted that its influence has been wide and beneficial. There is undoubtedly much that will have to be revised and some things will have to be dropped, but on the whole it is, both as theory and practice, a much-to-be-encouraged discipline. _____

28. Extrasensory perception, or the ability to perceive beyond the normal capacities of sense perception, is one of those areas in

* For the origin and development of the idea of the death instinct by Freud see his *Beyond the Pleasure Principle,* Hogarth Press, London, 1920.

which the open mind is indicated. Much scientific work requires still to be done before a general scientific judgment becomes possible. More research is needed. ⎯⎯⎯

29. Clinical psychologists desire to be licensed just as doctors, and, of course, they should be licensed in order that the public might distinguish between the properly qualified and the quacks. ⎯⎯⎯

30. Part of the training of the psychoanalyst must be the analysis of himself, so that he becomes aware not only of the nature of his own psychic development, but in the process learns how that development occurs in others. Furthermore, his own conflicts are brought to the surface and resolved, so that the chances are minimized that he will work them out on his patients. ⎯⎯⎯

Check Your References

1. Constance M. Winchell, *Guide To Reference Books,* published by the American Library Association, Chicago, 1951 (Supplements, 1954, 1956). ⎯⎯⎯

2. *Oxford English Dictionary,* 13 volumes, Oxford University Press, London and New York, 1933. ⎯⎯⎯

3. H. W. Fowler (1853–1933), *A Dictionary of Modern English Usage,* Oxford University Press, London and New York, 1926. ⎯⎯⎯

4. Margaret Nicholson, *A Dictionary of American-English Usage,* Oxford University Press, New York and London, 1957: based on Fowler's *Modern English Usage.* ⎯⎯⎯

5. *The Columbia Encyclopedia,* 2nd edition, Columbia University Press, New York, 1950; supplement, 1956. ⎯⎯⎯

6. Phyllis Hartnot (editor), *The Oxford Companion to the Theatre,* 2nd edition, Oxford University Press, London and New York, 1957. ⎯⎯⎯

7. *The Index Medicus,* American Medical Association, Chicago, Illinois. ⎯⎯⎯

8. Theodore Besterman, *A World Bibliography of Bibliographies,* 3rd edition, Societas Bibliographica, Geneva, Switzerland, 1955–56.

9. The Catalogue of the Library of Congress, Washington, D.C.

10. *Books In Print,* R. R. Bowker Co., New York, annually.

11. *Encyclopaedia of the Social Sciences* (edited by E. R. A. Seligman and Alvin Johnson), 15 vols., Macmillan, New York, 1930.

12. F. W. Bateson (editor), *The Cambridge Bibliography of English Literature,* 5 vols., Cambridge University Press, London and New York, 1941–57.

13. *The Dictionary of National Biography* (Macmillan, New York, 1900—63 vols.—and supplements), and *The American Dictionary of National Biography* (Scribner's, New York, 1928–44—21 vols.), respectively.

14. *The Oxford Dictionary of Quotations,* 2nd edition, Oxford University Press, London and New York, 1954, and John Bartlett (1820–1905), *Familiar Quotations,* Little, Brown & Co., 1948; 1st ed., 1855, at least, should be on your list.

15. William L. Langer (editor), *An Encyclopaedia of World History,* rev. edition, Houghton Mifflin Co., Boston, 1948.

16. Miles O. Price and Harry Bitner, *Effective Legal Research: A Practical Manual of Law Books and Their Use,* Prentice-Hall, New York, 1953; Carlton B. Putnam, *How To Find the Law,* 4th ed., West Publishing Co., St. Paul, 1949.

17. Paul Harvey (editor), *The Oxford Companion to English Literature,* 3rd edition, Oxford University Press, London and New York, 1955; E. Cobham Brewer, *The Reader's Handbook,* Chatto and Windus, London, 1925. See also the answer to question 29.

18. *Historical Atlas* by William R. Shepherd, 8th edition, Barnes & Noble, New York, 1956.

19. *Index Catalogue of the Library of the Surgeon-General's Office,*

First Series, 1880–1895; Second Series, 1896–1916; Third Series, 1918–1932; Fourth Series, 1936–   ; Washington, D.C.

20. Percy A. Scholes, *The Oxford Companion to Music,* 2nd edition, Oxford University Press, London and New York, 1943.

21. James D. Hart, *The Oxford Companion to American Literature,* 3rd edition, Oxford University Press, London and New York, 1956.

22. An almanac. Among the best known are *Whittaker's Almanac, Information Please Almanac, The World Almanac, The Old Farmer's Almanac,* and *American Ephemeris and Nautical Almanac.*

23. Peter Mark Roget (1779–1869), *Thesaurus of English Words and Phrases,* 1st ed., 1852; many editions since.

24. *Childcraft,* Marshall Field Enterprises, Chicago, 1949 and subsequently.

25. James Hastings (1852–1922), *Encyclopaedia of Religion and Ethics,* 12 vols., Scribner's, New York, 1908-27.

26. Maria Leach and Jerome Fried, *Dictionary of Folklore, Mythology, and Legend,* 2 vols., Funk & Wagnalls, New York, 1949–50.

27. Medicine: *Stedman's Practical Medical Dictionary,* Williams & Wilkins Co., Baltimore, 1957; *Blakiston New Gould Medical Dictionary,* McGraw-Hill Book Co., Blakiston Division, New York, 1956; *Dorland's Illustrated Medical Dictionary,* Saunders, Philadelphia, 23rd ed., 1957.

28. *The Concise Oxford Dictionary of English Literature,* Oxford University Press, London and New York, 1942.

29. Paul Harvey (editor), *The Oxford Companion to Classical Literature,* Oxford University Press, London & New York, 1954.

30. It is to be hoped that you always check your references.

Religion

1. Religion is the belief in a divine or superhuman power or powers to be obeyed and worshiped as the creator(s) and ruler(s) of the universe. _____

2. Abraham was born at Ur in Babylonia about 2153 B.C. _____

3. Abraham lived in Mesopotamia, Egypt, and Palestine. _____

4. The Old Testament is a work parts of which were written at different times. There is no certainty as to precisely when any part of the Bible was written, but it is considered among many scholars that Genesis, Exodus, Numbers, Joshua, Judges, Samuel 1 and 2, represent a combination of the history of a ninth-century B.C. writer called J or the Yahwist, and of an eighth-century B.C. writer called E or the Elohist. Deuteronomy is thought to be of late seventh-century B.C. authorship. Leviticus appears to have been composed soon after 570 B.C. Chronicles, Ezra, and Nehemiah, were composed about the late 4th century B.C. _____

5. Jesus (8–4 B.C.?–c. 29 A.D.) was somewhere between 31 and 36 years of age at his death. _____

6. The 27 books of the New Testament were written at different times and in different places. Most of the books appear to have been written between 50 and 100 A.D. _____

7. The Dead Sea Scrolls are a group of manuscripts, many in fragmentary state, found between 1947 and 1952 in caves along the northwest shore of the Dead Sea. These manuscripts date back to an age from about 170 B.C. to 68 A.D. The importance of the scrolls is that they throw much new light upon the beliefs and practices of Jewish sectarians of the last two centuries before Christ, and by their content serve to illuminate the sources of Christian doctrine. _____

8. The Sermon on the Mount is contained in the New Testament —Matthew 4:23 to 8:1. _____

9. Most people seem to be unaware of the fact that the Golden Rule, "Thou shalt love thy neighbor as thyself," is not Chris-

tian but Hebrew in origin. It is first stated in Leviticus 19:18, "Thou shalt not avenge, nor bear any grudge against the children of thy people, but thou shalt love thy neighbor as thyself: I am the Lord." Christian theologians have attempted to show that "neighbor" in the Old Testament here meant one's own people, that the love here enjoined is tribal, and that it becomes universal for the first time only in its Christian form. Unprejudiced study of the original Hebrew meaning of the word *rea* or neighbor, as well as the internal evidences of *Leviticus* itself, lends no support to the viewpoint of the Christian theologians. The homeless alien is to be loved just as much as any member of one's own people. This is clearly stated in *Leviticus*, 19:34, "But the stranger that dwelleth with you shall be unto you as one born among you, and thou shalt love him as thyself; for ye were strangers in the land of Egypt."*

10. The founder of Judaism was Abraham, its codifier Moses.

11. Christianity was first brought to England by St. Augustine (d. 604), first Archbishop of Canterbury (not to be confused with St. Augustine of Hippo (345–430), the famous author of the *Confessions* and *The City of God*). St. Augustine of Canterbury, a Roman Benedictine monk, was sent by Pope Gregory I with 40 monks as a missionary to England. He arrived in 597, and with his group was well received by King Ethelbert who gave them land at Canterbury. St. Augustine did not convert England to Christianity, but he prepared the way. It was at the Synod of Whitby in 664 that England may be said to have adopted the Roman form of Christianity as its official religion.

12. The founder of Protestantism, if a single man can be credited with that title, was Martin Luther (1483–1546). The term "Protestant" originates in the protest made by the German princes to the Diet of Spires (1529) against its decision to

* For a scholarly discussion of this matter see *Sayings of the Fathers or Pirke Aboth*, with a commentary by Chief Rabbi Joseph Hertz; New York, Behrman House, Inc., 1945.

uphold the edict of the Diet of Worms (1521) against the Reformation. _____

13. Protestantism was established as the religion of England by Henry VIII (1491–1547) in 1534. _____

14. The Reformation is the name given to the sixteenth-century religious movement that aimed at reforming the Roman Catholic Church and resulted in the establishment of the Protestant churches. _____

15. "Original sin" is the tendency to sin and depravity which, in Christian theology, is held to be inherent in mankind as a direct result of Adam's sin of rebellion and which, in Roman Catholicism, is held to have resulted in the loss of sanctifying grace. Baptism is a means of washing away original sin and restoring man to his innocent state, but even after baptism the tendency to sin remains. _____

16. "Original sin" is the invention of St. Paul in Romans 5:12. It is found in none of the words of Jesus. _____

17. A Unitarian is a member of a Protestant denomination which denies the doctrine of the Trinity, and while believing in the teaching of Jesus rejects his divinity, holding that God is a single being. _____

18. The idea of separation of Church and State implies the complete noninterference on each side in the affairs of the other. This idea is essentially American in its "complete" form. In other forms the idea is present in other countries. _____

19. *Agape* (pronounced a-gah-pay, the Greek word meaning *love*) is the form of love which is developed in the New Testament, to be distinguished from *Eros*. *Eros* is worldly or physical love, *agape* is otherworldly or spiritual love. The New Testament consistently uses *agape* and as consistently avoids the word *eros* which is the other Greek word for love.* _____

20. The first Pope was St. Peter (d. 67 A.D.?). _____

21. St. Ignatius of Loyola (1491–1556), was the Spanish founder of the Jesuit order, or the Society of Jesus. _____

* For a controversial discussion of *agape* see Anders Nygren, *Agape and Eros,* Society For the Promotion of Christian Knowledge, London, 1953; M. C. D'Arcy, *The Mind and The Heart of Love,* Meridian Books, New York, 1956.

22. The father and mother of King Solomon (c. 973–933 B.C.) were David and Bathsheba.   _____

23. The Pharisees were an ancient Jewish sect that rigidly observed the written law, but also insisted on the validity of the oral or traditional law that had grown out of popular usage. They aimed to keep everything non-Jewish apart from what they regarded as strictly Jewish. Their active period extended from about 135 B.C. to 135 A.D.   _____

24. Clericalism is the exercise of political influence or power on the part of the clergy.   _____

25. The Philistines were a people living in the southwestern region of Palestine from about 1200 B.C., who were constantly at war with the Israelites for control of the country. It is believed they were of Cretan origin. Samson, Saul, and notably David are the great antagonists of the Philistines presented in the Old Testament. The current usage of the word "philistine" to signify an uncultured person we owe to Thomas Carlyle (1795–81) who first used it in this sense in 1831, and to Matthew Arnold (1822–88) who made it popular from 1863 onward.   _____

26. Freedom of religious belief and practice is part of the credo of every civilized person.   _____

27. Every person has a right to believe exactly what he chooses to believe.   _____

28. The Old Testament attitude toward women is lamentable. The New Testament attitude is a considerable improvement— but leaves much to be improved.   _____

29. Whether secular beliefs can adequately replace religious beliefs is an open question, but one which every man who chooses to do so must in the interim decide for himself.

                    _____

30. Whether a secular religion is possible is a question which must be answered in much the same terms as the above.

                    _____

~·~

Scientific Method and Logic

1. Science is the systematized knowledge derived from observation, study, and experimentation carried on in order to determine the nature or principles of what is being studied.

2. Logic is the science of correct reasoning.
3. Truth is conformability to fact or reality. In scientific terms, the highest degree of probability that attaches to a judgment which can be verified.
4. If there is one word which best describes the method of science it is *verification*, principally by experiment.
5. A scientist is not interested in proving anything to be one way or the other. He is not interested in believing or in disbelieving, but in inquiry and the discovery of what *is*.
6. Induction is reasoning from particular facts or individual cases to a general conclusion. It is the method of science. Deduction is the process of reasoning from a general principle to a particular or specific conclusion.
7. A fact is something known to be true or existing as distinguished from conjecture or inference.
8. "A definition," according to Aristotle, "is a phrase signifying a thing's 'essence.'" In short, a definition is an exact statement which explains a thing in a manner that distinguishes it from everything else, by genus, species, property, differentia, and accident.
9. A syllogism is an argument or form of reasoning in which two statements, a major and a minor premise, are made and a logical conclusion drawn from them. Example: All men are mortal. John is a man. Therefore John is mortal.
10. Recent statistical studies do not prove that smoking is a cause of cancer. Statistics never prove anything, all that they do is to exhibit the degrees of association that exist between the variables examined. In the case of smoking, the association is so significantly great with cancer that there can be little doubt

that smoking is in some way significantly related to its causation.*

11. A cause is anything that produces an effect or result. A cause is usually made up of a complex of conditions, each condition is called a *necessary condition*. Necessary conditions alone or in combination with several others—but not all the other conditions—are alone insufficient to constitute a cause. It is the combination of all those conditions, no more and no less, which are sufficient to constitute the cause, that are known as the *sufficient conditions*.

12. The answer to this question depends upon what is meant by the words *going round*. If the cat's face is turned toward the dog all the time then the dog does *not* go round the cat, but if the dog passes in its orbit through all the degrees of the circle he describes, then he *does* go round the cat.

13. The Principle of Excluded Middle states that a thing is either *A* or a member of *A* or of *not-A*. A thing cannot be both *A* and *not-A* at the same time—except, possibly, in psychoanalysis.

14. The operational method or operationalism is the method or philosophy which holds that a concept is synonymous with the set of operations to which it corresponds. If one is dealing with the concept of weight the operations are those by which weight is measured. If the concept is mental, then the operations are mental operations. If we cannot give an adequate account of our ideas in terms of operations, we may be quite certain that those ideas are "fuzzy."†

15. Observation is the practice of noticing and recording facts or events.

16. Statistics is the branch of science which deals with the classification and frequency of occurrence of different kinds of things or different attributes of things, as a ground for inference and induction. Statistics "prove" nothing.

17. It was Francis Bacon (1561–1626), English philosopher, who

* See Sidney Russ, *Smoking And Its Effects,* Macmillan, New York, 1956; Alton Ochsner, *Smoking And Cancer,* Julian Messner, New York, 1954.

† See Percy W. Bridgman, *The Logic of Modern Physics,* Macmillan, New York, 1927; Anatol Rapoport, *Operational Philosophy,* Harper & Brothers, New York, 1953.

said "Truth grows more readily out of error than it does out of confusion."   _____

18. *Post hoc ergo propter hoc* means "after this, therefore on account of this": fallacy of logic, assuming that because two things occur in succession or in association one must therefore be the cause of the other.   _____

19. An experiment is a form of observation, it is observation under conditions produced or arranged by human action in order to discover the operative conditions; it is the process of undertaking to discover something not yet known or to demonstrate something known.   _____

20. A *petitio principii* is literally a begging of the question, and consists of smuggling an assumption into our premises and dealing with it as if it were a proved truth.   _____

21. The principle or law of parsimony enjoins us not to multiply hypotheses unnecessarily or to seek superfluous causes for natural phenomena: a form of "Occam's razor."   _____

22. A proposition is an expression in which the predicate affirms or denies something about the subject.   _____

23. The philosophy of science is concerned with the examination of the structure of science, that is, the method and form of scientific knowledge, and with the significance of science for practice and knowledge of reality.   _____

24. The scientific attitude of mind is the open-minded willingness to *inquire,* not either the willingness to believe or the willingness to disbelieve, but the willingness to make dispassionate inquiry into what is, not in proving anything to be this way or the other, but in discovering what *is,* and stating what is no matter how many orthodoxies may be outraged or tumbled in the process, and always to verify by inviting independent verification.   _____

25. The plausible is the seemingly true, but may or may not be so. The probable is what can be reasonably believed on the basis of the evidence.   _____

26. Scientific methods, it is believed by many students of the subject, *can* provide a basis for ethics.*   _____

* See Julian Huxley, *Evolution In Action,* Harper & Brothers, New York, 1953. Julian Huxley, *Religion Without Revelation,* Harper & Brothers, New York,

27. Almost anything read in a newspaper should be read with the reservation that it is subject to further confirmation. _____

28. As someone has remarked, it is desirable to have an open mind, but not so open that one's brains fall out. By the open mind one means a mind receptive to all ideas, but one so critical that it is able to evaluate and distinguish between ideas that are worth entertaining and those that are not. _____

29. Facts do not speak for themselves. They are always at the mercy of whoever chooses to interpret them. Facts are so only when they have been checked and verified. _____

30. Man is not descended from the chimpanzee or gorilla, as is popularly believed and too often stated, nor is he descended from any other living ape. In fact, the lines which led on the one hand to the living apes and to man diverged from their common ancestral stock in the Miocene period, some 35 million years ago. The living apes and men are, therefore, at nearest, collateral rather than linear relatives. Man *is* descended from an apelike creature, and the fact that he is so descended does not necessitate any assumption as to his inherited potentialities of behavior. When we attend to the study of the nature of man and the growth and development of his behavior we find that everything he knows and does as a human being he learns from other human beings, and all that he is born with are potentialities for such learning, potentialities which markedly distinguish him from all other creatures.

"Apelike potentialities of behavior" is a phrase which usually does service for a large number of myths about apes, such as their ferocious and dangerous assaults upon men, their continuous agressiveness. The truth is that apes are neither ferocious nor aggressive, and under natural conditions when they encounter a man, unless they are sorely provoked or

1957; Anatol Rapoport, *Operational Philosophy,* Harper & Brothers, New York, 1953; Louis O. Kattsoff, *The Design of Human Behavior,* Educational Publishers, St. Louis, 1953; Abraham Edel, *Ethical Judgment,* Free Press, Chicago, 1955; Ashley Montagu, *The Direction of Human Development,* Harper & Brothers, New York, 1955.

suddenly surprised, they will view him with curiosity and then go their own way.*   ———————

~~

Sex Differences

1. About 106 boys are born to every 100 girls that are born.
                                                              ———————

2. The bones harden earlier in girls than in boys.   ———————
3. The mortality rate for most diseases is higher for men than for women.   ———————
4. The female in virtually all the species of which we have knowledge lives longer, on the average, than the male because she is the biologically more valuable part of the species capital. The female must be preserved during the period of pregnancy, at the very least, and up to the time of delivery if the species is to be preserved, but the male may die at any time after he has fertilized the female and the species will continue. If all men were to drop dead at such a moment the species would not be seriously affected, but if the same full stop were to be put to women, the answer should be obvious and, it is to be hoped, clarifying.†   ———————
5. Men are weaker than women. Men are muscularly more powerful, heavier, and larger than women, and have a metabolic rate which is higher by some 5 to 6 per cent than that of women. This means that they must take in energy at a more rapid rate, burn it more rapidly, and expand it more rapidly, and go up in smoke, as it were, more rapidly than women. Hence, their greater muscular power is a source of constitutional weakness to men. Women are constitutionally stronger than men because, by virtue of their reproductive and maternal functions, they have to be.   ———————
6. The sex-determining mechanism in the human species is much the same as it is in all other species, namely, through the

* For the evidence see Ashley Montagu, *The Direction of Human Development*, Harper & Brothers, New York, 1955.
† See Amram Scheinfeld, *Women and Men*, Harcourt, Brace & Co., New York, 1944; Ashley Montagu, *The Natural Superiority of Women*, Macmillan, New York, 1953.

association of sex chromosomes called X and Y, with the non-sex chromosomes (the autosomes). The female in her ova caries only X chromosomes. The male in his germ cells carries 50 per cent of sperm cells with X chromosomes in them and 50 per cent of sperm cells with Y chromosomes. When a sperm carrying an X chromosome fertilizes an ovum two X chromosomes are associated and invaribly result in a female; but when a sperm carrying a Y chromosome fertilizes an ovum, the association is XY and invariably results in a male. Because the Y chromosome is incomplete the male falls so readily victim to all sorts of disorders that the female escapes, since the female in her chromosomes possesses a full complement of the necessary factors that the male lacks.   _____

7. In relation to total body weight the female brain weighs about 4 ounces more than that of the male.   _____

8. There are 8 times as many more color-blind males than females.   _____

9. Males at all ages constitute behavior problems more frequently than females.   _____

10. Girls achieve puberty earlier than boys. In the United States the figures are $13\frac{1}{2}$ years for girls, about 15 years for boys.

_____

11. The sickness rate is higher in females than in males, but the recovery rate is higher in females than in males.   _____

12. "It's a woman driver" is an old standby of the male, but it will not withstand critical examination. The evidence indicates that women are better drivers than men. For number of miles of driving they have fewer accidents than men, and the accidents they do have are less serious.* There are local differences in accident rates, but the insurance companies—who *should* know—believe women drivers under 25 to be better risks than men of the same age, and have, accordingly, lowered the insurance rates for women in this age group. Driving-education experts consider women safer drivers than men.†

_____

* See the chapter "Is It True About Women" in Ashley Montagu, *The Natural Superiority of Women*, Macmillan, New York, 1953, pp. 105-111.

† See Anthony Tramondo, "Female Drivers: Less Deadly Than the Male," *The New York Times Magazine*, 27 March 1955, p. 26.

13. Women are much more resistant to the effects of emotional strain than men.*

14. The female, in general, does better on intelligence tests than the male. _____

15. Diabetes is more frequent in the female. About five out of every eight diabetics is a female. It is, however, believed that there are probably more unrecognized diabetics among men than there are among females. _____

16. Male suicides outnumber women by more than three to one. More women attempt suicide than men, and are obviously less successful. It is, of course, an open question as to whether they intend to be successful or to precipitate a situation, or whether they are less successful because they prefer less violent means than men, and hence their acts are less likely to prove fatal. _____

17. Stuttering is eight times more frequent among males than females. _____

18. Women may overdraw their accounts, but the first time they are informed of the fact they tend to do so much less frequently than men.† _____

19. Males are more frequently hospitalized for mental illness than females. There are variations in different localities and in different years, but on the whole it is the male who is hospitalized more frequently than the female. _____

20. The Nobel prize has been awarded twelve times to women. _____

21. Marie Curie received the Nobel prize twice, the first time in 1903 jointly with her husband Pierre for their study of radiation, and the second time in 1911, alone, for her discovery of radium and polonium. _____

22. Males are vastly more occupied with sex than females, but cause females to make themselves sexually attractive in such a manner that most people have come to believe that women are more preoccupied with sex than males. _____

23. Some animals in which the males hatch the eggs are many

* For the evidence see Scheinfeld, and Montagu, books mentioned in note to question 4.

† Check with any bank.

frogs, the seahorse, the phalarope, and some penguins. Among marmosets the male often takes care of the young.   _____

24. Basal metabolism is the minimum rate at which the body produces energy when at rest. It is measured in terms of heat units (energy calories) per hour. In the male the rate is between 38 and 40 calories per hour, in the female between 36 and 38.   _____

25. Feminine intuition is merely the male's transparency, or rather, opacity. It is simply an evidence of the female's sharper mental awareness. What escapes the males does not escape the female. Since the male does not understand how this can be, he calls the process a mystery, "female intuition."*   _____

26. Human beings ought to be judged as human beings with a full right to the respect of their individuality as *persons,* and not be judged on the basis of their natural group membership, insofar as their rights as human beings are concerned.   _____

27. Women should not receive the same education as men, except, of course, in the fundamentals of a good all-round education. They should also receive an education which enables them to function more happily as women.†   _____

28. Certainly, all human beings ought to receive equal pay for equal work irrespective of their natural group membership, whether it be sex or ethnic group.   _____

29. Women should be at least adequately, if not proportionally, represented on all bodies having to do with their welfare.

_____

30. One should vote for the person, not for the group or party, hence, if a woman stood for the Presidency who possessed the necessary qualities, most certainly she should receive the votes that her merits have earned.   _____

* See Helene Deutsch, *The Psychology of Women,* 2 vols., Grune & Stratton, New York, 1945; Ashley Montagu, *The Natural Superiority of Women,* Macmillan, New York, 1943.

† See Kate Hevner Mueller, *Educating Women for a Changing World,* University of Minnesota Press, Minneapolis, 1954.

Social Questions

1. Our educational system requires a complete overhauling and revaluation from the beginning to the end, from top to bottom. We confuse *instruction* with *education*. Education, from the Latin *educare* (*not* educere), means to nourish, to cause to grow—to nourish and to cause to grow the potentialities of the human being for being a warm loving person who can relate himself to others in a creatively enlarging manner. This is education, all else is secondary to that one achievement. We need to reorganize our educational system in the light of that view.* _____

2. Cosmopolitanism is by no means a necessary step in the development of internationalism, but it is always a help._____

3. Force or violence can be justified only when it is used to repel force or violence, as Sir Norman Angell (1874–   ) pointed out in 1910 in *The Great Illusion*. _____

4. The idea of world disarmament is one that all good men would like to see turned into a reality, and for which all good men work. _____

5. Women should not be deprived of the right to serve on juries, but should be free to do so at all times. _____

6. The voting age could well be lowered to 18 years for many good reasons, chief among them being that since we require a certain amount of responsibility from eighteen-year-olds they should be further encouraged in that responsibility by being given the right to vote. _____

7. World federation is inevitable. World federation does not necessarily mean loss of sovereignty or cultural identity. It implies unity without uniformity. It is a goal to work toward.

---

* See Ashley Montagu, *Education And Human Relations,* Grove Press, New York, 1958; Robert M. Hutchins, *Some Observations on American Education,* Cambridge University Press, London & New York, 1956; David B. Dreiman, *How To Get Better Schools,* Harper & Brothers, New York, 1956; Earl C. Kelley, *Education For What Is Real,* Harper & Brothers, New York, 1947; Theodore Brameld, *Cultural Foundations of Education,* Harper & Brothers, New York, 1957; George Norlin, *Things in the Saddle,* Harvard University Press, Cambridge, 1940.

8. Pregnancy should be artificially terminated whenever the life or the health of the mother is endangered, and should be done, normally, on the advice of not one but of several physicians who are qualified to deliver a judgment. _____

9. The approach to the problem of juvenile delinquency should be on both a community and an individual level. It is the individual who needs immediate attention. The community must organize to see that he gets that attention, and to do whatever is necessary to eliminate those factors which produce juvenile delinquency.* _____

10. To enjoy anything one ought to be prepared for it. Hence we ought have education for the proper use of leisure before the leisure is thrust upon us. _____

11. The best age for conception for the human female is between 21 and 25 years inclusive.† _____

12. Integration of the schools is the law of the land and the constitutional right of every citizen of the United States is the freedom to education without discrimination. There can be not the least doubt as to the desirability of integration of the schools, just as there can be no doubt that millions will continue to object. _____

13. Equality is an ethical principal. And this is what is meant by the statement that all men are born equal, for they are obviously not born biologically equal, but by virtue of the fact that they are human they are born with the right to the development of their capacities as human beings. _____

14. Birth control means essentially the planning of births in such a manner that the children, the family, and society may enjoy the optimum benefits that life has to confer, instead of, by uncontrolled breeding, producing more children than can be properly cared for. Birth control should, usually, be left to the parents to decide. _____

15. Planned Parenthood is an organization which exists to advise

* See Milton L. Barron, *The Juvenile in Delinquent Society,* Knopf, New York, 1954; Albert K. Cohen, *Delinquent Boys,* The Free Press, Chicago, 1955; S. R. Slavson, *Re-Educating the Delinquent,* Harper & Brothers, New York, 1954; Frank J. Cohen, *Children In Trouble,* Norton, New York, 1952.

† See Ashley Montagu, *The Reproductive Development of the Human Female,* 2nd ed., Julian Press, New York, 1957.

on birth control and the planning of parentage. Its work is highly constructive.   _____

16. Socialized medicine simply underscores the fact that the health of the people is the interest of the nation, and should not be in the hands of a private monopoly.   _____

17. Women are still not regarded as "persons" in law. Their status, except for the Nineteenth Amendment, has scarcely been changed in so far as their constitutional rights are concerned since 1789. The Equal Rights Amendment, which reads, "Equality of rights under the law shall not be denied or abridged by the United States or by any State on account of sex," would greatly assist the establishment of constitutional and legal equality for women.   _____

18. Separate schools for boys and girls are an unnatural and short-sighted incursion upon the rights and needs of the sexes to get to know each other from the earliest possible age.   _____

19. Certainly, the expense should be taken out of divorce. But the law ought to be tightened.   _____

20. Special schools for bright children is a highly debatable question. The principle objection is that if such children are isolated from the not-as-bright children, they may eventually lose more than they gain by way of overdevelopment of the intellect and underdevelopment of the ability to relate themselves to human beings of every kind.   _____

21. Punishing the parents of juvenile delinquents is hardly likely to improve the situation. By the same logic, why not punish the delinquent society? Clearly, punishment of anyone is not indicated, but further research which will lead to a better understanding of the conditions producing juvenile delinquency, and thus enabling us to make the appropriate adjustments.   _____

22. The laws relating to alimony are anarchic and medieval. Alimony should be awarded on the basis of "net need," that is to say, according to the just needs of the spouse.
_____

23. Congressional investigating committees have a proper place in the investigation of federal offenses, as in the racketeering of unions, politics, and crime, and the like. But the freedom

to investigate the political beliefs of anyone should not be a right of any Congressional committee or of anyone else. A man's political and religious beliefs, so long as they do not interfere with or threaten the rights or freedoms of his fellow citizens, are his own affair. _____

24. Filibusters are a blot on the escutcheon of American government. _____

25. Euthanasia, or the putting of a person to death in order to end his suffering, is a practice that most right-minded persons would support in theory, but also realize that in practice the question "Who is to be the judge" is a very real one. And until that question has been adequately answered euthanasia remains a generous ideal.* _____

26. There is no such thing as a "clean bomb." This is madness. The words are mutually incompatible. Fallout of dangerous radioactive materials must be associated with every atom bomb. All atom bombs should be outlawed. _____

27. The 4-hour day for the working parents of young children would solve the problem (1) of returning the father to participation in the rearing of his own children together with his wife, and (2) help in the relief of the mother from labors which would benefit by an occasional change of scene and activity. _____

28. It is to be hoped that social problems are sufficiently important to share your attention, at least, with other interests._____

29. Our immigration laws are most unfavorable to ourselves and to other people desiring to become citizens of the United States. They work an unnecessary hardship upon untold thousands not only abroad but living in this country. For the story see J. Campbell Bruce, *The Golden Door: The Irony of Our Immigration Policy,* Random House, New York, 1954.

_____

30. War is collective insanity—a disease that should be forever made impossible. _____

* See Joseph Fletcher, *Morals And Medicine,* Princeton University Press, Princeton, 1954.

Sociology

1. Sociology is the science of society. _____
2. The family is the social institution developed around the child-mother relationship. The father is not an essential unit of family structure in all societies, and at least one society, the Nayar of India, declines to grant him any formal recognition. In numerous other societies it is the mother's brother who assumes the social role played by the father in our society. It is the *conjugal* or *biological family* that consists of parents and their children. _____
3. Anthropology tends to concentrate on the study of nonliterate peoples; sociology is more specifically devoted to the study of literate peoples. The distinction is arbitrary, but useful. _____

4. The state, process, or condition of being social is defined by or as the interaction of two or more organisms with each other. _____

5. Social Darwinism is the theory that the laws of competition governing the evolution and development of living organisms of every kind also prevail in determining the social development of individuals and social groups. _____
6. An institution is essentially an agreement to act in certain ways about certain things. More formally an institution may be defined as an enduring, complex, collectively integrated organized behavior pattern through which social control is exerted and by means of which fundamental and persistent social needs or desires are met. _____
7. It was Herbert Spencer (1820–1903), English sociologist, who likened society to an organism. _____
8. The function of ceremonial is to associate the group with a sense of tradition and continuity, and to invest the procedure with a dignity sufficient to impress and mark the importance of the event or occasion. _____
9. The word *civilization* refers to the late stages in the development of society. Civilization begins with writing and the organization of cities. _____

10. Competition is striving *against;* cooperation is striving *with* others to achieve the same or similar goals. _____

11. Propaganda is the conscious systematic effort to manipulate opinion and conduct through suggestion. _____

12. Society is the pattern of interrelationships existing between and among persons who are members of the same group. _____

13. The founder of sociology in America was Lester F. Ward (1841–1913). _____

14. Ethnocentrism is the attitude that one's own race, nation, or culture is superior to all others. _____

15. A revolution is a mass movement directed toward the changing of the social order or some part of it, usually involving an attempt to overthrow the existing government. _____

16. A caste is an hereditary class of persons marrying only within the limits of their own class. The insistence on marrying within the class may come exclusively from within, as among Brahmins, or be dictated by conditions from without, such as the prejudices and laws against marrying members of the lower castes. Thus, in many states of the Union there are strong prejudices *and* laws which render marriages between whites and nonwhites null and void. _____

17. War is the armed struggle of nations or other politically organized groups. _____

18. Man is the only creature who makes war upon his own kind. Ants may attack other species of ants, but man is the only living species that attacks and enters into conflict with members of his own species. _____

19. Custom is the manner of behaving in defined situations that has been set by the usage of the group, and is generally carried out with little or no deliberation. _____

20. Neo-Malthusianism is the late nineteenth-century term applied to the movement calculated to spread the knowledge of contraception in order to prevent the advent of the Malthusian checks to, and thus limit, population growth; the late Victorian term for "birth control." _____

21. A class is a group of people considered as a unit according to economic, occupational, or social status. _____

22. An individual is a person taken as a unit, but it is only for such census purposes that an individual, strictly speaking, may be said to exist. The person is, fortunately, too much interrelated with others to be considered as an entirely separable entity. _____

23. Ritual is a set form or system of rites, religious or otherwise.

_____

24. Sectarianism is the unreasoned and exclusive adherence to a doctrinaire belief or practice. _____

25. Social distance is the degree to which interaction and cooperation do or do not obtain between persons, groups, nations, or cultures; the set of attitudes which permits a person to allow only part of his personality to be involved in his relationships to others, determined by what he feels about them. _____

26. Sociology is a science in that it attempts systematic inquiry, analysis, and even experiment, in the attempt to order knowledge about the nature of society and to state the principles involved. _____

27. Progress is not automatic, but has to be cultivated. _____

28. History is the sociology of the past. Sociology is the history of the present. _____

29. We have Departments of Sanitation, Departments of Welfare, and Departments of Public Health—why not a Department of Human Relations, charged with the task of helping in the maintenance and development of good human relations between the various segments of a city population? _____

30. The value of sociology lies in the fact that it not only is the discipline which gathers together and systematically presents vast quantities of data on every variety of social phenomena, but in its analysis of such data enables us to obtain a firmer understanding and grasp upon the nature of human societies.

_____

The Theater

1. The first plays in Europe were Greek, originating in the ceremonial worship of Dionysus (Bacchus), god of wine and fertility. The earliest known example of such a play dates back to the middle of the seventh century B.C. The religious mystery plays of Europe proper, dating back to the fourth century A.D., were designed to spread the teachings of the Bible. _____

2. The proscenium is the front of the stage that is still visible when the curtain is lowered. _____

3. In the Elizabethan and early Restoration theater the musicians occupied a gallery, called the *musicians' gallery,* which was situated either at the back or the side of the theater. During the latter part of the Restoration period the musicians were brought down into the well in front of the stage. Since there were few musicians the well did not, as it does today, extend the full width of the stage, and hence afforded a grand opportunity for the witlings of the day to congregate in the corners—Fop Corner—and put on a play within a play. _____

4. To upstage means to hog a part in such a manner as to focus attention upon oneself and deprive others of the attention which is properly theirs. The acting area furthest from the audience is called the upstage, and an actor upstaging another forces him to turn away from the audience as he, the first actor, moves upstage. _____

5. The word "bloody" created a sensation when it was first used on the stage in George Bernard Shaw's (1856–1950) *Pygmalion,* 1912, when Liza Doolittle delivered herself of the now famous "Not bloody likely." _____

6. Thalia is the Muse of comedy. _____

7. George S. Kaufman (1889–   ) wrote, as sole author, *The Butter and Egg Man,* 1925. _____

8. A play written to be read but not to be performed is known as a closet drama. _____

9. Margaret Webster (1905–   ), American stage director, best known for her Shakespearian productions.   _____

10. Konstantin Sergeyevich Stanislavsky (1863–1938), Russian actor, producer, and teacher of acting.   _____

11. Guthrie McClintic (1893–   ), American director._____

12. Sir John Gielgud (1904–   ), English actor and producer.

13. *The Relapse, or Virtue in Danger,* was written and produced in 1696 with immense success by Sir John Vanbrugh (1664–1726).   _____

14. *The Inspector General,* 1836, is by the Russian novelist and playwright Nikolai Vasilievich Gogol (1809–52)._____

15. *Amphitryon,* 1667 is a comedy by Molière (1622–73), French comic dramatist. The original is by Plautus (c.254–184 B.C.), Roman comic poet, and there is another of the same title, based on both Plautus and Molière, by the English poet John Dryden (1631–1700), published in 1690.   _____

16. *Ghosts,* 1881, is by the Norwegian dramatist Henrik Ibsen (1828–1906).   _____

17. *Green Pastures,* 1930, is by the American dramatist Marc Connelly (1890–   ).   _____

18. *The Playboy of the Western World,* 1907, is by the Irish dramatist John Millington Synge (1871–1909).   _____

19. Percy Bysshe Shelley's (1792–1822) best known play is *The Cenci,* 1819.   _____

20. William Shakespeare (1564–1616) was a member of the Lord Chamberlain's Men, later known as the King's Men, which he had joined by 1595. He remained with them until 1610, when he retired to Stratford.   _____

21. Grand Guignol, a genre of plays specializing in violence, murder, rape, ghostly apparitions, and suicide, all calculated to chill and amuse the audience: so named from the theater in Paris where they were performed.   _____

22. The Green Room is the room behind the stage in some theaters, for use of actors and actresses when they are off stage.

23. Rachel (1820–58), one of the world's greatest actresses: of a poor Jewish French family. After singing in the streets she was rescued and sent to dramatic school, and from the age of

13 appeared in innumerable plays, traveling as far as Russia, London, and the United States.   _____

24. The rake is the slope of the stage upward from the audience.   _____

25. George Eliot's (1819–80) first husband, George Henry Lewes (1817–78), philosopher, scientific popularizer, and writer, had been an actor. He wrote many plays, but is principally remembered, in connection with the theater, for his admirable dramatic criticism. He was one of the most gifted men of his time.   _____

26. If you read the theater section of your newspaper, take full marks.   _____

27. If you read books on the theater, take full marks.   _____

28. Whether all plays should be passed by a state censor before being presented to the public, as is the custom in England and in the United States with respect to films, is a question which can be very easily decided with the example of the United States before us. The theater gets along quite well without benefit of a censor to advise it, and there seems, therefore, no necessity for such a functionary in this country.   _____

29. Of course there ought to be a national theater.   _____

30. It is to be hoped that you visit the theater as often as you please.   _____

~·~

Who Said It?

1. Alexander Pope (1688–1744) in the *Essay on Man* (1773).   _____

2. Voltaire (1694–1778).   _____

3. William H. Vanderbilt (1821–85), but also the policy of several of our railroads.   _____

4. John Randolph (1773–1833).   _____

5. Charles II of England, "Our sovereign Lord, the King, Whose word no man relies on, Who never did a foolish thing, and never said a wise one." The most slippery and treasonable character who ever occupied a throne.   _____

6. John Keats (1795–1821), in *Endymion,* Bk. 1. (1817).———

7. Aristide Briand (1862–1932), often inaccurately attributed to Clemenceau.

8. François de La Rochefoucauld (1613–80).———

9. *Qu'ils mangent de la brioche* (Let them eat cake): attributed to Marie Antoinette (1755–93) on being told that her people had no bread.———

10. Rev. Sydney Smith (1771–1845).———

11. Solon (c.640–c.558 B.C.), in Herodotus, *Histories,* i, 32.

12. Josh Billings (Henry Wheeler Shaw) (1818–85).———

13. Augustine Birrell (1850–1933).———

14. Oliver Cromwell (1599–1658), and later adopted by Valentine Blacker (1778–1803).———

15. The Duke of Wellington (1769–1852) to Harriette Wilson (1789–1846), the demi-mondaine, on declining her invitation to pay her for the privilege of being omitted from her *Memoirs.*———

16. Ben Jonson (1573?–1637) in *The Alchemist* (1610).

17. Lord Acton (1834–1902).———

18. George Santayana (1863–1952).———

19. Lord Acton.———

20. François de La Rouchefoucald.———

21. John Stuart Mill (1806–73).———

22. Samuel Johnson (1709–84).———

23. Cardinal Newman (1801–90).———

24. Blaise Pascal (1623–62.)———

25. George Bernard Shaw (1856–1950).———

26. Hilaire Belloc (1870–1953) in *On His Books.*———

27. Henry Clay (1777–1852) in a speech in 1850.———

28. Thomas Henry Huxley (1825–95) in *The Coming of Age of "The Origin of Species."*———

29. Thomas Hobbes (1588–1679) in *Leviathan* (1651).———

30. Samuel Johnson (1709–84).———

Words

1. A word is a speech sound or series of such sounds, having meaning and used as a unit of language. _____
2. Xenophobia, fear or hatred of strangers or foreigners. _____
3. Polyglot, spoken or written in many languages. _____
4. Perfunctory, without care or interest or merely as a form of routine. _____
5. Peremptory, in a commanding, dictatorial, or intolerantly positive manner. _____
6. Supererogatory, doing more than is required, beyond what is necessary. _____
7. Serendipity, an aptitude for making fortunate discoveries accidentally. _____
8. Fatuous, complacently stupid or inane, silly, foolish. _____
9. Unctuous, characterized by a smug, smooth pretense of spiritual feeling, fervor, or earnestness, especially in an attempt to influence or persuade. Perhaps the best literary example of this is Uriah Heep, in Dickens's *David Copperfield*, who was always washing his hands with invisible soap. _____
10. Historiographer, a historian; especially one appointed to write the history of some institution, country, or the like. _____
11. Polymath, a person of much and various learning. _____
12. (*a*) *Words, Words, Words!* by Eric Partridge, Methuen, London, 1933; (*b*) *The Romance of Words* by Ernest Weekley, John Murray, London, 1912, 1934; (*c*) *Language in Thought and Action* by S. I. Hayakawa, Harcourt, Brace & Co., New York, 1949; (*d*) *The Meaning of Meaning* by C. K. Ogden and I. A. Richards, Harcourt, Brace & Co., New York, 1923; (*e*) *Growth and Structure of the English Language* by Otto Jespersen, Anchor Books, New York, 1955, reprint of 1905 edition. Other good books on the subject are *The World of Words* by Eric Partridge, Scribners, New York, 1939; *History in English Words* by Owen Barfield, George H. Doran, New York, 1927; *Adjectives and Other Words* by Ernest Weekley, John Murray, London, 1931; *Semantics, The Nature of Words and Their Meanings* by Hugh R. Walpole, Norton, New

York, 1941; *The Tyranny of Words* by Stuart Chase, Harper & Brothers, 1938, 1945.

13. The word "eccentric" is derived from the science of astronomy.

14. The best source book for the origins and first usage of English words is the *Oxford English Dictionary*.

15. The earliest English dictionary is Robert Cawdrey's (fl. 1604) *The Table Alphabeticall of Hard Words,* London, 1604.

16. The standard work on the American language is H. L. Mencken's (1880–1956) *The American Language,* 4th edition, Knopf, New York, 1936, with *Supplements One* and *Two,* Knopf, New York, 1948.

17. A baker's dozen is thirteen, the number of rolls bakers used to give to purchasers of a dozen.

18. A single word apart from a context can often have a meaning, but quite frequently does not.

19. Tinkers in repairing pots and pans used to build a tiny mud dam around the hole to keep the molten metal in place. When the metal hardened, the dam was brushed away. Hence, not to give a tinker's dam was to indicate that one couldn't care less.

20. A word is a symbol, although it can act as a sign, as in "Stop, Look, Listen."

21. It was Johann Wolfgang von Goethe (1745–1832) who said "Where an idea is wanting, a word can always be found to take its place."

22. Words constitute a language by being endowed with agreed meanings in definite contexts used for the purposes of communication upon an abstract level.

23. It is impossible for a dictionary to keep up with the growth of words for the simple reason that language grows more rapidly than dictionaries do.

24. A bastard word is one that is formed from words originating in different languages. English is full of such words derived from Greek and Latin originals.

25. "Let thy words be few" is from Ecclesiastes 5:2.

26. To have a lively interest in the origins of words is to be in-

terested in the more refined use of language. It is one of the
marks of a cultivated mind.   _____

27. An unfamiliar word is always a challenge to increase one's
    knowledge and enlarge one's mind.   _____

28. A good vocabulary is the alphabet of the mind.   _____

29. Some men are better than others at spelling as in other things.
    The cultured man spells well willy-nilly.   _____

30. To take care in the choice of one's words is the respect that
    the mind pays to the instrument of its own being.   _____

ABOUT THE AUTHOR

Ashley Montagu was born in London, England, in 1905, and studied anthropology at the Universities of London and Florence, and Columbia University, where he was awarded the degree of Doctor of Philosophy for a thesis on the Australian aborigines. Professor Ashley Montagu has been scientific worker at the British Museum (Natural History), Curator of Physical Anthropology at the Wellcome Historical Medical Museum, London, Assistant Professor of Anatomy at New York University, Anthropologist to the Division of Child Research at the same university, Associate Professor of Anatomy at the Hahnemann Medical College and Hospital, Philadelphia, and Chairman and Professor of Anthropology, Rutgers University. He has also been a visiting lecturer and professor at Harvard University and the University of Delaware, Senior Lecturer in Anthropology on the Veterans Administration Postgraduate Training Program in Psychiatry and Neurology, and was Rapporteur of the UNESCO Committee of Experts on Race which drafted the famous UNESCO Statement on Race. He has been Family Affairs and Anthropological Adviser to NBC, and has appeared on many radio and television shows in his capacity as an anthropologist. He is Chairman of the Anisfield-Wolf Award Committee which awards annual prizes for meritorious works in the field of race relations, and he is an associate and advisory editor of *Isis* (The Journal of the History of Science), *Gemmologia* (the study of twins and twinning), and *Child-Family Digest*. Professor Ashley Montagu is a member of many scientific and learned societies, and is the author of some eighteen books, mostly in the field of anthropology, the best-known of which are *On Being Human, The Natural Superiority of Women,* and *Man: His First Million Years.* He has also contributed several hundred articles to the scientific and general periodicals of this and other countries. His hobbies are gardening and book collecting.

This book was set in
Garamond type
by The Haddon Craftsmen.
The paper is
Perkins and Squier Company's
RRR Smooth Antique
made by P. H. Glatfelter Company.
It was printed and bound
at the press of The World Publishing Company.
Typography and design are by
Lawrence S. Kamp